Rancière and Performance

Performance Philosophy

Series Editors:
Laura Cull Ó Maoilearca, Reader in Theatre and Performance, University of Surrey, UK
Will Daddario, Independent Researcher, Asheville, NC, USA
Alice Lagaay, Professor of Cultural Philosophy and Aesthetics, Design Department, Hamburg University of Applied Sciences, Germany

Performance Philosophy is an emerging interdisciplinary field of thought, creative practice and scholarship. The Performance Philosophy book series comprises monographs and essay collections addressing the relationship between performance and philosophy within a broad range of philosophical traditions and performance practices operating across multiple art forms and everyday life, including: dance, choreography, movement and somatic practices; music, sound and silence; drama and theatre; performance art; sport; meditation and spiritual practices. It also includes studies of the performative aspects of life and, indeed, philosophy itself. As such, the series addresses the philosophy of performance as well as performance-as-philosophy and philosophy-as-performance.

Books in the series both contribute to and critique the philosophy of music, dance, theatre and performance – raising important questions about the hierarchy of the relationship between philosophy and the arts; and advancing debates on philosophical method by examining performance as both object and medium of philosophical enquiry.

Comprising texts written by philosophers, researchers from multiple disciplines, and international arts practitioners, the series offers both academic and non-academic audiences the opportunity to engage with questions of how performance thinks and how thought is performed, from the ancient to the contemporary. The series supports diversely situated authors consider ideas and practices coming from various geographical and cultural contexts, particularly in solidarity with wider projects to address the Eurocentrism of Philosophy and the decolonization of knowledge-practices more generally.

Titles in the Series
Rancière and Performance
Edited by Nic Fryer and Colette Conroy
Experiments in Listening (forthcoming)
By Rajni Shah
The Critical Introduction to Salomo Friedlaender-Mnyona: 20th Century Performance Philosopher (forthcoming)
Edited by Detlef Thiel and Alice Lagaay; by Salomo Friedlaender/Mynona
Art Disarming Philosophy: Non-philosophy and Aesthetics (forthcoming)
Edited by Steven Shakespeare; Niamh Malone and Gary Anderson
Performance in the Age of Ecological Crisis (forthcoming)
By Tuija Kokkonen

Rancière and Performance

Edited by
Nic Fryer and Colette Conroy

ROWMAN & LITTLEFIELD
Lanham • Boulder • New York • London

Published by Rowman & Littlefield
An imprint of The Rowman & Littlefield Publishing Group, Inc.
4501 Forbes Boulevard, Suite 200, Lanham, Maryland 20706
www.rowman.com

6 Tinworth Street, London SE11 5AL, United Kingdom

Selection and editorial matter © 2021 by Colette Conroy and Nic Fryer
Copyright in individual chapters is held by the respective chapter authors.

All rights reserved. No part of this book may be reproduced in any form or by any electronic or mechanical means, including information storage and retrieval systems, without written permission from the publisher, except by a reviewer who may quote passages in a review.

British Library Cataloguing in Publication Information Available

ISBN HB: 978-1-53814-657-6

Library of Congress Cataloging-in-Publication Data

Names: Fryer, Nic, 1970– editor. | Conroy, Colette, 1973– editor.
Title: Rancière and performance / edited by Nic Fryer and Colette Conroy.
Description: Lanham : Rowman & Littlefield, [2021] | Series: Performance philosophy | Includes bibliographical references and index.
Identifiers: LCCN 2020040169 (print) | LCCN 2020040170 (ebook) | ISBN 9781538146576 (cloth) | ISBN 9781538146583 (epub)
Subjects: LCSH: Rancière, Jacques. | Theater—Philosophy.
Classification: LCC PN2039 R256 2021 (print) | LCC PN2039 (ebook) | DDC 792.01—dc23
LC record available at https://lccn.loc.gov/2020040169
LC ebook record available at https://lccn.loc.gov/2020040170

Contents

Introduction: Rancière's Theatrocracy Within and Beyond the Theatre   1
Nic Fryer

PART I: AESTHETICS AND POLITICS, POLITICS AND AESTHETICS   15

1. The Politics of Aesthetics, in a State of Disruption   17
   Ryan Anthony Hatch

2. Soft Shivers, Sweaty Politics: Dramaturgy, Politics of Perception and the Pensive Body   39
   Liesbeth Groot Nibbelink

PART II: THE ROLE OF THEATRE AND PERFORMANCE   57

3. Performing Philosophy: Rancière as Playwright, Director and Performer in *The Ignorant Schoolmaster*   59
   Shulamith Lev-Aladgem

4. Staging the People: Performance, Presence and Representation   81
   Adrian Kear

5. 'Apart, We Are Together. Together, We Are Apart': Rancière's Community of Translators in Theory and Theatre   101
   Nic Fryer

PART III: SPECTATORSHIP AND PARTICIPATION   123

6. Nights of Theatrical Labour in the Victorian Workhouse   125
   Jenny Hughes

| 7 | The Emancipated Educator: Chance, Will and Equality in Higher Education Role-Immersion Pedagogies
Will Shüler | 147 |

PART IV: PERFORMANCE AS POLITICAL DISRUPTION — 169

8	Resisting Rancière *Janelle Reinelt*	171
9	Dissensual Reproductions in You Should See the Other Guy's *Land of the Three Towers* *Caoimhe Mader McGuinness*	195
10	The Paradoxes of Performing Activism: Art, Oil and Liberate Tate *Stephen Scott-Bottoms*	215

| Index | 237 |
| About the Contributors | 245 |

Introduction

Rancière's Theatrocracy Within and Beyond the Theatre

Nic Fryer

Jacques Rancière's writing over the last fifty years offers a range of ways of reflecting on both the art form of theatre and of performance more broadly. The relationship between spectator and artwork, so central to much performance and theatre theory, has been core to his writing on aesthetics. And although Rancière has engaged directly with theatre less frequently than with other art forms, an interest in theatricality and performativity runs throughout his work to the extent that Hallward (2006) has described his work as proposing a 'theatrocracy'.

This collection was inspired by the implications of his interest in theatre, but also by the high level of interest many theatre and performance scholars have taken in his work. In this collection, we have sought to incorporate writings covering his work from a range of perspectives. We have sought to consider how the notion of theatrocracy in his work might enhance understanding of the potential and limitations of his wider philosophical project. We have also sought to consider how his ideas might be applied to and illuminate understanding of theatre, both generally as an art form and in relation to specific theatrical examples. Finally, we have sought to consider how specific examples of theatre and performance both within and beyond the theatre might in turn enrich understandings of his writing.

Before discussing the book itself, I begin with a historical event which offers rich opportunities for Rancièrian analysis. On Friday, 18 November 2016, two months before Donald Trump was inaugurated as the president of the United States, his running mate Mike Pence attended the celebrated musical *Hamilton* in New York. After a bruising and controversial election campaign, the country was in a state of high emotion. Pence's attendance drew attention from the audience: as Joanna Walters notes, 'Patrons did not lose sight of the irony of a strong conservative, with a record of opposition against gay rights, attending a hip-hop musical with a pointedly diverse cast' (2016). The audience both cheered and (more loudly) booed him, and 'certain moments in the play (particularly those that celebrated the power and influence of minorities and immigrants) garnered extended applause from the audience' (Gasoi 2017, 41). At the curtain call, the actor Brandon Victor Dixon, who played Aaron Burr in the show, delivered a scripted speech as Mike Pence got up to leave. I quote the speech in full because I want to return to its specifics, particularly its respectful tone, later:

> You know, we have a guest in the audience this evening. Vice-President Elect Pence, I see you walking out but I hope you will hear us just a few more moments. There is nothing to boo here, ladies and gentlemen, there is nothing to boo here, we are all here sharing a story of love. We have a bit of a message for you sir, and we hope you will hear us out. And I encourage everyone to pull out your phones and tweet and post because this message needs to be spread far and wide, OK? Vice-President Elect Pence, we welcome you and we truly thank you for joining the audience here at *Hamilton: An American Musical*, we really do. We sir, we are the diverse Americans who are alarmed and anxious that your new administration will not protect us, our planet, our children, our parents; or defend us and uphold our inalienable rights, sir. . . . But we truly hope that this show has inspired you to uphold our American values and to work on behalf of all of us, all of us. We thank you truly for sharing this show, this wonderful American story, told by a diverse group of men and women of different colours, creeds and orientations.

Pence then left, but Trump leapt to Pence's defence on Twitter, stating, 'Our wonderful future V.P. Mike Pence was harassed last night at the theatre by the cast of Hamilton, cameras blazing. This should not happen!', and in a second tweet stating, 'The Theater must always be a safe and special place. The cast of Hamilton was very rude last night to a very good man, Mike Pence. Apologize!' Needless to say, Dixon refused, stating, 'There's nothing to apologise for. If people are coming to see Hamilton to leave their politics behind, you came to the wrong show' (quoted in Jamieson 2016).

An obvious application of Rancière's ideas to Dixon's speech might be to see it as an example of Rancière's definition of politics. Rancière asserts that politics 'stands in direct opposition to the police' (Rancière 2010, 36). He uses the term 'police' not only in a literal sense. For him, institutions like the police symbolize authority and convention. They function to support what Rancière calls the 'distribution of the sensible'. This term reflects the ways in which authority, through the guise of what he calls the 'sensible order', 'parcels out places and forms of participation in a common world by first establishing the modes of perception within which these are inscribed' (Rockhill 2004, 85). These modes of perception normalize the assigning of social roles and the institution of social norms to the extent that what is actually a culturally specific 'parcelling-out' process is hidden. This is exemplified for Rancière in the police call to 'move along! There's nothing to see here!' (Rancière 2010, 37). Politics as Rancière conceives it, on the other hand, disrupts these modes of perception and renders them visible. It 'consists in transforming this space of "moving-along" [. . . and] is the instituting of a dispute over the distribution of the sensible' (2010, 37). Through doing and saying things beyond the normal order of things, the sensible is revealed as contingent, and other possibilities to the sensible are realized: 'Politics, before all else, is an intervention in the visible and the sayable' (2010, 37).

Dixon's action might also be seen as an example of this, with his intervention challenging what it is possible to do/say during the normal, 'sensible' theatrical convention of the curtain call. Dixon subverts the convention of the silent actor submitting to the audience with his subservient, respectful bow. Rather, he functions as an actor articulating a voice beyond his character in the theatrical space, insisting on the silent audience, including the vice-president, listening to him. Challenges to 'sensible' theatrical conventions viewed through a Rancièrian frame also occur in many chapters in this collection. Liesbeth Groot Nibbelink outlines challenges to conventions around bodies on stage, Adrian Kear outlines challenges to representations of community, Jenny Hughes outlines challenges to the spectator–performer relationship, Caoimhe Mader McGuinness outlines challenges to representations of class and gender representation, and Stephen Scott-Bottoms outlines challenges to the conventions of the art gallery. Each instance functions not only as novel but also as political: shifting the perspective of the spectator's relationship to what he is seeing.

In a statement that chimes with Hallward's depiction of Rancière as proposing a 'theatrocracy', Rancière further suggests that 'politics is the constitution of a theatrical and artificial sphere' (quoted in Citton 2009, 130). Dixon's act does not do away with the artifice of the theatrical relationship but draws on it to create a different artificial sphere beyond social norms: outside the theatre Pence would probably not listen to someone directly challenging him in silence. In this sphere the outside world intrudes into the theatrical space from which is usually clearly delineated; in this sphere the orator Mike Pence is turned into a listener. This sphere may only be temporary and artificial, but for a moment a different set of possible social relations are glimpsed. It is this breaking of theatrical convention that seems to most bother Trump: 'The Theater must always be a safe and special place,' he tweeted, outlining the sensible conception of theatre where normal relations are suspended in favour of the prevailing theatrical event. By contrast, reconstituting the space away from the event is seen as creating a lack of safety, specialness and is, in Trump's word, 'rude'. Yet since the courtesy of Dixon's speech is palpable both in terms of language and its delivery, it is arguably the performative breaking of the sensible, usually invisible, rules of theatrical engagement that most offends here. And the offence reveals the challenge that can be laid down when an 'intervention in the visible and sayable' occurs.

Perhaps another part of the 'rudeness' Trump detects is premised on the passivity of Pence as a seated spectator. On *Hannity*, a programme screened the day after the event by the famously pro-Trump Fox News, the presenter Ainsley Earhardt goes so far as to equate the treatment with bullying: 'Imagine sitting and you feel – it's kind of bullying a little bit. Imagine sitting in the audience and everyone is looking at you and booing you and *they're giving you a lecture when you're there to see them*' (quoted in International Wire 2016, emphasis mine). Larry Elder states on the same programme: 'The man is coming to see a play and an actor gives him a lecture about diversity and about protecting America? Are you kidding me?' (quoted in International Wire, 2016). For Trump and his supporters the poor defenceless Mike Pence, sitting there without power or a voice, is pitted against the angry active liberal mob, 'cameras blazing'.

This notion of the passive spectator as a distribution of the sensible is identified by Rancière as common in theatre discourse. In his well-known article 'The Emancipated Spectator', which explicitly discusses theatre, he suggests that in this conception 'to be a spectator is to be separated from both the capacity to know and the power to act' (Rancière 2009a, 2). According to Rancière, this has led theatre practitioners such as Brecht and Artaud to try to find ways of involving the audience: as Rancière puts it, theatre 'accuses itself of rendering its spectators passive' and 'assigns itself the mission of reversing its effects' (2009a, 7). However, Rancière challenges this presumption, suggesting that 'we need to recognise the [...] activity peculiar to the spectator' (2009a, 17). In other words, there is no reason to assume that Pence is inevitably passive during Dixon's speech. Regardless of his own capacity to talk back or walk out, there is an active processing as someone listens to and watches another, and spectators 'play the role of active interpreters, who develop their own translation in order to appropriate the "story" and make it their own story' (Rancière 2009a, 22). (Challenges to notions of the passive spectator are also taken up by Jenny Hughes and Will Shüler in part III, 'Spectatorship and Participation', of this volume.)

It is interesting that despite his political allies rushing to his defence, Pence is markedly less bothered by the speech than Trump: he said, 'I did hear what was said from the stage. [...] I can tell you I wasn't offended by what was said. I will leave to others whether that was the appropriate venue to say it' (quoted in Jamieson 2016). He also claimed he nudged his daughter after hearing the boos and cheers 'and I said, remember, Charlotte, that's what freedom sounds like' (quoted in International Wire 2016). Pence's uncompromising attitude to abortion and gay rights, among many other things, is well documented, but it is notable that here he seems to relish the debate. Perhaps, Rancière might argue, he did not experience passivity in his role as spectator. (One might indeed argue that, rightly or wrongly, Dixon's deferential tone could have led him to feel respected.)

Pence is of course an extremely privileged man used to experiencing power. But for Rancière the notion of the active spectator has political potential for all human beings. For example, he outlines workers recounting their experience of being spectators who stepped outside their sensible role: 'By making themselves spectators and visitors, they disrupted the distribution of the sensible which would have it that those who work do not have time to let their steps and gazes roam at random' (2009a, 19). Challenging a deterministic attitude to class consciousness, Rancière rather suggests that an aesthetic sensibility exists in all human beings. He writes about this at length in *Proletarian Nights* (originally published in English as *The Nights of Labour*), a book referred to by both Shulamith Lev-Aladgem and Jenny Hughes in this volume. In the book he outlines occurrences in nineteenth-century France where the working class' capacity to move beyond work, to dream and imagine, can be glimpsed. At one point he says, discussing a documentation of a performance, 'It is in the theater, the new temple of popular aspirations, that one can see the labouring class living its true life' (2012, 25). This notion that art can provide a radical space at a remove from the everyday occurs throughout his writing. Like his notion of the political outlined earlier, artistic events both stand at a distance from the everyday sensible order, and hence have the potential to imagine what might be possible, rather than what is. For him 'through the "free play" of aestheticization' the 'field of experience [is] severed from its traditional reference points' (Rancière 2010, 16). As such both politics and aesthetics can articulate the possibility of change.

However it is politics' and aesthetics' distinct characters that make this possible, and they should not, he warns, be collapsed into each other. For Rancière, according to Corcoran, 'To want to make politics and art disappear as singular processes is to miss the singular effects that they can bring about and to return them to the logic of consensus' (Corcoran 2010, 3). Therefore Rancière is suspicious of the notion of political art. 'Art is not, in the first instance, political because of the messages and sentiments it conveys concerning the state of the world. Neither is it political because of the manner in which it might choose to represent society's structures, or social groups, their conflicts or identities. It is political because of the very distance it takes with respect to these functions' (Rancière 2009b, 23). Hence in *The Politics of Aesthetics* it is the 'aesthetic regime' of art he valorizes, which 'strictly identifies art in the singular and frees it from any specific rule. [...] The aesthetic regime asserts the absolute singularity of art and at the same time destroys any pragmatic criterion for isolating this singularity' (2004, 23). This 'destroying' of criteria avoids art being sublimated into the sensible. He says, 'Police consists in saying: here is the definition of subversive art. Politics, on the other hand, says: no, there is no subversive form of art in and of itself; there is a sort of permanent guerrilla war being waged' (quoted in Battista 2017, 240). This war exists through the fight to maintain the alterity of art. Such a discussion is taken up by most of the writers in this volume, particularly Liesbeth Groot Nibbelink and Adrian Kear, who both identify the ways in which the performance events that they describe can reveal and/or create things invisible in normal discourse.

Rancière's notion of the constantly shifting aesthetic regime of art stands in contrast to political theatre that has a more direct intention, where politics are subsumed into the artwork. Dixon's assertion that 'if people are coming to see Hamilton to leave their politics behind, you came to the wrong show' perhaps suggests a very different conception of politics to Rancière's. *Hamilton* attempts to deal explicitly with politics through a range of elements: for example, its casting of minorities, its articulation of a female voice at the end of the show, its attempt to challenge conventional engagements with history or race. Rather than an example of the aesthetic regime, *Hamilton* might rather be read as having a well-intentioned desire to deal with 'the city's occupations' in a manner similar to that which Rancière identifies in the 'ethical' regime of art (2004, 21). By doing so, it arguably falls into the trap Rancière identifies in political art. For Rancière, by making its politics easily understood and contained, the work loses its power to provoke and question. It ultimately might also be seen as an example of an attempt to construct the spectator outlined in 'The Emancipated Spectator': someone who is assumed passive and in need of edification as she receives the parcelled out messages and issues that the performance outlines.

Therefore I think a Rancièrian analysis might be more interested in the moment of Dixon's speech and its fallout than by the elements of a musical which, however different to other musicals in musical style, ultimately has a relatively clear moral sense and intention. It might be more interested in the ambiguities and tensions created around Dixon's speech than his obvious attempt to challenge Pence which is clearly supported by a largely complicit audience. For example, a discussion of 'safety' in the theatre such as Trump's tweet presaged could be seen to destabilize assumptions about this word. How 'unsafe' is Dixon's speech, really? In what ways might a 'safe' theatre space be desirable, so that the spectator or participant can recognize a clearly demarcated space where normal relations can be suspended? Or might a 'safe' space suggest a lack of exploration or creative potential? How does

Dixon's polite articulation sit at odds with his implicit disagreement with Pence, and does this courtesy destabilize notions that they are only opposed? Is Dixon's suggestion to Pence that he is a 'fellow American' working for 'all of us' more destabilizing to Pence's normally divisive rhetoric than an openly hostile speech would have been? When questions such as these arise, certainties begin to be unsettled and 'truths' and clear hierarchies become unsettled. Hence this moment is political in the Rancièrian sense not because of its implicit challenge to Pence's politics but rather because of the *unfamiliarity of the moment*. And such moments occur as theatrical, or at least performative, in their occurrence as alternatives to current reality. In this volume, Caoimhe Mader McGuinness and Stephen Scott-Bottoms outline performances that are directly political not only in content but also in their aesthetic strategies. It is how these performances make things visible through the unfamiliarity of their aesthetic strategies that most evokes the interest of both writers. Indeed, Scott-Bottoms identifies how the activist collective Liberate Tate adapted their aesthetic strategies over time to avoid being co-opted by the very gallery they sought to confront. According to Peter Hallward, it is the unfamiliarity of performance and art that contains political potential for Rancière: he suggests that 'by refusing to speak in their own name, by acting at a distance from themselves or imitating the action of another, actors and poets threaten the very foundations of authority itself' (Hallward 2006, 113). To apply this to the *Hamilton* speech, Dixon is not only speaking as himself. He is drawing on a rhetorical device of courtesy within the artificial space of the theatre, developing a mode of speech and identity within a space that are all marked as beyond the everyday.

Eruptions of theatre, theatricality and performativity such as this are therefore at the centre of Rancière's political philosophy. Such occurrences of theatre and performance are specific moments in time and space that cannot be easily planned for or reproduced. However, this has led to Rancière's theatricality being identified as his problem. As Hallward notes, 'Its effects are unabashedly sporadic and intermittent' (2006, 123). Critics wanting to find a clear programme for political action in Rancière's writing are therefore likely to be disappointed. Indeed, Rancière himself explicitly disavows the likely effectiveness of political action: 'I don't think there are rules for good militant organisation. [...] All I can define are forms of perception, forms of utterance. As to how these are taken up by organisations, I must admit that I've never been able to endure any of them for very long, but I know I have nothing better to propose' (quoted in Battista 2017, 124–5). This refusal to articulate a clear sense of how his notion of art might be harnessed by politics has led to a great deal of frustration, including from Hallward as well as Janelle Reinelt and Ryan Anthony Hatch in this volume. Rancière offers a vision of sporadic resistance which has been labelled anarchic but ultimately rather limited. He is able to articulate the possibility of change but is not able to articulate sustainable solutions. Particularly in the current world climate, one might argue that developing sustainable alternatives is a key priority, not least in terms of environmental concerns. And theatre itself might want to claim a legacy beyond temporary change.

What remains is a set of writings which remain passionately committed to the possibility and power of human beings instigating performances of difference to the sensible; to their capacity to provoke and destabilize norms. The example utilized in this introduction is not a work of theatre but an event which I have called Rancièrian. I have done this not to move away from the art form of theatre but to recognize that the link between theatricality and politics in his work exists beyond as well as within the world of the arts. Despite his desire to place aesthetics as being discrete from politics, politics is always there in the analysis. What is important for him is that politics is not *collapsed into* aesthetics. Indeed, it is the aforementioned aesthetic regime of art which is most of interest to Rancière because it exists in its own irreducible unique space. In *Aisthesis*, for example, he takes a range of works of art that he sees as existing in the shifting aesthetic regime discussed previously, and locates them in 'the sensible fabric of experience within which they are produced' (Rancière 2013, x). His analysis outlines social and aesthetic conditions of the time, but also analyses the artworks as art, existing in their own discrete realm from these social conditions. And it is in the tension between the sensible world of the time and the artwork's potential to offer an alternative to this sensible world that his work remains political, in part at least: 'Art is inherently political for him insofar as it acts as a potential meeting ground between a configuration of the sensible world and possible reconfigurations thereof' (Rockhill 2009, 200).

If Rancière's commitment to committing to political structure remains vague, his commitment to art is much more palpable. Rancière said that his aim would be to speak of art providing 'a lightening, an alleviation. [...] The problem, first of all, is to create some breathing room' (Battista 2017, 234). This 'breathing room' is developed through 'aesthetic *separation* or aesthetic strangeness as that which alone can carry the promise of a new sensible world' (Rancière 2009b, 100–1). This separation or strangeness invites the spectator to place themselves in relation to the artwork and consider what it might offer. As he puts it, 'What interests me in the artworks that catch my attention is the problems they pose, and how they pose them' (Battista 2017, 266). Or, 'the aesthetic scene, properly speaking, thus turns out to be the scene of the irreconcilable' (Rancière 2009b, 103). For him it is in art that one best finds the potential to stimulate thought and debate: to instigate a process of the 'poetic labour of translation' (Rancière 2009a,

10) which is open to all human beings as they negotiate the artwork and its irreconcilable elements.

This focus on process emphasizes the specificity of the live event and the encounter between spectator and artwork so central to theatre and performance studies. Perhaps this desire to interrogate what is happening in the unique moment of each performance, or act, explains the mutual interest between Rancière and theatricality and Rancière and theatre/performance scholars. Throughout this book the chapters throughout reflect an interest in these specifics. Despite the very different works they discuss, throughout there is an engagement with both the politics of theatre and performance and the aesthetics employed in the works and ideas discussed. However, interest in the politics of performance events through a Rancièrian frame is articulated through a consideration of how the aesthetic strategies employed by the artwork provoke a relationship with the viewer, rather than how the artwork might provide an easily digestible reflection on the politics of the world. As such they also challenge the historical mode of theatre studies analysis, where work is there to be decoded and explained. Rather, the role of the critic might be to consider what the difficulty of decoding the performance creates in the spectator, how that which cannot easily be defined or contained is articulated, and what is created as a result of this articulation.

The importance of politics and its relationship to aesthetics therefore seemed to us to be a logical starting point for this collection, hence part I, 'Aesthetics and Politics, Politics and Aesthetics'. Here, writers seek to address some of the questions posed in this introduction about the relationship between politics and aesthetics, particularly Rancière's simultaneous insistence on both their independence and the ways in which politics 'has its own specific politics [... and] aesthetics itself has its own specific politics' (2009b, 46). The first chapter, Ryan Anthony Hatch's 'The Politics of Aesthetics, in a State of Disruption', poses a challenge to Rancière: Hatch suggests that Rancière's valorizing of the politically disruptive character of his aesthetic regime of art needs rethinking. He questions any notion that art is radical simply by virtue of its being art and suggests the need for a more complex analysis of the relationship between politics and aesthetics. He suggests that aesthetic disruption is often typical of contemporary capitalism rather than being a challenge to it, and instead asserts a need to 'think the politics of art beyond the spectacular logic of rupture'. Indeed, he suggests, politically there lies 'the difficult and mostly *unspectacular* work of formalization, the exigency of imagining and constructing a new order', which may be the most crucial job of politics in a fragmented dissonant world.

Liesbeth Groot Nibbelink's chapter, 'Soft Shivers, Sweaty Politics: Dramaturgy, Politics of Perception and the Pensive Body', also seeks to develop Rancière's notion of the politics of aesthetics. Noting Rancière's preference to 'analyse ideas or texts *about* the theatre rather than considering the embodied and experiential components that are also constitutive of the theatre event', she draws on analyses of three performance works which challenge neoliberal and rational notions of the body through a foregrounding of the corporeality of what she calls 'counter-bodies'. She suggests that an aesthetics which attends to such alternative corporealities provides space for the spectator through the difficulty of them finding a familiar reference point, and sees in such an aesthetics a development of Rancière's notion of the 'pensive image', where pensiveness goes hand in hand with the physical sensation and experience of sharing time and space with such bodies.

Part II, 'The Role of Theatre and Performance', brings the notion of theatre and performance themselves to the fore, considering how theatre and performance function in Rancière's writing as well as offering some specific examples of performances which seem to reflect some of Rancière's ideas. Shulamith Lev-Aladgem's 'Performing Philosophy: Rancière as Playwright, Director and Performer in *The Ignorant Schoolmaster*' draws on Mackenzie and Porter's notion of 'dramatization' to analyse the rhetorical devices Rancière uses in this early text. The book functions, she suggests, as an exemplar of his move from conventional political philosophy towards art and, specifically, performance: politically 'from criticism to activism'. She suggests that the book 'strives to appear as if it were an oral text – a live performance facilitated by a storyteller who is also playwright, director and performer'.

Taking Rancière's own notion of 'staging the people' as a starting point, Adrian Kear's 'Staging the People: Performance, Presence and Representation' looks at the impossibility of theatre ever fully representing any notion of 'the people'. Not only is such a task ontologically impossible, because it cannot contain all the variety within any notion of 'the people', the apparatus of staging itself further obfuscates any attempt. Yet embedded within any attempt to articulate the people exists real individuals and collective groups. The works Kear cites reflect this tension, drawing 'attention to the apparatus of representation as that which produces absence even as it claims presence as its effect'. The people remain staged but not fully represented.

My own chapter, '"Apart, we are together. Together, we are apart": Rancière's Community of Translators in Theory and Theatre', also seeks to suggest the complexity of community in theatrical representation and in the theatrical relationship between spectator and performer. Applying Rancière's ideas to a production of Duncan Macmillan's *People, Places and Things*, I suggest how the production, I saw revealed a desire to collectivize while retaining autonomy in the stage action, but also invited an individual response in the spectator within the community of the audience. In so doing, I seek to identify the importance of community and collectivity alongside an emphasis on individuality and rupture in Rancière's writing.

Arguably one of the most important contributions of Rancière's thought to theatre and performance studies has been his thoughts on how we view artwork, particularly theatre, and what any notion of 'participation' in artwork might mean. Part III of the book, 'Spectatorship and Participation', addresses this element of Rancière's writing. Jenny Hughes's 'Nights of Theatrical Labour in the Victorian Workhouse' looks at a theatrical entertainment given by a company of music hall performers from Collins' Music Hall to an audience of paupers in Islington workhouse in London in 1891. She outlines her intent to emphasize the paupers, 'silent witnesses' who were the spectators, as part of an attempt to develop a 'dissensual historiographical practice'. As a means to 'hear' the workhouse spectators, Hughes draws on historical accounts alongside Rancière's *The Philosopher and His Poor*, which outlined the limiting ways in which the working class were categorized and defined, and *The Nights of Labour*, in which he sought to outline the range of ways in which the working class participated in artistic activities. She uses Rancière's ideas to speculate on how this entertainment attempted to control the poor of the workhouse in its content while also offering dissensual elements that disrupted their everyday life: as she puts it, 'The performance provided a counter to the repressive context in which it occurred, while also subjecting both performers and audience to disciplining forms of performative social work.'

Will Shüler's chapter, 'The Emancipated Educator: Chance, Will and Equality in Higher Education Role-Immersion Pedagogies', takes Rancière's book *The Ignorant Schoolmaster*, and its theory of universal education, as a starting point to interrogate Shüler's own experiments with a role-immersion game approach in the classroom. In this approach, the teacher 'works to subvert or dissolve the classroom and institutional hierarchies which create distance between teachers and students' by facilitating creative play where students take on specific subject positions in a fictional scenario. Drawing on theories of play, he suggests that the open-ended nature of such activities and the opportunity for students to engage in 'reasoning between equals' create strong engagement and an understanding of a range of perspectives.

Part IV, 'Performance as Political Disruption', offers three responses to Rancière's provocation that politics is 'the constitution of a theatrical and artificial sphere' (quoted in Citton 2009, 130). The first chapter, Janelle Reinelt's 'Resisting Rancière', argues for a need to theorize politics beyond temporary theatrical/performative moments. Drawing on several contemporary real-world examples, she identifies a need for more nuance in politics than Rancière's binaries (such as dissensus/consensus or politics/police) offer. Doing so, she argues, could recognize the need to move beyond disruption towards the building of meaningful real-world change. Similarly, she sees a need for greater nuance from Rancière's theatrical acolytes who fear art being subsumed into political didacticism. She argues that it is perfectly possible for theatre to address politics in a range of varied ways, forming 'political affinities among diverse constituencies through performances that illuminate injustice, push back against power and evoke a political "we"', without descending into 'overly didactic messages directed at supposed ignorant spectators by presumptuous producers'.

Such an example might be seen in Caoimhe Mader McGuinness's 'Dissensual Reproductions in You Should See the Other Guy's *Land of the Three Towers*'. She discusses a protest by mothers in Stratford, London, who occupied a 'half-emptied housing estate' in protest at the local council's housing policy. She argues that their protest functioned as a realization of Rancièrian dissensus. She sees their protest, and open-mic nights and theatrical work developed in collaboration with the campaign, as manifestations of the kind of artistic labour Rancière outlines in *The Nights of Labour*: revealing the capacity of people normally considered absent from the artistic sphere. In this case, she argues, the campaign and its associated theatrical work made visible the often unseen nature of working-class women and their socially reproductive labour.

Stephen Scott-Bottoms's 'The Paradoxes of Performing Activism: Art, Oil and Liberate Tate' also outlines several performances/works which made visible what was previously hidden: in the case of the activist group Liberate Tate, the complicity between the Tate Gallery and the oil giant BP. Documenting their work over several years, he notes transitions in the aesthetic strategies employed in their work over time, and maps this on to the categories outlined by Rancière in 'The Paradoxes of Political Art'. Both drawing on and challenging different elements of Rancière's thought, he notes both the difficulty in claiming a direct political efficacy to their work while also making a claim for the political resonances that their work offers. Ultimately, in his conclusion, while avoiding any claim of direct causality between Liberate Tate's actions and the Tate's decision to stop their relationship with BP, he articulates the possibility of a relationship between politics and performance that is fruitful. The creation of a theatrical and artificial sphere here is indeed political – but not necessarily in a direct sense. Indeed, it is partly the very autonomy of the theatrical and artificial sphere that has political potency.

We hope that this collection embraces a range of varied and sometimes conflicting perspectives on Rancière's relationship to performance. With Rancière's own celebration of dissensus, any Rancièrian approach would arguably embrace such heterogeneity. Hallward's description of Rancière's work as proposing a 'theatrocracy' draws on Plato, for whom the term (according to Hallward) imagines 'a regime of unlicensed ignorance and disorder that has its source in a "universal confusion of musical forms" initiated by irresponsible artists' (Hallward 2006, 112). We might not go that far in our claims for this book (for good or ill). Nonetheless, in addition to the range of perspectives offered here, something common emerges across the chapters: a shared sense that theatre and performance, which in their very essence exist in space marked as beyond or separate from the everyday, can offer a stage when all sorts of new possibilities can be glimpsed. Such possibilities may only be temporary, inadequate or unhelpful, whether onstage or off. Yet the possibility of change will persist as what theatre and performance offer keeps shifting, continuously constructing what Rancière defined in relation to the politics of art as 'sensible landscapes and the formation of modes of seeing that deconstruct consensus while forging new possibilities and capacities' (Rancière quoted in Battista 2017, 246).

REFERENCES

Battista, Emiliano, ed. 2017. *Dissenting Words: Interviews with Jacques Rancière*. Translated by Emiliano Battista. London/New York, NY: Bloomsbury.

Citton, Yves. 2009. 'Political Agency and the Ambivalence of the Sensible'. In *Jacques Rancière: History, Politics, Aesthetics*, edited by Gabriel Rockhill and Philip Watts, 120–139. London: Duke University Press.

Corcoran, Steven. 2010. 'Introduction to Jacques Rancière'. In *Dissensus: On Politics and Aesthetics*, 1–24. Cambridge/Malden: Polity.

Hallward, Peter. 2006. 'Staging Equality: On Rancière's Theatrocracy'. *New Left Review* 37 (January/February), 109–129.

International Wire. 2016. 'Interview With Vice President-Elect Governor Mike Pence …'. [Online]. https://search.proquest.com/docview/1842667028?accountid=7179. Accessed 11th September 2019.

Jamieson, Amber. 2016. 'Hamilton Actor Defends Speech to Mike Pence: "There's Nothing to Apologize For"'. *The Guardian*. https://www.theguardian.com/stage/2016/nov/21/hamilton-actor-defends-speech-mike-pence-donald-trump. Accessed 11th September 2019.

McWhorter, Jon. 2016. 'Will *Hamilton* Save the Musical? Don't Wait for It'. *American Theatre*, March, 48–52.

Panagia, Davide. 2018. *Rancière's Sentiments*. Durham, NC: Duke University Press.

Rancière, Jacques. 1999. *Disagreement*. Translated by Julie Rose. Minneapolis, MN: University of Minnesota Press.

Rancière, Jacques. 2004. *The Politics of Aesthetics: The Distribution of The Sensible*. Translated by Gabriel Rockhill. London/New York, NY: Continuum.

Rancière, Jacques. 2009a. *The Emancipated Spectator*. Translated by Gregory Elliott. London/New York, NY: Verso.

Rancière, Jacques. 2009b. *Aesthetics and Its Discontents*. Translated by Steven Corcoran. Cambridge/Malden: Polity.

Rancière, Jacques. 2010. *Dissensus: On Politics and Aesthetics*. Translated by Steven Corcoran. Cambridge/Malden: Polity.
Rancière, Jacques. 2012. *Proletarian Nights: The Workers' Dream in Nineteenth Century France*. Translated by Zakir Paul. London/New York, NY: Verso.
Rancière, Jacques. 2013. *Aisthesis: Scenes from the Aesthetic Regime of Art*. Translated by David Fernbach. London/New York, NY: Verso.
Rockhill, Gabriel. 2004. 'Glossary of Technical Terms'. In *The Politics of Aesthetics: The Distribution of the Sensible*, edited by Gabriel Rockhill. London/New York, NY: Continuum.
Rockhill, Gabriel. 2009. 'The Politics of Aesthetics: Political History and the Hermeneutics of Art'. In *Jacques Rancière: History, Politics, Aesthetics*, edited by Gabriel Rockhill and Philip Watts, 195–215. London: Duke University Press.
Walters, Joanna. 2016. 'Trump Demands Apology from Hamilton Cast After Mike Pence Booed'. *The Guardian*. https://www.theguardian.com/us-news/2016/nov/19/mike-pence-booed-at-hamilton-performance-then-hears-diversity-plea. Accessed 11th September 2019.

Part I

AESTHETICS AND POLITICS, POLITICS AND AESTHETICS

Chapter 1

The Politics of Aesthetics, in a State of Disruption

Ryan Anthony Hatch

Evading a certain type of critique often occurs at the cost of satisfying criticisms of a different kind, so that opponents find themselves disoriented, even making common cause with a capitalism they earlier claimed to be contesting.

—Boltanski and Chiapello 2005, 167

We start to think we are doing something new only to realize that capitalism shares our fascination with novelty.

—Dean 2018, 115

The requirement to innovate is, if one likes, the only reality manifested in culture.

—Groys 2014, 7

The significance of Jacques Rancière's contribution to the theory and practice of art would be difficult to overstate. Taken together, his investigations of literature, cinema, performance and the visual arts amount to a reconceptualization of the work of art, in terms of both its ontological status and the kind of work it can perform in the world. What distinguishes this rethinking is the specific, and radical, gesture of historicization from which it sets out. Art, Rancière argues, must not be considered a neutral, transhistorical name for designating a common field of objects and events; rather, it delimits a specific and fundamentally historical form of experience, the contours of which come into being only at the dawn of our own era. Prior to the second half of the eighteenth century, what we talk about when we talk about art simply did not exist, because the complex conditions on account of which things of art show up did not yet exist.

Rancière calls the perceptual framework to which these conditions give shape the *aesthetic regime*. It is from within this regime alone that art as we know it (along with the very possibility of speaking of *art* in the singular, rather than of *the arts*, each with its own well-defined parameters) emerges in its conceptual specificity. Yet, as he is keen to emphasize, this specificity turns on a paradox: art can be said to exist as an autonomous field precisely insofar as it is constituted by the absence of a limit, the absence, that is to say, of any fixed criteria by means of which one would be able to legislate what does and does not belong to it (Rancière 2013, x). Indeed, works 'count' as works of art within the aesthetic regime in part because they blur the boundary that would separate art from non-art.

More is at issue here than one might first suppose. For one thing, Rancière's approach would seem to undo, in a single stroke, the binary opposition of autonomy (*art is a distinct domain*) and heteronomy (*because it is that domain to which nothing doesn't potentially belong*) on which a great deal of modern aesthetic theory depends. More important still, the contrast between this new framework and the one it sublates – what he calls the mimetic or representative regime of the arts – gives a clear indication that something irreducibly political is at stake in the 'aesthetic revolution' that gives rise to art as an experiential category at once singular, generic and heterogeneous. Prior to this revolution, classical thought apprehended the various fine arts as arranged in a fixed, hierarchical schema and expressive of a fixed social hierarchy, in so far as each art forged an 'organic' link between its specific mode of representation and the subject matter considered proper to it. Thus, as Rancière explains in *Aisthesis: Scenes from the Aesthetic Regime of Art*, the superiority of the dramatic poem was bound up with the established superiority of the 'men of action' to whose exploits the poet devoted, as a matter of course, the mimetic powers of his craft:

> The representative order [...] defined discourse as a body with well-articulated parts, the poem as a plot, and a plot as an order of actions. This order clearly situated the poem [...] on a hierarchical model: a well-ordered body where the upper part commands the lower, the privilege of action, that is to say of the free man, capable of acting according to ends, over the repetitive lives of men without quality. (Rancière 2013, xiv)

The poem mattered, we can say, because its subject belonged to the class of men that mattered in and to the classical world. Within the representative regime, the work was therefore mimetic *twice over*: beyond deploying the conventional techniques of figuration we continue to refer to as mimetic today, its *treatment* of its subject was in imitative harmony with the way such a subject was to be treated in the world. Plainly put, the fine arts participated in a logic of inequality, as its supposedly 'natural' expression and as its effectively naturalizing instrument: the heightened language through which the poet disclosed the noble protagonist's thoughts, speeches, and deeds was taken for granted as the sign and consequence of this figure's stature. It is against this background that the emergence of art at the dawn of modernity takes on its full significance. For, if the representative regime amounts to a schema of fixed correspondences – 'of concordance between sense and sense', that is, 'between the complex of sensory signs through which the process of *poiesis* is displayed and the complex of forms of perception through which it is felt and understood' (Rancière 2009b, 60) – then the aesthetic regime is what happens when these links are finally broken. In their place is established a new and differently ordered sensorium, founded on a principle of radical equality. Glossing Schiller, Rancière asserts that the 'aesthetic free appearance and free play' that constitute the aesthetic regime 'challenge [...] the distribution of the sensible that sees in the order of domination a difference between two humanities' (Rancière 2009, 32). That any material whatsoever can belong to the sensory field of art means, of course, that nothing in particular belongs there more than any other thing – and, by extension, that there can no longer be any determinate ratio between the work's 'content' and how it makes this content available to us. Hence Wordsworth's exemplary declaration, in the 'Preface' to the second edition of *Lyrical Ballads*, that what distinguishes his (and Coleridge's) poetry as truly modern is the fact 'that the feeling therein developed gives importance to the action and situation, and not the action and situation to the feeling' (Wordsworth and Coleridge 2013, 99). One can scarcely imagine a more compact and precise formula for what in Rancière's view constitutes the political essence of aesthetic revolution: the unique powers of the work of art are emancipated from their historical obligation to harmonize with social power.

It should hardly come as a surprise that, especially where the heterogeneous objects, practices, situations and events gathered under the equivocal name 'contemporary art' are concerned, Rancière's interrogations of the nature and stakes of aesthetic experience have become indispensable reference points – not only, and perhaps not even principally, within the restricted sphere of academic philosophies of art. Conceptual artist Liam Gillick considers Rancière's work 'compulsory reading' and speaks of his ideas as 'a structural justification' (Gillick 2007, 268) for his own practice. In a breathless paean, Thomas Hirschhorn declares that 'Jacques Rancière gives me the *strength* to keep my *eternal flame* burning for art' (Hirschhorn 2007, 261, emphasis in original). It bears mentioning that the texts from which these statements are sourced appeared together in a special issue of *Artforum* devoted to Rancière, which brought together major artists, curators and scholars to reflect on his place in the art world. Included in this special issue is a brief text by interdisciplinary artist Paul Chan, in which, reflecting on the political implications of certain artistic gestures as well as on the aesthetic implications of certain political strategies, Chan asks, 'How do we verify, following Rancière, the efficacy of our practice' (Chan 2007, 261)? That Chan would speak of Rancière's theorizations of the aesthetic not only as an evaluative metric for his and others' practice but moreover in the decidedly prescriptive and instrumentalizing terms of establishing, or opening the question of, that practice's efficacy underscores the extraordinary position his texts occupy in the broader apparatus of contemporary art.

The central aim of this chapter is to elaborate a critique of what I take to be the essential claim in Rancière's aesthetic theory. As such, it will have important implications for how we situate this theory in relation to the medium of performance and within the field of performance studies. Beyond these, I am even more interested in the capacity of this critique to occasion, or at least participate in, a broader critical reassessment of the politics of performance – both in the realm of aesthetic practices and as a dimension of collective emancipatory struggle. Yet what follows must be understood mainly as the critical prolegomenon to any such reassessment, wherein I hope to present a sufficiently developed framework for further inquiry, and to suggest some of the paths further inquiry might take. Their originality and subtlety notwithstanding, Rancière's often pathbreaking reflections ultimately depend on a sweeping central premise about the relation of art to politics the soundness of which has been neither effectively demonstrated nor sufficiently put into question.

Not incidentally, this foundational premise is precisely what accounts for his unique appeal in and to the contemporary art world, where, as Bettina Funcke has observed, his statements have become useful at a suspiciously intuitive level. 'Perhaps the biggest problem with the art world's reception of Rancière's ideas', Funcke writes, 'is that they are often applied in an overtly direct way. They're handy' (Funcke 2007, 284). Granted, if certain not altogether disinterested readers come away from his texts with a handily simplified misprision of the shape and stakes of his thought, he is not entirely to blame. But neither is he entirely innocent, for it strikes me that the central premise I wish to interrogate here does in fact lend itself to just such a too-simple 'application' – it makes itself a little too handy. In navigating the space between what Rancière's text 'really' declares and the 'practical' uses and misuses to which some of his interlocutors have put these declarations, I in fact borrow the spirit of my critical approach from Rancière himself, who began *Althusser's Lesson* – his trenchant critique of his former teacher's theoreticist Marxism and its profound failure to account for the uprisings of May 1968 – by announcing that his text was intended to be a commentary on the lesson in Marxism that Louis Althusser gives to John Lewis. It is a reflection on what this lesson wants to teach us, and on what it actually teaches us, not about Marxist theory itself, but about the present reality of Marxism, that is to say, about what constitutes the discourse of an acknowledged Marxist in 1973. (Rancière 2011, xix)

I am similarly concerned here both with what Rancière's text wants to teach us and what, in excess of and perhaps in contradiction with this textual will, it in fact teaches us about what can show up at the intersection of politics and aesthetics from within the confines of our present reality. The point is to arrive at a more complex understanding of Rancière's central declaration, not in order to redeem it but instead to articulate as precisely as possible what within it makes it problematic, and thus to avoid replacing vague celebration with vague condemnation. My wager is that the ease with which Rancière's thought has circulated among artists and curators, the placid enthusiasm of its reception, needs to be approached as a symptom. It needs to be read, that is to say, as indexing a crucial moment at which the theory fails to address one of the most urgent questions facing contemporary art and aesthetic thought today: namely, how to think the politics of art beyond the spectacular logic of rupture, given the degree to which neoliberal capital has co-opted and neutralized this once-subversive logic.

Of course, the rapport between Rancière and his objects of inquiry – the fact that he has 'become increasingly interested in contemporary art, even as the art world, in neat symmetry, has become increasingly interested in him' (Funcke 2007, 283) – could in part be considered a practical consequence of his commitment to the axiom of the equality of intelligences. Rancière discovered this axiom in the course of his research on the obscure nineteenth-century pedagogue Joseph Jacotot, who bore witness to it when he found he was capable of effectively teaching to others what he himself did not know. This key discovery, which gains its full significance against the backdrop of Rancière's break with Althusser in the wake of the events of May 1968, has determined not only the diverse topical foci of his investigations but also and more importantly the singular method by which these investigations unfold and address themselves to what is theorized there. Rancière rejects the model of theoretical work whereby the philosopher-expert explains to and on behalf of the artist the truths latent in what she is doing and making but that she is incapable of understanding on her own, in the expert's absence. 'I never say what should be done or how to do it,' he declares (Carnevale and Kalsey 2007, 269). This may well be true – though Paul Chan's characterization of Rancière's text as containing something against which the artist verifies the efficacy of his practice seems to complicate things – and yet, what in fact sets his work apart is not that it eschews prescriptiveness but rather that it refuses the symptomatizing-explanatory gesture that would reveal the ideas the artist transmits on the condition that they remain opaque to her, that she transmits them by accident.

While the egalitarian dimension of his inquiry thus surely figures in the 'neat symmetry' of Rancière's relationship with contemporary artists, what seems truly decisive here is the rather more banal fact that his account of the relation of art to the political has the effect of gratifying its artist-addressee. His analyses suggest to the contemporary artist an ennobling, idealizing image of her practice to the extent that they depend on the remarkable presupposition that the work of art 'does' politics *simply in so far as it is a work of art*. That is, if the work of art can be said to have something to do with politics, this is not thanks to its engagement with any particular political content (progressive, reactionary or otherwise), nor even to the 'politics' of the formal resources it deploys (unless, as we shall see, we conceive of form in the most basic sense): 'Art is not, in the first instance, political because of the messages and sentiments it conveys concerning the state of the world. Neither is it political because of the manner in which it might choose to represent society's structures, or social groups, their conflicts or identities' (Rancière 2009, 23). Rancière's text effectively declares that, from within the field of the aesthetic regime of art, whatever the artist brings into being will be political, full stop. That there is nothing but political art means, for one thing, that the various frameworks through which artists and scholars of art alike have established criteria to identify 'political art' as a particular subset of artistic production, or distinguish between different politico-aesthetic orientations ('bourgeois', 'radical' and so on), in fact entail a fundamental misapprehension regarding the nature of the aesthetic. 'There is', Rancière proclaims, 'no conflict between the purity of art and its politicization' (Rancière 2009, 32). To properly situate the singularity of this position, it will be worth underscoring that Rancière is *not* making the by-now fairly common claim that any work of art, no matter how little it concerns itself with politics, can be shown to have political 'implications', that is, can be read in such a way that the political assumptions or orientations inscribed and dissimulated therein are brought to the light of day. Such a claim depends on a concept and framework conspicuous in their absence from Rancière's discourse in the wake of his break from Althusserianism – namely, the notion of ideology and its attendant mode of critique, whereby the theorist-master decrypts the ideological mechanisms that function through the work only as long as they remain concealed on its surface. Again, the symptomatizing-explanatory gesture has no place in a Rancièrist approach.

A matter of neither implications nor unconscious inscriptions, the artwork's politicity is, in Rancière's thought, located in the fundamental action it always already performs, the way that its being in the world acts on the world. The aesthetic is directly, immediately political. One can see quite clearly in what sense this framework might run the risk of becoming 'handy' to the art world. It imputes a certain prestige to the labour of the artist that at once signals and forestalls the anxiety that the idea of the aesthetic itself continues to provoke in us. Claire Bishop has persuasively argued that this theorization of the politics of aesthetics entails at least two major drawbacks: first, as we have observed, 'it opens the door for all art to be political' and second, it 'tends to sidestep the question of how we might more specifically address the ideological affiliations of any given work' (Bishop 2012, 28–30). Even Rancière's most zealous disciples are conscious of such problems. Thus, for instance, Liam Gillick observes 'the danger' of this theory's currency in the art world: 'We [...] might be ascribing an excess of potential to his reassuring assertion that visual contributions at the root of certain familiar artistic strategies transcend modernism's endgames and postmodernism's perpetually circling relativisms' (Gillick 2007, 265). One might well ask, transcends these endgames and relativisms in order to arrive at what, exactly? 'We're relieved,' Funcke writes, wagering an answer, 'to [...] conclude that a particular work of art is indeed political art, because that gives a more concrete sense to what otherwise is an amorphous debate about aesthetics and politics based on ill-defined criteria' (Funcke 2007, 284). Ill-defined criteria are thus replaced not by new, more rigorous criteria but by an absence of criteria, which, in turn, seems to have both a palliative and a redemptive effect, in so far as it exempts us from the formidable task of thinking the singularity of *a* work's engagement with the political. This absence of criteria, which, if taken seriously, delegitimates the critical question of art's ideological commitments, must itself be understood as ideological, to the extent that it founds and frames contemporary consensus. Speaking to this consensus, and echoing Bishop's critique, Bruno Bosteels speculates that its strength 'depends on the necessary erasure of [a] second aspect, that is, the specific ideological nature of certain art forms, in favour of a sweeping and always vaguely celebratory generalization of the first aspect, that is, the fact that all art is in some way political and all politics in some way aesthetic. Today,' Bosteels avers, 'such inversions of the politics of aesthetics and the aesthetics of politics have turned into automated gestures that are as rhetorically pleasing as they are conceptually empty' (Bosteels 2012, 8).

Beyond its therapeutic function in the art world, how might we make sense of Rancière's formidable claim that art does politics simply in its being art? Rancière duly recognizes that contemporary art operates under the sign of a 'post-utopian' present, and that the work of art does not and cannot act within the space of politics 'proper' in any recognizably instrumental sense: 'What aesthetic education and experience do not promise is to support the cause of political emancipation with forms of art' (Rancière

2009, 33). The question, then, is how to reconcile this post-utopian realism, which would seem to lead to a thoroughly depoliticized notion of art, with the claim that the artwork is *directly* political. What will it mean to speak of the aesthetic as a mode of being that is as such also a mode of doing, a mode of political activity that takes the paradoxical form of an irreducible passivity? Rancière's way out of this apparent impasse (but for him, it is no impasse at all) is to argue that *art does politics on its own terms by occasioning a redistribution of the sensible* – by proposing a new way of apportioning the common sensorium. The introduction of this concept is, I want to claim, the essential moment in his aesthetic theory, insofar as it marks the point at which aesthetics and politics do not so much intersect as enter into a relationship of radical affinity, becoming structurally indiscernible. The singular power of the artwork, so the argument goes, resides in its capacity to engender a rethinking or renegotiation of the limits of the sensible: to make visible what was hitherto (determined) invisible, to make heard what was hitherto (determined) inaudible. That is to say, aesthetic experience implies a specific kind of rupture. But a rupture with *what*, exactly? With a prior distribution of the sensible, of course: the politics of contemporary art 'consists in suspending the normal coordinates of sensory experience' (Rancière 2009, 25). It is by interrupting 'the everyday distribution of the sensible', as Joseph Tanke puts it, that the work of art performs the politics proper to it (Tanke 2011, 84).

That the encounter with an artwork always involves a more-or-less challenging suspension of the norms that frame 'ordinary' sensory experience seems anodyne and, indeed, obvious to the point of going without saying. Oliver Davis points to the weakness of this formulation of art's political efficacy, noting that Rancière 'seems almost to fall back on the' patently liberal-humanist 'idea that art broadens the mind' (Davis 2010, 157). What *is* interesting, however, is that this modest claim about aesthetic experience would mark the point at which art connects with politics – would, in fact, be *all* that connects art to politics. To understand the logic of this connection, we must come to grips what is meant here by politics. 'Politics', Rancière writes,

> is not the exercise of, or specific struggle for, power. It is the configuration of a specific space, the framing of a particular sphere of experience, of objects posited as common and as pertaining to a common decision, of subjects recognized as capable of designating these objects and putting forward arguments about them. [...] This distribution and redistribution of places and identities, this apportioning and reapportioning of spaces and times, of the visible and the invisible, and of noise and speech constitutes what I call the distribution of the sensible. (Rancière 2009, 24–25)

The conceptual novelty of Rancière's aesthetic thought is *not*, it turns out, in his conception of the artwork itself but instead in its linking this to an original and counterintuitive notion of politics. Or, to put this more precisely, politics is not so much linked to Rancière's account of art as it is shown to be *homologous* with it: aesthetic experience always already bears upon politics, because politics itself is, finally, a question of aesthetics, of the *redistribution of the sensible*: 'art and politics are simply two forms' of this redistribution (Funcke 2007, 283). It is crucial to note how strong a claim Rancière is making in the previous passage. It is not merely an exhortation not to underestimate or forget the aesthetic dimension of politics; rather, we are in a sense being asked to screen out everything *save for* the aesthetic dimension of politics, save for politics as a mode of sensorial redistribution. This is made absolutely clear at the outset of Rancière's 'Ten Theses on Politics', where the exposition of his first thesis begins with the claim that 'politics, when identified with the exercise of power and the struggle for its possessions, is dispensed with from the outset' (Rancière 2010, 27). The seizure of a factory by the workers who labour in it is a phenomenon that, if we accept this analysis, does not strictly speaking belong to politics. What *does* belong is the fundamentally aesthetic matter of a *re*arrangement in or of the common sensory field, whereby factory workers 'show up' in a (symbolic) space other than the one to which they have been assigned, making visible what was invisible, making audible as speech what hitherto registered as noise. In that this approach is exclusively concerned with 'the system of forms that governs what is seeable and sayable – the world, in other words, of perception', it involves the reduction of politics to its aesthetic valence (Ross 2007, 255).

There is, I want to suggest, rather more to be said for the politics of aesthetics than that the work of art precipitates a redistribution of the sensible, in large part because there is a great deal more to say about the politics *of political struggle itself* than Rancière's aesthetic reduction grants. As an essential aside, let us note that this reduction raises an important set of questions pertaining to the *subject* of politics-as-perception. For, to claim that politics amounts to 'making visible what was invisible' begs the question: *To whom* does what was once invisible become visible in the moment of politics, and what circumstances condition this sensorial transformation? Which is also to say, *on whom and what does the visibility of the hitherto invisible actually depend*? Whose sensory experience truly matters here? The 'Ten Theses' glosses Aristotle's well-trodden definition of humans' properly political being as constituted, Rancière writes, 'by their possession of the *logos*, which is alone able to demonstrate a community in the *aisthesis* of the just and the unjust, in contrast to the *phonê*, appropriate only for expressing feelings of pleasure and displeasure' (Rancière 2010, 37, emphasis in original). It is precisely this difference between sound and sense to which Rancière refers when he speaks of the 'apportioning and reapportioning [...] of noise and speech' that the redistribution of the sensible enacts. And yet, on this point, his argument takes a curious turn, which bears citing at length:

> The only practical difficulty lies in knowing in which sign this sign [of the political nature of the human] can be recognized; that is, how can you be sure that the human animal mouthing a noise in front of you is actually articulating a discourse, rather than merely expressing a state of being? If there is someone you do not wish to recognize as a political being, you begin by not seeing him as the bearer of signs of politicity, by not understanding what he says, by not hearing what issues from his mouth as discourse. [...] Traditionally, in order to deny the political quality of a category – workers, women and so on – all that was required was to assert that they belonged to a 'domestic' space that was separated from public life, one from which only groans or cries expressing suffering, hunger or anger could emerge, but not actual speech demonstrating a shared aesthesis. (Rancière 2010, 38)

Two things ought to strike us about this passage. First, its slippage (really, its *leap*) from an epistemological question – the 'practical difficulty' of knowing how to distinguish between political speech and extra-political noise – to one concerning the subject, not of knowledge but rather of power. In this second moment, failing to hear the speech coming from the disenfranchised other as speech is never a neutral epistemological phenomenon, but in fact forms part of a strategy whereby the ruling order maintains the other in her disenfranchisement: this order *wishes* to deny the political quality of, say, women, *and so* it 'fails to understand' what they have said as bearing on politics. That the emissaries of this order, which Rancière refers to simply as *the police*, have little to gain from actually inquiring whether what has issued from the others' mouths is speech or noise is perfectly obvious. Conversely, whether they have made claims or noise is certainly not in question for workers and women *themselves*. Indeed, the question 'was that *logos* or *phonê* we just heard?' makes sense only from the perspective of an embattled dominant order.

Thus it is not only that Rancière fails to account for the slippage his text performs. In so doing, he also fails to make explicit that the second moment of this passage actually nullifies the first: the 'practical difficulty' of discovering a way to distinguish between political discourse and animal noise and the refusal to recognize a certain other as belonging to the order of politics are, obviously, mutually exclusive concerns. Yet what is more striking is that this key moment in the argument implies that politics itself (again, in so far as it is coterminous with the redistribution of the sensible) ultimately pivots not on the *actor* in a given event – women marching, workers striking at the factory gates and so on – but rather on the *spectator* to whom the event is (supposedly) addressed, a subject position that, located at a distance from the march or the strike, can thereby take such events as objects of aesthetic experience and judge them accordingly. This addressee is the subject implied in or, rather, present-as-absent from, the various passive grammatical constructions by means of which Rancière develops the redistribution of the sensible. This amounts to a problem, for, even if we were to accept the premise that politics hasn't anything to do with the seizure of power, we would need to ask: What about something like visibility? Is it seized or conferred? And how, precisely, might a subject seize a place in the sensible without seizing some form or measure of power? Of course, a great deal of what concerns both politics and art hinges on such questions.

The centrality of this spectatorial perspective leads Slavoj Žižek to charge Rancière's conception of politics with a certain 'liberal leftist "irresponsibility"', by which he means that it depends, in a way that it cannot avow, on the preservation of the very order it sets out to subvert (Žižek 1999, 236). This is the case simply insofar as the spectator in question, the 'Master' to whom the eventual rupture of politics is supposedly addressed, always spectates from within this order. Pushing back against this critique, Rancière scholar Oliver Davis contends that 'it is not clear on what grounds Žižek thinks the mere fact that Rancière's concept of politics stands in structural opposition to the police order implies that it has a problematic, secret dependency on that order. [...] Žižek presents no argument in support of his assertion that Rancièrian politics '"*needs*" the Master' (Davis 2010, 95, emphasis in original). This is not altogether accurate; Žižek does in fact present a detailed argument in support of his assertion. But to make sense of his critique, we need not look any farther than what we have already cited of Rancière's first thesis on politics – which, to repeat, declares that politics vanishes as soon as it is identified with the struggle for or exercise of power. Žižek thus observes that 'we are dealing here with a logic which includes its own failure in advance, which considers its full success as its ultimate failure [...] and thus entertains an ambiguous attitude toward its politico-ontological opposite, the police Order of Being' (Žižek 1999, 234). The 'pure' (i.e. non-dialectical) opposition that pits politics-as-rupture against order-as-police in itself already is an admission of the former's dependence on the latter; we are dealing with two ways of articulating the same phenomenon. Davis misses the point when, in his defence, he credits the limits of Rancière's thinking to his 'account [being] more interested in some aspects of emancipatory politics' than in others (Davis 2010, 95). What this defence fails to grasp is that, for Rancière, the subversive moment of rupture with the police order is not merely the aspect of emancipatory politics that most interests him; it simply *is* emancipatory politics tout court. Any attempt to transpose this event-rupture into the framework of a new sociopolitical order ultimately involves its betrayal; the 'mastery' of order itself corrupts what is essentially political in the event. It follows that, *in its very subversiveness*, Rancière's politics not only requires but, in a sense that the theory itself must disavow, further entrenches the order in relation to which it shows up as a redistribution. It is in fact no more in structural opposition to the police order than an intermission is in structural opposition to a play.

Yet the problem with this articulation of politics involves something other than its overvaluation of subversive rupture; beyond this, it also implies a misunderstanding of the nature of the order in question. For Rancière, 'the police' names not the men and women the state employs to protect the interests of capital through force but rather the basic fact of 'a symbolic constitution of the social'. According to his argument, this fundamental logic engenders the social field by immobilizing it; it constitutes the social as a fixed structure from which the empty space, or void, necessary for mobility is lacking (Rancière 2010, 36).

> The essence of the police lies in a partition of the sensible that is characterized by the absence of void and supplement: society here is made up of groups tied to specific modes of doing, to places in which these occupations are exercised, and to modes of being corresponding to these occupations and these places. In this matching of functions, places and ways of being, there is no place for any void. (Rancière 2010, 36)

A structure without void, from which absence is itself absent, would necessarily be one in which movement is not so much forbidden as simply impossible, in which one cannot but stay in (one's proper) place. Let us bracket for now the question of whether any such social structure can or does exist. Or, better, let us hold this question open by observing that it is Plato's *Republic* that furnishes Rancière with the prototypical police order: he traces a line from the text's proposal that the worker's time-consuming labour 'naturally' prohibits him from participating in political assembly to its ban on the dramatic poem and its theatrical performance. Performing a critical breach of its perfect closure, the artwork is supposed to undermine the hyperstability of this symbolic formation, and thereby affirm and reintroduce the possibility of movement to the social field.

Thinking the politics of a performance or the aesthetics of an uprising effectively comes down to the same thing here: both bear witness to the rigid opposition between, on the one hand, the police as an immobilizing formal principle and, on the other, politics as the subversive destabilization of any such form – a moment that puts form in flux. We thus find in Rancière something like a photographic negative of Plato's argument. In his view, redistributive rupture falls squarely on the side of emancipatory promise, while the imposition of a new formal logic cannot but be a repressive police measure in service to the state (of things). The question is whether this framework, with its conceptual alignments that double as political alliances, is adequate to the contemporary situation it is marshalled to clarify and potentially transform. Granted, policing (in the more common and restricted use of the term) frequently deploys repressive violence to 'restore order'. It is an explicit aim of the police to maintain people where, according to the state, they belong and to force them back when they show up elsewhere. One need only recall with what lawless, militarized brutality cops and privately contracted security firm personnel collaborated to crush the occupation of Standing Rock by indigenous activists protesting the construction of the Dakota Access Pipeline (see Estes 2019). Recent history offers us no shortage of such events. And while they deserve our serious attention, such instances cannot, I think, be taken as representative of the broader logic by means of which the aesthetic coordinates of the social field are ordinarily constituted. It is not *primarily* through acts of violent repression that our day-to-day sense of our world is policed into being – which is not to deny that this 'ordinary' policing is itself a formidable form of violence. At the level of their structure, such spectacular instances are exceptions that both express and obscure something crucial about the rule. Nonetheless, Rancière's notion of the police is modelled after such exceptions. One could say that, on this point, he makes it only halfway through the classic Foucauldian critique. In referring to the logic or force constitutive of social order as such as 'the police', he affirms, *à la* Foucault, that modern power's operation well exceeds the scope of the state apparatuses explicitly tasked with governing (see Foucault 1990). And yet, in a second step that parts with Foucault's theory (of modern power as biopower), he accounts for this more expansive domain of power's exercise in largely the same repressive terms as are used to characterize the operations of official (sovereign, juridico-political) power. That they may not function according to the same logic is left unexamined; the policeman and the police principle are taken to 'say' the same thing.

Rooted as it is in the opposition between 'police' as fixed distribution of places and 'politics' as destabilizing/redistributive moment, Rancière's approach to the politics of aesthetics ultimately proves incapable of discerning, and so of effectively addressing, the most formidable political-aesthetic challenges that the contemporary situation poses. For, on its own, the mere fact of sensorial rupture is insufficient to meaningfully qualify the artwork as political. Indeed, to discern in the redistribution of the sensible the political promise of emancipation, one must ignore what strikes me as an increasingly inescapable fact, perhaps the one fact that should most concern contemporary aesthetic theory, namely, that the forces of global neoliberal domination operate precisely through an unceasing and increasingly frenzied sensorial redistribution. Far from throwing a wrench in the works, an ever more pervasive experience of aesthetic flux forms an essential part of contemporary global capital's arsenal and indexes the 'health' of its policing mechanisms. Consider again the example of Standing Rock. In this struggle, it was the police who sought to redistribute the sensible, to place a social order in flux, so as to clear a path for neoliberal capitalism's barbarous project of accumulation through extraction, while indigenous activists and their allies, fighting against the construction of the Dakota Access Pipeline, essentially demonstrated for the sovereign right of the Dakota and Lakota nations that comprise Standing Rock reservation to remain in place, that is, to preserve their land as inhabitable. Given a global situation governed by the anarchic law of capital's accumulative flow, it should come as no surprise that, in such an instance, the police come to perform the 'subversive' role.

Hence what Rancière identifies as the politics of aesthetics is not just no guarantee of politics after all. The problem with which we are confronted is graver still, for it may well be that aesthetic disruption is precisely what the domain of art and the forms of contemporary power that police us hold most in common, and, therefore, what most threatens to nullify the critical difference between them. Not only has it been co-opted to serve the very forces it was supposed it would undermine. In an era of ubiquitous advanced digital and network technologies, in which any approach to the common sensorium must consider the extent to which the latter extends into cyberspace, the forces of domination have dramatically expanded the scope and radicalized the logic of rupture, deploying strategies of 'innovation' at such breathtaking speeds that the very notion of a common sensorium seems a quaint relic from a simpler time. Of course, the point is not to turn away from the pressures of the present and look to the time before our own to discover and recover some supposedly more authentic articulation of politics and aesthetics, comparatively simpler because less fully implicated in the police logic in question here. Tempting though such nostalgic gestures may be, they can only disappoint, for, looking back, one faces the lurid spectacle of a consumer 'culture' that already functions according to a logic of disruptive innovation, one which *seems* largely appropriated from the discourses and practices of aesthetic modernism. More precisely still, one faces the emergence of what capitalism's in-house ideologues have called 'the experience economy' (see Pine and Gilmore 1998). This stage in the development of capitalism, at which (in 'developed nations', at least) the event or, better, the *atmosphere* of consumption itself becomes the primary object of commodity fetishism, very clearly rhymes with the turn in contemporary art from object to process – that is, to 'immaterial' practices that prioritize process, or in which performance, event, environment or relation *is* the object.

Isomorphisms such as these serve to complicate Rancière's political valuation of aesthetic disruption. Yet I have in mind another sort of counterevidence, which more precisely indexes the specificities of the contemporary moment. Consider the pressing problem of bot armies, which have come to play (and, it is all but certain, will continue to play) an outsize role in contemporary politics. Bots are software applications programmed to run autonomous, repetitive scripts, for instance, on social media platforms like Twitter, where they are capable of composing original tweets, retweeting, posting links, liking, following other accounts, spamming hashtags with content and direct messaging other Twitter accounts. Crucially, these little bits of code posing as human users execute such tasks at superhuman rates and volumes, crowding the digital sensorium with semblances of human 'communication' and thereby crowding out the 'speech' of actual users. This is by design: bots exist to flood, crowd out, overwhelm. And, as we know, when enough are set to work in concert – as, say, when a critical mass of bots is programmed to appear to express enthusiasm for Trump's performance in the wake of a presidential debate – they effectively perform a disruption that, though at a basic level 'fake', has real political consequences (see Guilbeault and Woolley 2016).

In *Duty Free Art: Art in the Age of Planetary Civil War*, transdisciplinary artist and critical theorist Hito Steyerl argues that bot armies are fundamentally a matter of aesthetic concern: they perform a redistribution of the sensible, disrupting established apportionments of invisible and visible, inaudible and audible. By introducing a surplus (here, of tweets) linked to a lack (of real human users tweeting), they bring about a new apportionment of the common (digital) sensorium. Yet, in a techno-dystopian perversion of the dialectic of *phonê* and *logos* central to Rancière's thought, bot armies disseminate sublime quantities of algorithmic noise on behalf of this or that political party, oligarch, or would be demagogue, and, often enough, this noise is taken for the speech of 'the people'. Hence they are also a political concern, though not in the sense in which Rancière imagines that the aesthetic 'does' politics. Rather, they demonstrate that the disruption of the sensorium has nothing necessarily to do with power's subversion; they are in fact exemplary proof of how useful a tool such disruption can be for further entrenching the hierarchies of oppression.

Bot armies demand our critical attention because, as an exemplary instance of what Steyerl calls 'proxy politics', they demonstrate with particular clarity that contemporary political struggles tend to unfold in a zone beyond the framework of representation – the very framework which, she claims, Rancière's political thought inhabits. For, to imagine politics as still turning on the division between speech and noise, or visible and invisible, is effectively to imagine that 'if everyone is aurally (or visually) represented, and no one is discounted as noise, then equality might draw near' (Steyerl 2017, 37). Yet the situation with which the digital age confronts us would seem to undermine this hypothesis, not least because it is constituted by the extreme discrepancy between 'cultural' and 'political' representation. 'There is', Steyerl writes,

> an overabundance of representation of almost anything and anybody: in commercial as well as social media. This avalanche of representation has increased a great deal with digital technologies. [...] While cultural representation of everything is undergoing massive inflation [...] political representation is not only uneven, it is also less and less relevant. The two realms also seem to be running wildly out of sync. If one were to push the point, one could conclude that there is almost an inversely proportional relationship between political and cultural representation. (Steyerl 2017, 174–75)

The point is an important one that seems difficult to contest. In the first decades of the twenty-first century, the tools necessary to transform the aesthetic fabric of the commons – to disrupt social hierarchies by insisting on the inclusion in the field of representation of the hitherto excluded – have become widely, almost universally available. And yet, this unprecedentedly widespread and increasingly immediate access to the means of aesthetic disruption has not led to a newly emancipatory era (see Alkousaa 2016). 'The internet', Steyerl reminds us, 'spawned Uber and Amazon, not the Paris Commune' (Steyerl 2017, 187). Indeed, the very tools we use to try to make the invisible visible are succeeding, though not as the techno-utopians among us had hoped: that is, they are making us visible to power as so much data, hence evermore calculable and governable. At present, to use social media platforms to raise awareness or register dissent is to volunteer oneself as an object for surveillance by corporations and a target for authoritarian political regimes' armed forces. Hence in her critique of communicative capitalism, Jodi Dean argues that 'the displacement of political conflict to the terrain of networked media has the perverse repercussion of perpetually expanding the topography of struggle even as it constantly signals the locations, intentions, and associations of those who are fighting' and so 'increases the vulnerability of those engaged in active protest and resistance on the ground' (Dean 2018, 110).

That aesthetic redistribution would spell crisis for power is ultimately, the bot armies tell us, little more than a modernist myth – the one such myth Rancière seems unready to upend. Beyond the narrow view of this myth, there is a vast, grim reality: the architects and beneficiaries of global capitalism's breakneck expansion are only too happy to allow for the dissolution of all sorts of aesthetic and cultural hierarchies, so long as this redistribution of the sensible has nothing to do with, say, the redistribution of the edible. Or, more precisely – because there *is* in fact a relation between them – so long as aesthetic redistribution functions as a substitute for, hence an obstacle to, the struggle for the equitable distribution of material resources. This is precisely the reality Luc Boltanski and Eve Chiapello map in their landmark sociological analysis of capitalism's transformations in the wake of the revolts of May 1968. *The New Spirit of Capitalism* demonstrates that what made the radical upheavals of *les années soixante-huit* so singular, in themselves and in terms of their consequences, was how they wove together two distinct and not altogether complementary levels of critique. On the one hand, the 'social critique' articulated by workers involved both 'classical' socialist/unionist demands to limit economic exploitation of the proletariat and more radical, properly communist efforts to seize control of the means of production. On the other hand, what Boltanski and Chiapello call 'artistic critique' launched a series of attacks, not on the exploitative 'law' of private interest intrinsic to capitalism but rather on what we might call the repressive 'culture' of its implementation. Articulated not only by artists but also and, more consequentially, by intellectuals and professionals belonging to the managerial class, it was essentially a libertarian line of critique that took aim at those rigid hierarchies, modelled on paternal authority, that structured the world of work. Against this alienating 'police order' capitalism, it demanded greater autonomy, flexibility, horizontality and mobility. Thus confronted with the singular and sometimes precarious coalition of these two lines of critique, capitalism made a remarkable move: *it answered and assimilated the demands of the artistic critique and, in so doing, altogether disarmed social critique.* 'It was by recuperating some of the oppositional themes articulated during the May events', Boltanski and Chiapello write, 'that capitalism was to disarm critique, regain the initiative, and discover a new dynamism' (Boltanski and Chiapello 2005, 168). Demanding that capitalism liberate them from its oppressive and alienating structures, what the agents of artistic critique unwittingly participated in was *the liberation of capital itself* from the regulatory structures that 'oppressed' it, precipitating the emergence of a new era of deregulation, expansion and exploitation. 'Formulated in a libertarian rhetoric, the critique […] was apt not to perceive its proximity to liberalism: it was, as it were, liberal without knowing it' (Boltanski and Chiapello 2005, 202). One of the great political lessons of May 1968, which any serious attempt at thinking the politics of aesthetics must confront, is that artistic critique's attack on capitalism's oppressive forms not only did not imperil capitalism. In satisfying its demands, capitalism found itself immunized, for a time at least, against any meaningfully radical action to arrest the global spread of its creative destruction (see Schumpeter 1994).

On the occasion of its fortieth anniversary, Alain Badiou wondered whether some weren't commemorating the events of May 1968, not for the still unrealized revolutionary promise they bodied forth but instead 'because the real outcome and the real hero of '68 is unfettered neo-liberal capitalism', because 'the transformation of the way we live, the individualism and the taste for *jouissance* have become a reality thanks to post-modern capitalism and its garish world of all sorts of consumerism' (Badiou 2010, 44). Discouraging though the proposition is, and although Badiou will go on to affirm another, properly radical legacy of May '68, it nonetheless points to the fact that artistic critique, detached from the concerns of social critique, cleared a path for capitalism to arrive at what Boltanski and Chiapello call a 'new spirit', but which we, remembering Marx and Engels's well-known characterization of capitalism as constant revolutionizing, might instead call its spirit tout court (Marx and Engels 2017, 54).

These critical reflections lead us to put a question to Rancière's thought: How might we differentiate between a properly political redistribution of the sensible – never mind whether this politics is potential or realized – and the sort of aesthetic redistribution that in fact characterizes and drives late capitalism? As Samo Tomšič argues, 'In the capitalist-scientific universe where reality essentially comes down to permanent change, the latter loses its a priori revolutionary character. The structural change that could bring about a new social link [...] presupposes a correct interpretation of the given logic of change, the conditions of the permanent capitalist revolution' (Tomšič 2015, 95). If Rancière can claim that art does politics simply by being art – hence, that in the age of the aesthetic regime, art in a sense always does politics – this is because the disordering gesture of the aesthetic is mobilized in relation to his conception of a police order that always operates via an immobilizing logic of proper places. Yet such solid stasis is precisely what the oppressive dynamism of capitalism by definition melts and profanes, and so Rancière's police principle seems more apt a description of the 'traditional' sociopolitical formations that predate the emergence of capitalist modernity. Artist John Kelsey, in a published exchange, challenged the theorist on this very point:

> You use the word *police* to identify all the social and political forces that constantly try to keep things, activities, and people in their proper places. ... But doesn't it sometimes seem that in our times 'police' might describe instead the forces that demand and facilitate constant circulation, that promote the efficiency of a boundary crossing that no longer produces problems for the existing order? A circulation where nothing really moves? In any case, some might say these are the conditions under which contemporary art attempts to define and think itself. (Carnevale and Kelsey 2007, 264)

In the absence of a theorization of the different *forms* the distribution of the sensible can take, we are ill-equipped to conceptualize with real precision art's capacity to intervene on or subtract itself from the conditions Kelsey outlines. Yet the question of differentiating between forms of aesthetic rupture consistent with 'permanent capitalist revolution' and those that might operate otherwise is pre-empted in Rancière, insofar as the 'power' of form is for him inextricable from the aesthetico-political inequality of the representative regime of the arts, that is to say, analogous to 'the power of the class of intelligence over the class of sensation, of men of culture over men of nature' (Rancière 2009, 31). In this key question's place, we have an ascription of politicity to art that, in its breadth, seems to lose its conceptual value. This antipathy to the 'discipline' of form speaks to the central limitation of Rancière's approach to the politics of aesthetics, which (as I suggested earlier) echoes and expands the central limitation in his approach to politics as such. The sweeping attribution of politicity to art in general must ultimately be read as the underside of Rancière's narrow identification of politics with the event of rupture with the dominant order. To be sure, this moment of upheaval is precisely the part of the political process (considered broadly) that is most *spectacular* and, one might even risk saying, most *beautiful*. It is the dimension of politics most available and amenable to the theatricality of scenic representation, not least because, in itself, it is often already structured by the logic of the scene. And yet, beyond the beauty of demonstrations, marches and riots, there lies the difficult and mostly *unspectacular* work of formalization, the exigency of imagining and constructing a new order. That this whole horizon of collective thought and action would somehow fall outside the frame of politics seems an altogether insupportable claim. Likewise, a theorization of the politics of aesthetics that wants to do justice to its object's contemporary situation must move beyond reassuringly generic affirmations of the value of sensorial redistribution. It must concede that, in an era dominated precisely by capitalism's pernicious and widespread instrumentalization of constant aesthetic revolutionizing, we must once again take up the question of the politics of aesthetic forms. That is, we must reconsider, perhaps even begin to reinvent, the capacity of art's modes of formalization to *arrest the flow* – not once and for all, and not from the vantage of some 'pure' outside, of course, but long enough to render what polices by disorientation newly legible, thinkable and contestable.

REFERENCES

Alkousaa, Riham. 2016. 'How Facebook Hurt The Syrian Revolution'. *Al Jazeera*, 4 December 2016. https://www.aljazeera.com/indepth/opinion/2016/12/facebook-hurt-syrian-revolution-161203125951577.html.
Badiou, Alain. 2010. *The Communist Hypothesis*. London: Verso.

Bishop, Claire. 2012. *Artificial Hells: Participatory Art and the Politics of Spectatorship*. London: Verso.
Boltanski, Luc and Eve Chiapello. 2005. *The New Spirit of Capitalism*. Translated by Gregory Elliott. London: Verso.
Bosteels, Bruno. 2012. *Some Highly Speculative Remarks on Art and Ideology*. Berlin: Hatje Cantz.
Carnevale, Fulvia and John Kelsey. 2007. 'Art of the Possible: Fulvia Carnevale and John Kelsey in Conversation with Jacques Rancière'. *Artforum International* 45.7, March 2007.
Chan, Paul. 2007. 'Fearless Symmetry'. *Artforum International* 45.7, March 2007.
Davis, Oliver. 2010. *Jacques Rancière (Key Contemporary Thinkers)*. Cambridge: Polity.
Dean, Jodi. 2018. *The Communist Horizon*. London: Verso.
Estes, Nick. 2019. *Our History is the Future: Standing Rock Versus the Dakota Access Pipeline, and the Long Tradition of Indigenous Resistance*. London: Verso.
Foucault, Michel. 1990. *The History of Sexuality, Volume 1: An Introduction*. Translated by Robert Hurley. New York, NY: Vintage.
Funcke, Bettina. 2007. 'Displaced Struggles: Bettina Funcke on Rancière and the Art World'. *Artforum International* 45.7, March 2007.
Gillick, Liam. 2007. 'Vegetables'. *Artforum International* 45.7, March 2007.
Groys, Boris. 2014. *On The New*. Translated by G. M. Goshgarian. London: Verso.
Guilbeault, Douglas and Samuel Woolley. 2016. 'How Twitter Bots are Shaping the Election'. *The Atlantic*, 1 July 2016. https://www.theatlantic.com/technology/archive/2016/11/election-bots/506072/.
Hirschhorn, Thomas. 2007. 'Eternal Flame'. *Artforum International* 45.7, March 2007.
Marx, Karl and Friedrich Engels. 2017. *The Communist Manifesto*, edited by Jodi Dean. Translated by Samuel Moore. London: Pluto Press.
Pine, B. Joseph and James Gilmore. 1998. 'Welcome to the Experience Economy'. *The Harvard Business Review* 76.4 (July–August), 97–105. Gale Academic OneFile.
Rancière, Jacques. 2009. *Aesthetics and its Discontents*. Translated by Steven Corcoran. Cambridge: Polity Press.
Rancière, Jacques. 2009b. *The Emancipated Spectator*. Translated by Gregory Elliott. New York, NY: Verso.
Rancière, Jacques. 2010. *Dissensus: On Politics and Aesthetics*. Translated by Steven Corcoran. New York, NY: Continuum.
Rancière, Jacques. 2011. *Althusser's Lesson*. Translated by Emiliano Battista. New York, NY: Continuum.
Rancière, Jacques. 2013. *Aisthesis: Scenes from the Aesthetic Regime of Art*. Translated by Zakir Paul. London: Verso.
Ross, Kristin. 'Kristin Ross on Jacques Rancière'. *Artforum International* 45.7, March 2007.
Schumpeter, Joseph A. 2008. *Capitalism, Socialism, & Democracy*, Third Edition. New York, NY: Harper Collins.

Steyerl, Hito. 2017. *Duty Free Art: Art in the Age of Planetary Civil War*. London: Verso.

Tanke, Joseph J. 2011. *Jacques Rancière: An Introduction (Philosophy, Politics, Aesthetics)*. London: Continuum International.

Tolokonnikova, Nadezhda and Slavoj Žižek. 2014. *Comradely Greetings: The Prison Letters of Nadya and Slavoj*. London: Verso.

Tomšič, Samo. 2015. *The Capitalist Unconscious*. London: Verso.

Žižek, Slavoj. 1999. *The Ticklish Subject: The Absent Centre of Political Ontology*. London: Verso.

Chapter 2

Soft Shivers, Sweaty Politics

Dramaturgy, Politics of Perception and the Pensive Body

Liesbeth Groot Nibbelink

SOFT SHIVERS

Slowly moving towards the front of the stage, nine dancers line up in a row close to the audience, modestly lit by a darkish purple light that covers the entire stage. It is the opening scene of *Dança Doente*, by Marcelo Evelin/ Demolition Incorporada (2017). The dancer's bodies seem strained and tense; there is a sense of anticipation of things to come. Yet nothing comes. Nothing happens. Or so it seems. While pulsating music fills the theatre space, the dancers stand still, the audience is silent, and quietly waits. Then, after quite a while, one dancer moves her arm a little. Another dancer shifts the weight of his body. Other bodies seem to move marginally as well. An arm crawls upwards, a leg briefly escapes control, a torso trembles, ensuing small displacements of bodies or body parts. Through these minimal tremors, vibrations and spasms the performance unfolds. The show lasts about 1.5 hours, mostly without significant changes in dynamics, slowing down even more towards the last half hour, when the performers (including the light and sound engineer) walk downstage to leave the stage one by one, at an extremely quiet pace.[1]

Dança Doente is a dance performance without stylized or explicitly choreographed movements, without the type of movements we tend to call 'dance'. All dancers are professionally trained, yet there are no overt demonstrations of technical virtuosity. What we see, instead, are bodies that seem resilient to performing 'well': in *Dança Doente*, meaning 'sick dance', we look at *inoperative* bodies, bodies that refuse to produce 'dance' and live up to expectations. Non-moving or non-functioning bodies that question what dance is are no new phenomena (Cvejić 2016; Georgelou 2011; Lepecki 2006). Expectations regarding the fully functioning, productive body, however, are persistent and stubborn – both inside and outside the context of theatre. Authors like Jon McKenzie, in *Perform or Else* (2001), Lepecki in *Singularities* (2016), or Byung-Chul Han, in *The Burnout Society* (2015), have convincingly shown that performance and productivity are the dominant parameters of our neoliberal 24/7 society. On his website, Marcelo Evelin indirectly seems to allude to the depredations of advanced capitalism when stating that *Dança Doente* 'stages a body that is infected by the world and dominated by external forces that are wearing it out to the point of ruin'.[2] Neoliberalist economies require productive and healthy bodies. The shivering bodies in *Dança Doente*, instead, are antithetical to the 'corpus economicus'. They are in fact a welcome antidote to the overabundant fitgirls of Instagram or the worked-out bodies at the gym, exponents of a rapidly proliferating fitness and health culture (Sassatelli 2014). They are sick bodies perhaps, or they are just sick of it all: sick of the imperative to perform, weary of the demand to function as effective, labouring forces of production.

This refusal (or incapacity) to function 'properly' questions how we look at bodies on stage, what we expect from dancer's bodies and those of our own, and how we treat (inoperative) bodies in daily life. Put differently, a performance like *Dança Doente* broaches a *politics of perception* in its critical exploration of perceptual habits and ensuing horizons of expectation. By presenting us with vulnerable bodies instead of productive ones, the performance implicitly asks what bodies we dominantly get to see in a capitalist and media-saturated society: which bodies are seen as 'common' and which as deviant. A politics of perception may alert us thus to wider societal, ideological or political implications of how things are presented and perceived.

This bond of perception and politics is precisely at the heart of Jacques Rancière's concept of the *distribution of the sensible*. In *The Politics of Aesthetics* (2004), he argues that our perception and therefore our conception of the world is first and foremost a product of a certain division of what is visible or audible, and therefore, of what is thought, done and imagined (12). This distribution of the sensible establishes what is shared and what is excluded from communality; it asks what is 'common to the community' and who is in the position or function to decide so (13). The concept helps to investigate what is present in the world and what is made imperceptible: to seek the exclusions within the inclusions, to focus on what is ignored, misrepresented or even removed from consciousness. Rearranging or redistributing the sensible, therefore, can be understood as a critically surveying and reframing of what we think we know, of rendering perceptible how we perceive and what strategies make us see what we think we see.

In this contribution, I suggest that Rancière's distribution of the sensible is of great value for the performing arts and may help to elaborate what a politics of perception could entail. Theatre and performance scholars occasionally refer to such a politics, yet usually the term remains little reflected upon (Read 2008; Lehmann 2006; Van Kerkhoven 2005). Yet in order to fully 'adapt' Rancière's concept to theatre as a live event, I would like to 'tweak' the concept a little as well. As I will argue more fully later, Rancière's aesthetics seems to pivot around the visible and the audible, the text and the (moving) image. Subsequently, spectatorship is often discussed in terms of storytelling, translation, visual analysis and other semiotic-cognitive processes of meaning-making and interpretation (Rancière 2009). In response to this optico-logocentric regime of signification, I would like to extend his aesthetics to incorporate bodies as well, since I think it is remarkable that Rancière's distribution of the *sensible* pays little attention to *corporeal* intelligence: to embodied knowledge that is present in affects and sensations. A shiver down the spine can be a very evocative sign! This shift in focus seems even more relevant in view of contemporary (postdramatic) theatre, dance and performance, where next to the text, also bodies, objects, space, time and media play an equally prominent role (cf. Lehmann 2006).

Consequently, I will test Rancière's concept by analysing three performances that put the body centre stage. They each practice a politics of perception by presenting us with specific 'counter-bodies' in view of neoliberalism, rationalism and postcolonialism. Next to the fragile bodies of Marcelo Evelin's *Dança Doente*, I will discuss *Bacchae – Prelude to a Purge* (2017), in which the Capeverdian choreographer Marlene Monteiro Freitas stages bodies in between discipline, chaos, play and ecstasy. In *Solar: A Meltdown* (2014), the artist Ho Rui An presents a critical postcolonial perspective on colonial bodies, in an ingenious lecture-performance on a (counter)history of sweat. By also attending to the *dramaturgy* of these performances, I suggest that Rancière's politics of aesthetics may benefit from a dramaturgical perspective that is inspired by a material rather than a discursive engagement with theatre, that is, by an approach that focuses on theatre as a live performance and subsequently, on the role of audience address. Lastly, I will briefly discuss Rancière's use of the term 'pensiveness', which seems to cover an interesting middle ground between Rancière's distribution of the sensible and my approach to dramaturgy. In this chapter, I will argue that regarding theatre's politics of perception, we should not limit ourselves to texts or images but also attend to the corporeality of bodies, and to physical sensations and experience. Bodies, whether sweaty, soft or shivering, are exquisitely capable of sharpening our perception. Such a 'sweaty politics' not only generates exciting aesthetics but above all places living bodies and animate things at the core of commonality.

SWEATY POLITICS

As mentioned previously, there is a close alliance between theatre's *politics of perception* and Rancière's distribution of the sensible. Alan Read briefly hints at this connection, in *Theatre, Intimacy and Engagement* (2008, 12–13). Whereas Read aligns such politics of perception with an ethics of association that renders visible those who usually have no part, Hans-Thies Lehmann and the Flemish dramaturge Marianne van Kerkhoven locate theatre's political potential in its critical assessment of a media-saturated society. For Lehmann, a 'politics of theatre is a politics of perception' (2006, 185). In *Postdramatic Theatre*, he asserts that media massively shape our perception and create a constant caesura between what appears on screen and the lives we live in front of those screens. The live performance ideally generates an aesthetics of 'response-ability', by which Lehmann alludes to theatre's capacity of restoring the bond between the sending and the reception of signs and images (ibid.). Almost two decades later, we are witness to an algorithmic turn in a datafied society (Schäfer and Van Es 2017; Uricchio 2011), which probably impacts perception even more. Big data and algorithmically defined relations channel information through personal customization and on-demand streams. Because of those filter bubbles, or 'echo chambers', the information we acquire about the world increasingly confirms what we already know or believe, while other perspectives are pushed out of sight (Sunstein 2017; Flaxman et al. 2016). When devoid of alternative viewpoints, we are also bereft of opportunities to develop coping strategies. Negotiating or acknowledging opposing opinions is a way of exercising empathy, which, looking at the current increase of polarization, populism and nationalist sentiments, is a vital necessity.

Van Kerkhoven (2005), although addressing different media technologies, engaged with similar concerns. To reduce the field of vision and to limit choices is ultimately a form of de-politicization, in her view. Politics, instead, involves the creation of an arena for critical and independent thinking, where one can test one's observations and viewpoints in exchange with others. For Van Kerkhoven, the critical assessment of how we are made to look, see and think is perhaps the biggest task that contemporary theatre and performance could set for itself. By actively analysing how spectatorship is organized, composed, orchestrated and manipulated – both inside and outside the theatre – theatre might be able to re-politicize our mode of looking.

Such a politics of perception closely aligns with Rancière's *(re)distribution of the sensible*, through which he surveys systems, strategies and power relations that determine what is to be seen in the world, and what is made imperceptible. The distribution of the sensible is a key concept in Rancière's work. It has been extensively described in *The Politics of Aesthetics*, resurfaces in many of his essays and is also the undergirding logic of *Aisthesis: Scenes from the Aesthetic Regime of Art* (2013). In both books, Rancière distinguishes between two regimes of art, the mimetic and the aesthetic.[3] Whereas mimesis involves the illustration of an idea, aesthesis involves perception directly, referring to what renders itself perceptible to the senses. It is this regime of aesthetics, specifically, that Rancière is interested in, since to Rancière, there is an intrinsic bond between aesthetics and politics. In pointing out this connection, he does not address the aestheticization of politics that draws on mass culture spectacle, but the perceptual order itself, which is inherently political: 'Politics revolves around what is seen and what can be said about it, around who has the ability to see and the talent to speak, around the properties of spaces and the possibilities of time' (2004, 13). The distribution of the sensible not only defines what is visible or audible but extends itself as well to what can be said, thought, made or done (85). The concept thus reveals patterns of inclusion and exclusion, and hence forms of societal and political organization.

For Rancière, art's capacity to question and challenge our perception and understanding of history, society, commonality or thought itself is inherently political (42–45). Art is capable of rearranging the distribution of the sensible, of creating ruptures in what we think we understand. Such (re)arrangements expose the intrinsic bond between perception, knowledge and understanding. A certain distribution of the sensible not only decides what can be seen or heard, it also defines what we think or are able to conceive or conceptualize. Rancière thus creates a thorough awareness of the far-fetching (epistemic) consequences that a particular distribution of the sensible may have. When recalling the fragile bodies in *Dança Doente*, for example, the distribution of the sensible may help to understand that Evelin's inoperative bodies not only disrupt conventions of dance but also address socio-economic processes at large.

In *Dança Doente*, the resistance to perform 'well' may spur a range of other refusals in the spectators' minds, from Oblomov's inertness to Bartleby's 'I prefer not to', from Christoph Marthaler's sleeping characters to stillness in conceptual dance, from strikes to standing still as a form of protest.[4] In an after-talk, the performers and the audience jointly addressed the connection between neoliberalism and the emergence of a fitness and health culture. The slim and well-trained body, whose value is reduced to the capacity to work or to appear as (spectacular) image, is the ultimate example of twenty-first-century Foucauldian biopower, in my view.[5] *Dança Doente* initiates a *re*distribution of the sensible by presenting bodies that escape this imperative to perform 'properly'. Rancière remarks that the partition of the sensible 'reveals who can have a share in what is common to the community' and what are the means through which 'something in common lends itself to participation' (2004, 12). Likewise, *Dança Doente*'s inoperative bodies redefine what is common to the community and widen the perceptual coordinates of communality.

Foucault's disciplined bodies also reverberate in Marlene Monteiro Freitas's *Bacchae – Prelude to a Purge*, although through rather different means. Freitas is known for being inspired by elements that deviate from well-organized everyday life, such as the carnivalesque, madness, dream logic or play. In *Bacchae* we see thirteen performers (including five trumpet players) involved in a disorderly confusion of events, balancing, in words of Freitas, 'as funambulists over the wire of intensity'.[6] Through an amalgam of loosely connected scenes, the (musical) mayhem on stage conjures up loose associations with Euripides's *Bacchae*, where Dionysian desire is pitted against Apollonian reason and discipline. On the one hand we get an impression of a festive, noisy, playful and particularly energetic party or bacchanal, while on the other hand this energy is explicitly suppressed, the outburst withheld, in scenes that loosely refer to an average-day-at-the-office. We see distorted versions of driving a car, cycling, typing, sitting behind a desk, and the occasional boredom, (social) competition and (sexual) frustration at the workplace. This distortion is caused by the strained and staccato movement style through which all scenes are delivered. Both performers and musicians move like animated figures from a comic book. With some exceptions, it seems they are constantly stuttering, physically. *Bacchae*'s redistribution of the sensible primarily resides in the impossibility to grasp the performance entirely. Rancière has described this as *heterology*, referring to instances in which 'the meaningful fabric of the sensible is disturbed: a spectacle does not fit within the sensible framework defined by a network of meanings; an expression does not find its place in the system of visual coordinates where it appears' (2004, 63). Heterology is 'a rupture with the very logic of meaningful situations' (63). Freitas's cartoonesque figures elicit a sense of free-floating energy which generates a feeling of unbound freedom, an 'anything goes' one may know from experiences of flow or when absorbed in play. *Bacchae* distinctively speaks to the sensitive body rather than the decoding mind.

Rancière further remarks that this play of heterologies 'undoes the sensible fabric – a given order of relations between meanings and the visible – and establishes other networks of the sensible which can possibly corroborate the actions of political subjects to reconfigure what are given to be the facts' (64). The establishment of such 'other networks of the sensible' thus instigates a process of *political subjectivation*. This perfectly characterizes Ho Rui An's *Solar: A Meltdown*, a lecture-performance on Western representations of colonialism in popular culture. Ho Rui An is a visual artist based in Singapore, who provides a resourceful counter-reading of paintings, pictures, films and musicals that are set somewhere in 'tropic countries'. He starts with a dissection of the Tropenmuseum's exhibition in Amsterdam, a museum dedicated to representing life in the 'tropics' and now struggling with its not yet critically assessed colonial history. The exhibition stages 'daily life in the tropics' and shows a scene of the anthropologist Charles LeRoux 'at work', photographing pygmies in Papua New Guinea. In a light-humoured tone, Ho Rui An invites us to look closely at this extraordinary scene. While pointing to the sweaty back of the white colonialist, he subtly enquires how often do we see a colonial officer as a labouring body, suffering under the merciless sun, meanwhile suggesting that this sweat can also be read as an index of the museum's anxiety towards its colonial past. From hereon he embarks upon a history of colonial sweat, in which he replaces the dominant idea of the Western colonialist, dressed in stainless white costumes and holding postures that suggest survey, overview, discipline and control, with that of the white Western male as a labouring, perspiring, suffering and occasionally delirious body, melting away under the merciless tropical sun. Ho Rui An thus redistributes the sensible by reframing stories of colonial adventure and heroism, creating a pictorial counter-narrative. *Solar: A Meltdown* disturbs what Rancière calls the *police*, a system of organization or 'law' that establishes a sensible order and privileged positions (2004, 3). In the introduction to *The Politics of Aesthetics*, translator Gabriel Rockhill remarks that the 'essence of *politics* consists in interrupting the distribution of the sensible by supplementing it with those who have no part in the perceptual coordinates of the community, thereby modifying the very aesthetico-political field of possibility' (3, emphasis in original). Ho Rui An revises history by rearranging the images and stories that account for the colonial past, changing perspectives and offering alternative viewpoints. Here, *political subjectivation* takes shape by dismantling the order of the police, by reclaiming a position of equality and the right to speak, by appropriating and changing the coordinates of the aesthetico-political field.

DISTRIBUTIONS OF THE SENSIBLE

As suggested in the introduction, Rancière often explains the distribution of the sensible by referring to the visible or the audible, to text and the image – mostly in relation to art, photography, film and literature, next to macrohistorical issues such as democracy or modernity. One can also notice that he sparsely engages contemporary theatre in his reflections. His well-known essay 'The Emancipated Spectator' features Brecht and Artaud; in *Aisthesis*, some chapters are devoted to theatre and dance but largely relate to the early modernism of Ibsen, Maeterlinck, Appia or Craig or, in dance, of Loïe Fuller and Isadora Duncan. In line with his focus on the audible and the visible,

Rancière often grounds his arguments in a close reading of either texts or images, while subordinating other elements that are equally key to (postdramatic) theatre and the live performance, such as space, time or bodies. In 'The Emancipated Spectator', for instance, he equates (looking at) theatre with (reading) a book and compares spectatorial activity with 'the gaze focused on an image' (2009, 22). We may observe, then, that with regard to theatre, Rancière's primary mode of engagement is a discursive rather than a materially oriented one, since he tends to analyse ideas or texts *about* the theatre rather than considering the embodied and experiential components that are also constitutive of the theatre event.[7] Even when studying artworks that easily exceed textual or visual registers, like the dances of Loïe Fuller, he mainly seems interested in the *ideas* about the body in her work. For sure, in *Aisthesis*, Rancière does speak of affects, percepts, energy, movement and rhythm, yet the body remains a symbolic abstraction.

This becomes apparent in his discussion of Loïe Fuller, who is known for creating organic figures such as waves, butterflies or flowers by manipulating large volumes of textile, in relation to bodily movement and innovative lightning techniques. Analysing her serpentine dance, Rancière appreciates the work because it questions the aesthetics of symmetric harmony: Fuller's asymmetric, curved lines oppose the perfect circle which captures Da Vinci's Vitruvian man. Fuller's dance redistributes the sensible by adhering not to geometric balance but to a 'perpetual variation of the lines who accidentally merge' (2013, 95). Above all, Rancière values Fuller for communicating these ideas not by imitation but through abstraction. In the serpentine dance, 'the body abstracts from itself. It dissimulates its own form in the display of veils sketching flight rather than the bird, the swirling rather than the wave, the bloom rather than the flower. What is imitated, in each thing, is the event of its apparition' (100). In emphasizing the fabric's operations, Rancière undoubtedly evokes a performative rather than a representational register (although not using the word as such), yet his agenda is a different one. For Rancière, Fuller's serpentine dance produces an abstract, non-psychological body, 'a pure display of a play of forms' (ibid.), in which the aesthetic outmanoeuvres the mimetic.

Rancière's partition of the sensible in principle addresses all the senses, yet his emphasis is on abstractness and form, and sides with the visible and the audible. This optico-logocentric distribution of the sensible has some repercussions for his view on spectatorship as well, which seems to favour rational-cognitive processes over material-sensory imprints.[8] In 'The Emancipated Spectator', for instance, he asserts that all spectators 'learn' something different from a theatre performance, by means of active interpretation, meaning-making, translation and storytelling, thus explaining what they perceive in their own way (2009, 14–17). In these acts, Rancière's emancipated spectator actually comes quite close to Erika Fischer-Lichte's description of the spectator as a 'master of semiosis', already in 1997. In 'Discovering the Spectator', Fischer-Lichte observes how throughout the twentieth century, theatre history shows a series of recurring attempts to activate the spectator (for a variety of ends), until postmodern performance takes the stage, and spectators are 'given back' their role as spectators again. Evoking Robert Wilson's theatre of images specifically, Fischer-Lichte sees spectators as creative masters of semiosis, who produce their own show, so to say, by deciding where to look, what associations to make, which fragments to select or what meanings to ascribe. This is why Fischer-Lichte regards looking on as a creative act – quite similar to Rancière. This idea of the freely interpreting spectator, however, tends to overlook that a performance always employs certain forms of audience address and that this same theatre history has provided theatre makers with a range of artistic strategies that deal with steering the gaze, and with managing attention.

In *Visuality in the Theatre* (2008), Maaike Bleeker convincingly argues that each performance functions by way of address, whether hardly perceptible or persistently present, and points to the body as the locus of looking. Elsewhere I already observed that what Rancière tends to neglect, in my view, and what Bleeker purposefully emphasizes is precisely this (corporeal) address (Groot Nibbelink 2019, 2012). This is why I think it is helpful to present another way of thinking about (politics of) perception in the theatre, by attending to the *dramaturgy* of performance events. Revisiting the distribution of the sensible through a dramaturgical perspective will also make clear that a politics of perception does not need to be restricted to visual analysis or the reading of signs but also involves embodied experience.

DRAMATURGY

There are of course many ways of analysing dramaturgical strategies in the theatre. My approach to dramaturgy is inspired by postdramatic theatre, performance installations and the live performance (although not excluding plays), which has led to identifying three planes of dramaturgy.[9] These planes or layers continuously inflect and interfere with each other, evidently. They are, respectively, the *plane of composition*, the ensuing *modes of audience address*, and the *social and artistic context* of a work in case. I will briefly explain these layers and point out how they inform a dramaturgical analysis.

First, I distinguish the *plane of composition*, comprising of all the tools and tactics used to create, design and structure a performance, to organize space and arrange time so that the performance is carried across from a begin-point *a* to an end point *z*, according to a specific, idiosyncratic logic that provides structural coherence. This is the 'internal fabric' or texture of the performance event (Turner and Behrndt 2008, 3). In my approach, this can involve the plot structure of a well-made play, but as well *Dança Doente*'s refusal of progress – where the principle of inertia defines the logic of the event and its consistency – or *Bacchae*'s playing with the tension between Dionysian drives and Apollonian reason. This dramaturgical plane also involves the use of (theatrical) means to create such scenes or situations. In a scene in *Bacchae*, one of the dancers climbs on a chair and temporarily adopts a convulsive bodily posture that sits somewhere between an exotic bird and a very old lady. Her words are rather rude and horny, as if plucked straight away from a B-film or an obscure internet chatbox, while she stutters extremely. This leads to hilarious situations: while stuck in this physical corset, she screams, 'I-i-i-i-i w-a-a-a-a-nt t-o-o-o f-f-f-f-u-c-k-k-k-k you, I-i-i w-w-i-i-i-i-i-l-l-l-l-l c-c-c-c-co-o-me a-a-a-a-and g-e-e-et you,' while not going anywhere of course. Here it is not the primacy of the word or the act of intentional speaking that defines the scene, instead, the sputtering voice, the warped posture and the facial expression together mount to an impression of a fantastic animal, which creates an imprint on the retina and produces a tension one feels in one's body. In all its chaotic turmoil, *Bacchae* resists the linear structure of conventional tragedy. In an after-talk, Marlene Freitas remarked that she is interested in dream logic, since in dreams, one can combine people or situations and shift from one place or person to the other, without wondering how or why one gets there. She seeks to create a similar freedom on stage. From a logocentric perspective, watching the 2.5-hour show could cause some annoyance, when wanting to know what this show is 'exactly about'. Yet when accepting Freitas's redistribution of the sensible, it can also put one on track of this free-floating associative logic, and touch upon the liberty of children's play or, indeed, dreams.

A second layer in dramaturgical analysis pertains to *modes of audience address* – this is an element that Rancière largely ignores or discusses in very general terms only. Spectators do not just look at a theatre performance. Whether 'en groupe' or singled out, whether seated or walking around, they are addressed in specific ways, and positioned through address: they are perhaps confronted or aroused, they can be treated as guests or as outsiders, as sensitive bodies, as citizens, and so on. In *Visuality in the Theatre*, Maaike Bleeker observes that through this address, spectators are invited to adopt a particular point of view from which to look at what is presented on stage. Bleeker terms this presented viewpoint the 'subject of vision', to be distinguished from the subject seeing and the performance event as the subject seen (2008, 80). Bleeker's subject of vision does not imply that spectators (the subjects seeing) always accept or identify with the presented or implicated perspective. In fact, Bleeker's theory precisely helps to explain how experiences of frustration, annoyance or displacement are the product of a collision between the subject seeing and the subject of vision. *Dança Doente* takes such a collision quite literally. Throughout the full duration of the show, a large rectangular screen covers much of the top-right half of the stage, displaying only the legs of the performers who regularly position themselves behind the screen. The screen obviously obstructs the view, adding up to the logic of resisting the spectacle that governs the entire performance. About halfway the show, Marcelo Evelin briefly changes the dynamic of small-scale tremors by inserting a fierce and highly sexually charged duet aka fight between a younger and an older male dancer.[10] Here, not only heteronormativity but also the 'imperative of youth' enter the performance's canvas: to present an aged body as a sexual body is to ask who takes part in defining how a desiring body (on a stage) looks like. And how it feels. Neither of the dancers holds back, while grappling and wrestling forcefully. The scene is of such intensity that the red welts in their bare chest and back are almost felt within one's own skin.

Both *Dança Doente* and *Bacchae* are not very forthcoming, in terms of audience address, as they both avoid clear signals of what the show is 'about'. I deliberately chose these works because they can easily be regarded as either hermetic or completely open to everyone's interpretation, which is also reflected in reviews.[11] *Dança Doente* is qualified as dark and abstruse, *Bacchae* as resisting clear description and rational interpretation. These are works in which the emancipated spectator has free rein, so to say. Both performances, however, still do address spectators in specific ways. When adopting the subject of vision presented through gestures and movement, these bodies speak to us from an other-than-daily consciousness. Fragile in *Dança Doente*, frantic in *Bacchae*, it seems as if these bodies reach out to us from within another time, another world, another awareness. *Bacchae* swings back and forth between coded action and profuse cacophony; *Dança Doente* may evoke the kind of outer-world-ness that illness or extreme fatigue can create. These works redistribute the sensible through 'irresponsible' play and by persevering weakness, by persistently acting against readability and transparency, and instead presenting us with bodies that are concerned with existence itself, with desire, drifts and drives. This redistribution establishes a process of political subjectivation, yet different than in Ho Rui An's case, and perhaps in a more subtle way. A remark by dramaturg Stephanie Carp will help explaining this. She once gave a beautiful description of Christoph Marthaler's non-active, because sleeping, characters: 'Sleep refuses to be fixed in time. Sleep relieves the strain of meaning. In sleep and dreams [one can express different possibilities of existence]: what else people could be, if they could. Sleeping, dreaming, daydreaming .... Sleep relieves the burden of intentional speaking; it has no goal; it dilates time' (Carp 1997, 72). Although employing different means and strategies, both performances equally produce a radical openness, which creates a sense of freedom, a 'what else people could be, if they could'. This glimpse of potentiality is intensely political, in my view, directed against the 'police' of normativity and standardization. To me at least, seeing bodies that are distinctively 'other' – without this otherness being defined exactly, hence remaining radically open – generated an experience of intense consolation and relief. In *The Politics of Aesthetics*, Rancière remarks that political art does not employ clear messages that create 'awareness' on the side of the spectators but rather is achieved through an active negotiation between the readability of a message and 'a sensible or perceptual shock caused, conversely, by the uncanny, by that which resists signification' (2004, 63).[12] In both performances, precisely the uncanny becomes significant. These fragile and frantic bodies remind us of our own vulnerability and free us from the imperative to perform – if only temporarily.

Taking quite a different stance towards readability, Ho Rui An explicitly shows how popular imagery may be read *differently*. With a great sense of wit, he introduces the colonial wife next to the imperial ruler (or the female teacher, in *Anna and the King*), who comes to the rescue by never sweating at all. Her coolness functions as a safe haven for the colonial enterprise; she reproduces the house by occupying the heart of what Ho Rui An terms 'the global domestic: an all-encompassing, air-conditioned planetary interior'.[13] Also present in this fanned interior, usually in the shadow but now put in the spotlights, is the figure of the punkawala, the servant who manually operates the fan that is to provide fresh air and solace to the sweaty imperial back. Ho Rui An's dissection of both colonial women and the punkawala is full of ambiguity as he portrays them as both heroically tasked with being in the centre of the global domestic and being confined to the colonial house. *Solar* thus resets the perceptual coordinates of commonality and disrupts the hierarchies of knowledge brought about by colonialism.

Ho Rui An's epistemic interventions put us on track of the third layer of dramaturgical analysis, which attends to the *social and artistic context* in which a work is being made and presented. This wider context always resonates within a work – even when obscured or when a performance pretends not to. We might regard this work-world connection as 'the crossing and re-crossing of intensities across and between these surfaces' (Read 2008, 37). *Solar* is full of such intensities. Ho Rui An decolonializes power relations, by exposing the vulnerability of the men (formerly) in power, while recasting the women and the punkawalas from the shadow into the light. He does not replace the one position with the other but shows how these positions are deeply entangled, and how politics and power are essentially also embodied affairs. Meanwhile his story is full of absurdist twists and little jokes. This preference for certain styles or materials is part of the artistic context, which also works its way through in an artwork, similar to preferences for certain working methods, materials, recurring themes or motifs, affinities with certain ideas or people, and so on. One can think of Marcelo Evelin's kinship with butoh, or of Marlene Freitas's personal repertoire of affinities, materializing in her 'stage figures' who act like wind-up dolls, tinkering with stage objects and self-fabricated music instruments, while manifesting all sorts of uncontrolled behaviour. This highly contrasts with what is usually required from employees at the office, where rationality, control-ability or calculation are favoured over playfulness, intensity, animalistic drive or physical vulnerability. And yet, it is precisely in these ambiguous, embodied domains that corporeal intelligence emerges. It is the domain where all three performances tap into, each in their own way, all using the body as a motor for political subjectivation.

PENSIVE BODIES

By attending to the dramaturgy of performances, one takes into account, among other things, the significance of audience address. This notion seems rather antithetical to Rancière's resistance to artistic intentionality, in 'The Emancipated Spectator', where he states that spectators should not adopt the 'messages' conveyed by directors (2009, 14).[14] Address, however, is not the equivalent of a (univocal) 'message'. Acknowledging the role of address, instead, helps to make clear that a performance is not a neutral surface on which the spectator projects her associations, and that interpretation, in turn, does not exist independently from address. Rancière's resistance is also a little surprising when considering his essay 'The Pensive Image', where Rancière analyses photographs and other artworks in a way rather close to dramaturgical analysis.[15] In turn, his understanding of pensiveness, referring to a zone of indeterminacy in how a viewer is invited to relate to the work, provides a useful perspective on the 'pensive bodies' in the performances discussed in this contribution, and brings together various strands of argumentation in this chapter.

Rancière describes pensiveness as something that manifests itself in those moments in artworks when two aesthetic registers interfere with one another. This creates a certain ambiguity – an impossibility to decide on how to read or understand the work. Such pensiveness can arise when an artwork uses both representational and abstract strategies, for instance, or when at the (open) end of a narrative an element is introduced that does not bring the action to a close but instead replaces the action for an affect. Similarly, a work may hover in between thought and sensation, in between art and reality, or in between the literal and the figurative. The interference precisely is the 'effect' and occasionally the 'affect' of the work (2009, 124–25).

Rancière arrives at this sense of indeterminacy through a critical reading of Barthes's distinction between punctum and studium, respectively indicating the affective and informational layers through which art communicates. Rancière analyses in detail the well-known picture of the handcuffed soldier who is about to be executed. Rancière notes that Barthes locates the punctum partly in the eyes of the soldier, sentenced to death; we are struck by the eyes of the man who is about to die (112). Rancière, however, aptly remarks that nothing in the picture tells us that this man is going to die. In order to be affected by the picture (the punctum), we need to rely on external information, which is outside of the image and belongs to the studium. The picture's affect, argues Rancière, resides in the entanglement of punctum and studium, in how they operate in and through one another. Rancière provides many examples of pensiveness that arise from colliding expressive registers. Next to the photographic work of Rineke Dijkstra and Walker Evans he mentions the films of Abbas Kiarostami, whose work sits in between cinema, photography and poetry. Rancière describes how the roads and landscapes in his films simultaneously can be seen as belonging to the regime of representation, depicting a route leading from one point to another, and as operating on a plane of abstract composition, producing a play with lines, figures and spirals (125).

Pensiveness is basically about the tension between aesthetic regimes: 'The pensiveness of the image is [...] the latent presence of one regime of expression in another' (124). Pensiveness arises when Barthes's studium shimmers through the punctum but can also be located in Loïe Fuller's serpentine dance, when the mimetic vibrates within the abstract form. Pensiveness, then, perhaps describes the actual experiencing of a distribution of the sensible at work. We may recognize such pensiveness in the three performances discussed here, since they too provoke a sense of indeterminacy regarding what bodies we see on stage and how we are invited to look at them. Marcelo Evelin's *Dança Doente* operates in between the representational and the performative. Its resistance to perform produces a relief from the strain of meaning, while we continue to ask what 'sickness' in this context may entail. *Bacchae* hovers in between discipline and desire, between rationality and sensory experience, and also its reception swings back and forth between the hermeneutic impulse and the excess of indulgence. In those fluctuations we can recognize the never-ending struggle between Dionysian and Apollonian drives that are at the heart of Euripides's *Bacchae* (in this sense, Freitas *does* stay close to tragedy). In *Solar: A Meltdown*, Ho Rui An inserts a sense of vulnerability in uneven power relations. The sweaty colonialist appears to have an internal weakness; he survives due to his wife and the efforts of the punkawala. Ho Rui An reads and rewrites these bodies for us, yet these corporeal palimpsests also exceed writing. The clash of expressive registers is exquisitely captured in the 'image' of sweat. We can see sweat but it also escapes the image: thinking of sweat we can almost smell it; we engage our flesh memory or revisit personal moments of physical exertion or social anxiety. In sweating, interiority becomes exteriority, as bodily fluids pour out of the body and into the world.

These colliding aesthetic registers instigate a return to the politics of perception, which, concludingly, may be regarded as an invitation to engage with pensiveness. In *Aisthesis*, Rancière refers to art encounters and theatre scenes as 'little optical machine[s]' that show us thought; they are concepts at work that allow us to think (2011, xi). Thinking, in turn, is 'always firstly thinking the thinkable – a thinking that modifies what is thinkable by welcoming that what was unthinkable' (ibid.). Not only images or 'optical machines' make us think. Bodies do this as well. Theatre's politics of perception, then, does not need to be restricted to texts or images but instead opens up the thinkable to the corporeality of bodies and to visceral experiences of the flesh. To fully appreciate such embodied perceptions, I suggest to move beyond logocentrism or the domain of opsis, and instead employ the perspective of dramaturgy. Dramaturgy provides ample space for pensiveness. Pensive bodies, whether controlled or uncontrolled, sweaty, soft or shivering, do address us. They are capable of instigating a redistribution of the sensible, of generating a sensitivity for our corporeal existence, and posit physicality and vulnerability at the heart of commonality.

NOTES

1. *Dança Doente* draws inspiration from the Japanese choreographer Hijikata Tatsumi, key figure in the development of butoh dance. See https://www.demolitionincorporada.com/danca-doente (accessed 22 September 2020).

2. See https://www.demolitionincorporada.com/danca-doente (accessed 22 September 2020).

3. In *The Politics of Aesthetics*, Rancière actually distinguishes three regimes, that is, the ethical regime of images, the mimetic realm of (poetic) representation and the aesthetic regime of the arts (2004, 20–22). Since his argument primarily focuses on the difference between the latter two, I do so as well.

4. For other examples and a thorough theoretical underpinning of the resistance to perform (based on Bataille and Agamben), I warmly recommend Konstantina Georgelou's PhD dissertation *performless* (2011).

5. Biopower, briefly put, entails the exercising of power through the controlling and disciplining of bodies. Foucault specifically addressed military training, schools, prisons and hospitals, but the concept can be widely applied to any process in which power relations are enacted through the social body. One can think of assembly line

work, the skinny models of the fashion industry, genetic modification, bioweaponry and more. See Foucault (2003) and Lazzarato (2002).

6. See Marlene Monteiro Freitas's page on Key Performance, at http://www.keyperformance.se/?page_id=5498 (accessed 20 July 2018).

7. When discussing Appia's innovations in scenography, for instance, Rancière focuses on his visionary ideas, and less on the theatrical event itself. In Appia's case, this is hardly surprising of course, since many of his ideas only materialized in sketches and writing (2013, 121–31).

8. Logocentrism entails the primacy of the word or text, which brings in a set of other values as well, such as structure, order, hierarchy, causality, rationality or telos (orientation towards a clear goal or end) (see Lehmann [1997]). There is also a considerable history of visuality in which vision is paired with objectivity, rationality, transparency and truthfullness (Bleeker 2008).

9. This approach also evolved out of a collaborative teaching practice, connected to BA and MA dramaturgy classes at Utrecht University.

10. Marcelo Evelin himself is the older dancer.

11. This was in particular the case in Dutch reviews in newspaper journals.

12. To Rancière, political art ideally produces an effect that is 'a negotiation between opposites, between the readability of the message that threatens to destroy the sensible form of art and the radical uncanniness that threatens to destroy all political meaning' (2004, 63).

13. See http://horuian.com/solar-a-meltdown/ (accessed 22 September 2020).

14. In his prelude to *Aisthesis*, however, Rancière makes room for the possibility of an artwork or theatre scene being an 'artistic proposition' (2013, xi).

15. This essay is included in *The Emancipated Spectator* (2009).

REFERENCES

Bleeker, Maaike. 2008. *Visuality in the Theatre: The Locus of Looking*. Basingstoke: Palgrave MacMillan.

Carp, Stephanie. 1997. 'Slow Life is Long: On the Theatre of Christoph Marthaler'. *Theaterschrift* 12: 65–78.

Cvejić, Bojana. 2015. *Choreographing Problems: Expressive Concepts in European Contemporary Dance and Performance*. London: Palgrave Macmillan.

Fischer-Lichte, Erika. 1997. 'Discovering the Spectator: Changes to the Paradigm of Theatre in the Twentieth Century'. In *The Show and the Gaze of Theatre: A European Perspective*, 41–60. Iowa, IA: University of Iowa Press.

Flaxman, Seth, Sharad Goeld, and Justin M. Rao. 2016. 'Filter Bubbles, Echo Chambers, and online News Consumption'. *Public Opinion Quarterly* 80 (Special Issue): 298–320.

Foucault, Michel. 2003. *'Society Must Be Defended': Lectures at the Collège de France, 1975–1976*. New York, NY: Picador Books.

Georgelou, Konstantina. 2011. *Performless: The Operation of l'Informe in Postdramatic Theatre*. PhD Dissertation, Utrecht University.

Groot Nibbelink, Liesbeth. 2012. 'Radical Intimacy. Ontroerend Goed meets The Emancipated Spectator.' *Contemporary Theatre Review* 22.3: 412–420.
Groot Nibbelink, Liesbeth. 2019. *Nomadic Theatre: Mobilizing Theory and Practice on the European Stage*. London: Bloomsbury Methuen Drama.
Han, Byung-Chul. 2015. *The Burnout Society*. Stanford, CA: Stanford University Press.
Kerkhoven, Marianne van. 2005. 'De herpolitisering van de blik. Naar een nieuwe relatie met het publiek'. In *Theater moet schuren! Essays over de maatschappelijke opdracht van het theater*, edited by Pol Eggermont et al., 104–115. Amsterdam: Boekmanstudies.
Lazzarato, Maurizio. 2002. 'From Biopower to Biopolitics'. *Pli: The Warwick Journal of Philosophy* 13: 99–113.
Lehmann, Hans-Thies. 1997. 'From Logos to Landscape: Text in Contemporary Dramaturgy'. *Performance Research* 2.1: 55–60.
Lehmann, Hans-Thies. 2006. *Postdramatic Theatre*. Translated and introduced by Karen Jürs-Munby. London: Routledge.
Lepecki, André. 2006. *Exhausting Dance: Performance and the Politics of Movement*. New York, NY and London: Routledge.
Lepecki, André. 2016. S*ingularities: Dance in the Age of Performance*. London and New York, NY: Routledge.
McKenzie, Jon. 2001. *Perform or Else: From Discipline to Performance*. London: Routledge.
Rancière, Jacques. [2000] 2004. *The Politics of Aesthetics*. Translated and with an introduction by Gabriel Rockhill. London: Continuum.
Rancière, Jacques. 2009. 'The Emancipated Spectator'. In *The Emancipated Spectator*. Translated by Gregory Elliott, 1–23. London: Verso.
Rancière, Jacques. 2009. 'The Pensive Image'. In *The Emancipated Spectator*. Translated by Gregory Elliott, 107–132. London: Verso.
Rancière, Jacques. [2011] 2013. *Aisthesis: Scenes from the Aesthetic Regime of Art*. Translated by Zakir Paul. London: Verso.
Read, Alan. 2008. *Theatre, Intimacy and Engagement: The Last Human Venue*. Basingstoke: Palgrave Macmillan.
Sassatelli, Roberta. 2014. *Fitness Culture: Gyms and the Commercialisation of Discipline and Fun*. Basingstoke: Palgrave Macmillan.
Schäfer, Mirko Tobias, and Karin van Es. 2017. *The Datafied Society: Studying Culture through Data*. Amsterdam: Amsterdam University Press.
Sunstein, Cass R. 2017. *Republic: Divided Democracy in the Age of Social Media*. Princeton, NJ: Princeton University Press.
Turner, Cathy, and Synne K. Behrndt. 2008. *Dramaturgy and Performance*. Basingstoke: Palgrave MacMillan.
Uricchio, William. 2011. 'The Algorithmic Turn: Photosynth, Augmented Reality and the Changing Implications of the Image'. *Visual Studies* 26.1 (March): 25–35.

Part II

THE ROLE OF THEATRE AND PERFORMANCE

Chapter 3

Performing Philosophy

Rancière as Playwright, Director and Performer in **The Ignorant Schoolmaster**

Shulamith Lev-Aladgem

One of Jacques Rancière's most celebrated texts today is, indubitably, *The Ignorant Schoolmaster: Five Lessons in Intellectual Emancipation* (1991 [1987]). From my very first encounter with it I have been particularly drawn to its singular and different style of writing, in comparison with other books by this author. Rather than his usual intellectual mode of writing, which at times is highly complex, here Rancière writes as if he were talking enthusiastically to a group of ordinary people. Such awareness of the exceptional literariness of this book has already been noted by several scholars. Yves Citton points to the 'tentative', 'experimental' and 'provisional' nature of the book and indicates that 'rarely has he [Rancière] been as literary as in this early book, which takes the form of a narrative' (Citton 2010, 26). Maarten Simons and Jan Masschelein emphasize the storytelling quality of the lessons, which 'do not explain, but tell a story' (Simons and Masschelein 2011, 4); while Kristin Ross, in her Introduction to the English version of the book, recognizes more specifically the affinity of the book with theatre: 'His [Rancière's] commentary contextualizes, rehearses, reiterates, dramatizes [...]' (Ross 1991, xxii). However, Ross, like the other above-noted intellectuals, provides only a general comment without looking more thoroughly at the theatre-like nature of *The Ignorant Schoolmaster* – a project indeed better suited to a theatre scholar.

My attention to the theatre-likeness of *The Ignorant Schoolmaster* was further heightened by Peter Hallward, who had already emphasized how 'the most fundamental, and illuminating, dimension of Rancière's anarchic conception of equality is that which relates to theatre – in both the literal and metaphoric senses of the term' (Hallward 2006, 110). As a political philosopher,

Hallward's main interest lies indeed in posing strategic questions and concerns that Rancière's 'theatrocratic configuration raises' (122). However, as a theatre scholar, I was drawn rather to how, by teasing out the ways in which Rancière employs theatre to elucidate his political theory, philosophy comes close to theatre. Thus, undertaking this study of the theatre-likeness of *The Ignorant Schoolmaster* was triggered by the attempt to determine what kind of theatre is embedded in the book, and how it heralds and germinates Rancière's singular way of thinking theatre-and-politics.

Looking at Rancière's entire oeuvre, and specifically at its recent publications on the aesthetic regime of art and its politicity, it seems that he favours other artistic forms than theatre such as cinema, installations, photography and above all literature. Thus, surprisingly enough (particularly from the viewpoint of a theatre scholar and practitioner) while on the one hand, as already noted, Rancière envisages the political moment as a theatrical event, on the other hand, his attitude towards theatre in general and certain notable theatre artists in particular is complex and paradoxical. It is precisely this attachment–detachment relationship between Rancière and theatre that also drew me to *The Ignorant Schoolmaster* as an early text by this writer, in which there is as yet no clear sign of this complexity and which reveals even at first glance Rancière's deep understanding of how theatre works, especially the practice of storytelling.

Such an intellectual journey of fleshing out the theatre-likeness of *The Ignorant Schoolmaster* necessitated an appropriate analytical model, which I found when I encountered the works of two English political philosophers, Mackenzie and Porter (2011a, b), who provide a detailed 'method of dramatization' for the reading of political philosophy. It is important to note here that although Mackenzie and Porter usually employ the word 'drama' and its variations, they refer by it to both drama (play/script) and theatre (performance), as construed from their method presented in the following.

THE METHOD OF DRAMATIZATION: THE POLITICAL PHILOSOPHER AS PLAYWRIGHT AND DIRECTOR

In their article 'Dramatization as Method in Political Theory' and their book *Dramatizing the Political: Deleuze and Guattari*, both published in 2011, Mackenzie and Porter draw on Gilles Deleuze's individual work and Deleuze and Felix Guattari's joint work, and present the method of dramatization as an artistic system of engaging with both the writing and reading of political theory. Deleuze and Guattari's basic provocative contention is that the political concept would not function 'in the world of representation *without the dramatic dynamisms*' (Deleuze 2004, 98, emphasis mine). Mackenzie and

Porter's unique contribution, particularly for theatre scholars, lies is their ability to translate Deleuze and Guattari's idea into a detailed accessible analytical method in which *dramatic* refers to both drama (play/script) and theatre (performance). Its main claim is that what is important for the philosopher is not so much to explain a concept empirically but to 'bring the concept to life' as forceful, vivid, vital, bold and attractive. At the heart of this method lies the assumption that in order to bring a political concept to life and render it compelling and striking for the readers, the philosopher has to look for means 'outside the confines of the discipline' – in theatre (Mackenzie and Porter 2011a, 498). The philosopher has to act as both playwright and director, conceptualizing his theory as a play/script 'with characters and roles that the readers can and must re-enact' (488) and thus become 'readers-performers' (498). Thus, 'dramatization' for the philosopher is a method of both scripting and staging his political idea in order to collaborate and attract the readers.

Mackenzie and Porter draw attention to the 'surprising forms' that this method can take (485), such as slogans, characters/roles, humour and irony (Mackenzie and Porter 2011b, 75–76; 2011a, 485, 494), all planned to induce in the reader such emotional reactions as excitement, sadness, happiness, laughter, puzzlement or confusion (Mackenzie and Porter 2011b, 75–76). I shall appropriate all these components as anchors in the following demonstration of how Rancière brings to life his radical ideas in *The Ignorant Schoolmaster*. I shall also show how Rancière even extends the method, since he not only offers the reader a script to be acted out in order to better internalize and more easily accept his radical ideas but even participates himself in the event as the leading character who directs the entire performance.

Accordingly, Mackenzie and Porter's method facilitates the following discussion on why and how *The Ignorant Schoolmaster* is a written text that strives to appear as – if it were an oral text – a live performance facilitated by a storyteller who is also playwright, director and performer.

A SHORT SYNOPSIS OF THE BOOK

Rancière found the writings of Joseph Jacotot when, around 1974, he turned to the archives in order to study the conditions and consciousness of French workers in the mid-nineteenth century. The book, *The Ignorant Schoolmaster: Five Lessons in Intellectual Emancipation*, is Rancière's sympathetic reading of Jacotot's work. Ross (1991), the translator of the book into English, indicates in her Introduction that the book can be understood as Rancière's intervention in the debates on education in France in the mid-1980s. On the one side there were the Republicans with their idea of the rationality of knowledge, taught by teachers who found no interest in the sociopolitical background of their students. On the other side stood prominent sociologists, such as Pierre Bourdieu and Jean-Claude Passeron, who advocated a system of education that would address social differences and inequalities. Although there is no direct indication as such in the book, Ross suggests that Rancière presented Jacotot's educational model in order to criticize both sides. However, what truly fascinated Rancière was the new theory on equality that he found in Jacotot's writings, which led him to think anew about equality not as an end to be achieved in the future but as a starting point or presupposition to be continually practised. Accordingly, Rancière was drawn to the pedagogical model of Jacotot not as an optional model to be adopted by the Ministry of Education but as a clear example of equality in process – a radical novel idea that in fact dismantles the accepted basic rule of Western thought, culture and life from Plato until today, which according to Rancière is based on inequality. This revolutionary assumption of equality in process would become the core of Rancière's entire philosophy on both politics and aesthetics (Rancière 1992).

Jacotot, as presented by Rancière, was a lecturer and teacher of French literature, whose ideas about intellectual emancipation had caused a brief scandal in Holland and France around 1830 and who was then forgotten. Jacotot had participated in the French Revolution as a soldier, administrator and teacher. Following the restoration of the Bourbon monarchy in 1818, he was exiled from France and became a teacher in Louvain (Belgium). There he faced a problem, since he did not speak Flemish while some of his students could not speak French. In order to overcome this obstacle, he recommended, through a translator, that they take the popular bilingual novel by Fénelon, *Télémaque*, and read and recite it, while also writing about it in French. The success of this chance proposal led Jacotot, as Rancière narrates, to realize that he had managed to teach something that he himself did not know, and in this respect was an ignorant teacher. Second, he realized that his students were thereby encouraged to learn by themselves, and that this process reactivated their innate ability to learn their first language as infants, on their own (Rancière 1991, 5). For Jacotot, the ability of young children to acquire their mother tongue by themselves became evidence for his presupposition that all human beings share equal intelligence. Following this premise, he proposed an educational model based on the principle that everyone can learn anything new by comparing and relating it to what he or she already knows. Thus, the teacher's vocation is first and foremost to encourage self-confidence among his/her students by guiding them to realize their own intellectual capacities and power as intellectual subjects (15, 108). Such a pedagogy, which is based on the equality of intelligence, was therefore defined by Jacotot as 'universal teaching' (16), and such a teacher, who reminds his students that they are already capable of learning by themselves, was defined by Jacotot as an 'emancipatory master' (12).

Discussing this book through 'the method of dramatization' reveals, I contend, a drama in its two meanings: The first is the drama as play/script and performance by which Rancière brings his radical idea to life. Rancière writes as if he were talking directly to a group of people. Thus the text largely resembles a live performance facilitated by a skilled storyteller. However, he not only recounts the five lessons that were constructed by an ignored teacher from the past (Joseph Jacotot), but he himself takes on the role of that teacher as if he were an actor or performer, and stages both himself and the reader within a fictional theatrical event. Thus, Rancière manages in a dramaturgical move both to conceptualize Jacotot's ideas as if they were his own and to equate between the content of his idea – an alternative pedagogical model, and the form by which he delivers this model – a theatrical, pedagogical event, enabling the reader to experiment and directly experience the exceptional model. In other words, by using the means of the theatre, as detailed in the following, Rancière presents as well as activates the model through its own principles. He thus stages a unique encounter between philosophy and theatre, transforming philosophy into literature into theatre/performance, providing optimal access to his novel thought. The second meaning of a drama is that of the exciting and crucial moment in Rancière's intellectual itinerary. If until then Rancière had been mainly preoccupied with criticizing and denouncing the accepted leftist thinking of his contemporaneous intellectuals, in *The Ignorant Schoolmaster* he offers the anchors of a new, radical philosophy based on a novel presupposition of equality. The singular literariness of *The Ignorant Schoolmaster* signals the in-between, liminal phase in which Rancière has just begun to formulate his new theory, still looking for his own voice, and thus engaging with a means 'outside the confines of [his own] discipline' – in theatre (Mackenzie and Porter 2011a, 498) in order to deliver his novel thinking as safely as possible, persuading and keeping his readers connected and attentive.

SLOGANEERING THE TITLE: ENCAPSULATING THE CORE IDEAS IN THE TITLE

Rancière begins to dramatize directly from the title, which he posits in the form of a slogan. A slogan is a form of writing that 'does not represent something familiar and easily communicable' (Mackenzie and Porter 2011a, 495), nor does it operate on the basis of facts or in accordance with a logic or the truth, but, rather on the basis of its appropriateness' (Mackenzie and Porter 2011b, 85). The slogan is a collective, challenging assemblage meant to change or arrange things so as to intensify the argument by producing first confusion and then 'compel[ling] obedience' (85).

The title, *The Ignorant Schoolmaster: Five Lessons in Intellectual Emancipation*, is a provocative assemblage in which appropriateness is constructed upon a symmetry of apparent contradictions: (1) between the first and the second parts, and (2) between the two sub-parts of each part of the title – an ignoramus and a schoolmaster are usually two opposite subjects, while lessons are usually associated with formality and discipline and not with emancipation. This multiplicity of oppositions creates concomitantly an effect of confusion, puzzlement and shock, while at the same time it also arouses curiosity and a sense of suspicion that the apparent, straightforward reading of the title might be a manipulation that implies a totally different and novel relationship between these words and their meaning.

Thus, by sloganeering the title, Rancière provides a subversive statement, producing a shocking effect that provokes questions such as how and in what way does Rancière think of ignorance, who is the ignorant schoolmaster, why five lessons, what kind of lessons and what is the reason for the strange connection between the words 'intellectual' and 'emancipation'? Moreover, if an ignorant teacher can teach lessons in emancipation, does this mean that a master of knowledge cannot? Does not such a title invert our usual way of thinking? The title indeed encapsulates the entire book through the play of sloganeering, compelling the reader to move curiously and attentively into the text in order to seek the logic behind the contradictions in general, and the answers to the above questions in particular.

The title as a slogan is also a condensed, multi-layered text by which Rancière encodes a huge drama – an exciting and extremist event in his life. The words 'five lessons' evoke another title, that of *Althusser's Lesson* (1974), Rancière's first book, which also comprises five lessons. The first lesson of this latter book echoes yet another lesson – that of Althusser's lesson offered to John Lewis (Althusser 1976 [1973]). This playing with the echo effect through the literary device of intertextuality is purposely deceptive, drawing the reader into interpreting the resemblance between the two titles as an allusion to continuity between the books, probably focusing on the same (school)master (Althusser). However, this impression is soon thwarted. Reading the first line of *The Ignorant Schoolmaster* immediately clarifies that the echo effect aims at dramatizing an additional radical contradiction, that between the 'Old Master' (Rancière 1991, 16) – Althusser (and all those like him) – and the new schoolmaster – Joseph Jacotot.

As the following reading of the text will reveal, this multiplicity of contradictions exposes the title as an assemblage of intensive relations, not of mere oppositions but of 'pure difference' (Mackenzie and Porter 2011b, 491), which in fact means a complex kind of contradiction: 'Instead of something distinguished from something else, imagine something which distinguishes itself – and yet that from which it distinguishes itself does not distinguish itself from it' (Deleuze 1994, 28).

In *Althusser's Lesson* Rancière publicly distinguishes himself from Althusser. In a polemic, poignant writing he expresses his dramatic break from his eminent teacher, for whom he was one of the favourites chosen to continue his master's intellectual heritage. Althusser's fierce denouncement of the uprising of May 1968 in France for not being led by the French Communist Party totally shook Rancière, who read the event differently, as an autonomous, spontaneous grassroots protest, thus completely against the grain of his own structuralist Marxist belief. This dissonant experience directed Rancière to publicly rebut his intellectual mentor through five lessons in orthodoxy, politics, self-criticism, history and discourse, each criticizing an aspect of Althusser's ideology. The aim of these lessons was to sharply expose the oppressive presupposition of Althusserianism, which perceived the proletariat as a single unit of the masses in need of the leadership of intellectual masters in order to act out a political revolution. What Rancière realized and rejected was Althusser's elitist and hierarchical thinking, devoid of any reflexivity, and differentiating between thinking and manual labour, science and ideology, workers and masters, and thus perpetuated oppression by establishing a class division that preserved the privileged position of the intellectuals/bourgeoisie. The deep recognition that rather than emancipating the workers, Althusserian Marxist science took away their voice, and actually advocated a contemporary version of Plato's philosopher-king idea, led Rancière to cut himself off from the left. Furthermore, as he told Peter Hallward in an interview in 2003, it was not so much the shock but the aftershock of 1968 that forced him to give up (temporarily) on philosophy as well. Not only could he not accept the philosophical stand developed at Paris VIII University, elevating the position of scholarly knowledge and turning the teachers into masters, but also his own doubts regarding his practice as a researcher and the problem he faced due to the invalidation of his diploma in philosophy at Paris VIII led him eventually to isolate himself as an archive consultant (Rancière 2003, 195).

His encounter with the archive stimulated Rancière to spend about ten years seeking the proper voice of the people. Investigating documents and chronicles on French factory workers in the 1830s, he did not find, as he might have expected, ignorant masses of the tired proletariat, complaining about their harsh conditions, awaiting the bourgeoisie intellectuals to show them the route to emancipation. Instead, he found autodidact workers engaged by night in aesthetic activities of writing poetry, prose, letters and newspaper pieces, all of which Rancière read as a poetic transgression thwarting the accepted contradictions between labour and leisure, workers and bourgeoisie, and mostly between people of logos (those who act rationally) and people of pathos (those who act only emotionally). He formulated his research in two subsequent books: *The Nights of Labour* (1981), which presented a new way of thinking the worker, based on his empirical archive findings, and *The Philosopher and His Poor* (1983), which outlined the traditional, hierarchical approach to thinking the worker from Plato and Aristotle to Marx and Sartre.

Although the seed of his political theory had already been geminated in *The Nights of Labour*, until then Rancière had primarily been occupied with criticism, delivering lessons on cases of inequality, but still without presenting any alternative, new lessons on equality. This was to occur when Rancière ran into Joseph Jacotot and his educational model of universal teaching/learning. This was a moment of revelation for Rancière, in which he found a new way of rethinking equality as an a priori starting point, the axis around which all his theoretical oeuvre would revolve. Thus, all these milestones of Rancière's intellectual itinerary before writing *The Ignorant Schoolmaster* are in fact embedded and encoded in the title. It would seem that Rancière's momentous and transformative encounter with Jacotot, temporarily situating him in a liminal phase, in between two fathers-masters, encouraged Rancière to employ the domain of theatre in order to bring to life his singular voice as also an echo or double of Jacotot.

SCRIPTING THE DRAMA/PLAY: THE APPEARANCE OF THE THEORY THROUGH STORYTELLING

While the earlier five lessons against Althusserianism had constituted a written frontal attack, the five new lessons of the ignorant schoolmaster appeared through a different strategy. The appearance of the new, radical idea of equality, for the first time, necessitated a virtuosic vehicle by which it would be safely received. The term 'appearance' is employed here deliberately, since my suggestion is that the choice of Rancière in this book to use devices from the domain of theatre in general and storytelling in particular was not only in order to bring his theory to life but more than that to continue to formulate his alternative idea on appearance through appearance itself. As Rancière had already realized in *The Nights of Labour*, the political is especially embedded in a moment of appearance 'when the real world wavers and seems to reel into mere appearance' (Rancière 1981, 19), such as when the French workers of the nineteenth century affirmed their ability to achieve appearance in the public sphere through artistic manifestations. Appearance for Rancière, as further configured in his later texts, is not an illusion of the surface that must be penetrated in order to expose the real and the true, as his Old Masters claim but, as underlined by Lewis E. Tyson, 'an event of sensation that disarticulates the order of things' (Tyson 2012a, 36) thus 'engendering profound [political] disruptions' (Tyson 2013, 56). The choice to dramatize *The Ignorant Schoolmaster* can therefore be construed as political from the outset, verifying Rancière's own idea regarding the politicalness embedded in the aesthetics of appearance, while at the same time demonstrating a sensitivity to the power of theatre in general to engender such an appearance. Accordingly, Rancière chose the theatrical 'as-if' principle, by which he appears in the text as if he were an actor playing a storyteller who throughout the story plays interchangeably Rancière, Jacotot and several other secondary roles. Rancière writes not only a script to be played out by the reader (Mackenzie and Porter 2011a, 488) but an entire participatory theatre in which he plays the protagonist who facilitates the collaboration of the readers as participants-students. The theatrical 'as-if' principle bears however an additional politicalness, since, as Tyson, following Rancière/Jacotot, indicates, the educational process itself is based 'on a will to experiment, perform and play' (Tyson 2012b, 8), which is, according to Tyson, '"the theatrical will" as a will to act "as-if"' (17).

In order to reinforce storytelling, as a specific appearance of the theatrical will to experiment, perform and play and thus as an aesthetic-political action, Rancière attacks rhetoric, the usual device of the philosopher, which has always been accepted as 'the art of *reasoning*' (Rancière 1991, 83, emphasis in original). For Rancière rhetoric is neither an artistic nor a truthful practice but only 'a control of reason over the intention to speak' (84), a 'perverted poetry', which disguises itself as truth and 'speaks in order to silence' (85). Towards the end of the book he also posits a strong self-reference to his aesthetic-political choice of acting a storyteller by citing Jacotot: 'Come and we will make our poetry. Long live the panecastic philosophy! It's a storyteller who never runs out of stories' (138).

The story of Jacotot, by which the educational model, as already indicated, is intended both to be fleshed out and tested/experienced by its own principles, is particularly interesting in its opening and ending moments. Rancière dramatizes them on the one hand as a contradiction of mood and atmosphere while on the other hand as a completion of the main radical idea. The opening of *The Ignorant Schoolmaster* already presents the important details of the story: the time, the identity of the protagonist, the place and the genre of the story. The choice of time is critical, since rather than adopting an exposition and/or a chronological recounting of the story, Rancière chooses to open with the turning point when the 'adventure' begins, seeking to arouse his readers' curiosity to hear more about who this unknown Jacotot was, and what adventure had brought him from France to Belgium. Therefore, Rancière goes back in time and provides a few more details about the important stations in Jacotot's biography. He delivers a short, focused characterization of a very interesting and attractive young teacher, not at all ignorant, whose life circumstances during the Revolution and then the restoration of the Bourbon monarchy brought about his encounter with unusual experiences, until he was forced into exile. Following this and using another tension-creating sentence, 'Chance decided differently' (1), Rancière moves on to tell us how when Jacotot became a teacher in Louvain (Belgium), he faced a problem, since he did not speak Flemish while his students could not speak French. By repeating the word 'chance', Rancière deliberately emphasizes the accidental nature of Jacotot's solution, who recommended that the students take the popular bilingual novel by Fénelon, *Télémaque*, and read and recite it, while also writing about it in French. This repetition enables Rancière in the role of the storyteller to emphasize briefly the moment of 'sudden illumination' (4) that had propelled Jacotot to enthusiastically compose a new pedagogical model. Such a legendary opening, which also generates a distancing of time, provides, I suggest, the receptive atmosphere into which Rancière immediately inserts Jacotot's/his radical theory of equality: 'The minimal link of a *thing in common* had to be established between himself [the teacher] and them [the students]' (2, emphasis in original). In other words, the basic anchor of intellectual emancipation, which is the vocation of the alternative pedagogical model, is a presupposition that there should always be some point of equality to be shared from the outset between two or more subjects.

Approaching the end of the theatrical event, the storyteller, who begins his story high-spirited and full of energy, becomes somewhat sombre, gloomy and tired. He recounts the entire scandal that Jacotot had caused and how unfortunately his opponents and allies alike had in fact all misunderstood the radical, political core of his model. Then, finally, Rancière completes Jacotot's/his idea of equality. Interestingly, he speaks this time not in the past tense as he does throughout the story but in the present tense while repeating what he has already sloganeered several times during the theatrical event: 'Equality is not given, nor it is claimed; it is practiced, it is *verified*' (137). Rancière, it is important to note, reiterates throughout the text those parts of Jacotot's method that he finds most important, and scores them *in italics*, as if they were slogans to be memorized. Moreover, the use of *italics* is also similar to the mode in which stage directions are written in a play/script, differentiated from dialogue, indicating changes of tone or intensity of speech, as well as referring to the bodily gestures of the character. Here, approaching the end of the book, the repetition is delivered as a declaration, affirming the message through the present tense and a change of voice highlighting the most important word (*verified*). However, the full meaning of the idea, which is concluded for the first time only here, at the end of the event, is delivered, in contrast, in the past tense, but again with one word in *italics*: 'Equality was not an end to attain, but a point of departure, a *supposition* to maintain in every circumstance' (138). This is the novel, original idea for which Rancière chose dramatization in order to conceptualize it in a form that would make it intelligible from its very first appearance. In his later publications he would reiterate it ceaselessly in various present-tense phrasings (Equality is an end to attain). Here, however, the storyteller prefers to leave the most important message still in the past (Equality was not an end to attain), sufficiently protected from those readers who might accept the collaborative extravaganza of the book as an intellectual-enough adventure but not yet a relevant-enough theory for the present.

THE STORYTELLER AND THE PARTICIPANTS: EXPERIENCING/ EXPERIMENTING THE NOVEL THEORY

Scripting a live performance of storytelling, including audience participation, supports the spontaneous, repetitive, improvisatory, disordered and non-edited nature of the text. This, however, is only the first impression that the text produces, while looking at it more attentively reveals that Rancière employs a basic dramaturgical principle by which he constructs the text in a spiral mode. The first chapter/lesson is a condensed synopsis of the theory. Hereafter, the storytelling extends its appropriation of characterization and the asides to the implied audience/readers, while it is also transformed into various types of role-playing, guided affective imagery and audience participation, including humour and irony, all of which are intended to reinforce the live and improvisatory appearance of the book in order to compel the readers to be attentive, focused and emotionally responsive. Above all Rancière seeks to facilitate the radical pedagogical model by means of its own poetic tool, so that the readers/implied audience will accept the new idea as much as possible through direct sensuous experience and experimentation.

Characterization

Mackenzie and Porter contend that the character/s of the scripted drama 'must not be read as everyday, 'more-or-less' human beings but as the outcome of 'a process of intense characterization' (Mackenzie and Porter 2011a, 488). Rancière indeed follows this requirement in his characterization of Jacotot, the protagonist, to the extent that he scatters throughout biographical details and historical scenes, probably fictional in part, in order to present an outstanding character that will retain his audience's involvement.

In the opening scene, Jacotot is characterized as a very intelligent and educated young man, who at the age of nineteen was already a teacher of rhetoric and a lawyer. A few years later, after succeeding in different employments, attained not by an ambitious ego but due to the tumultuous circumstances of the Revolution, he even taught 'analysis, ideology, ancient languages, pure mathematics, transcendent mathematics, and law' (1). Through this exaggerated, legendary characterization, Rancière manages immediately to present an appealing, intellectually gifted character, whose adventurous life was not an outcome of his will or personality but a coincidence of the historical circumstances that he had accidentally experienced. Rancière thereby indirectly emphasizes not only that Jacotot was not at all ignorant (and thus, following the sloganeering of the title, as already discussed, further propelling the readers into confusion regarding the identity of the ignorant teacher and the meaning of ignorance) but also that the radical, pedagogical model was not intentional but happened 'by chance' (3). This line of characterization, including the indication that Jacotot had once been a quiet, ordinary, traditional professor for thirty years (4), intends to intensify the effect of the 'accident' as a grand discovery and a miraculous-like inversion of Jacotot's thinking. It also underlines the transformative process that Jacotot underwent from the moment of his 'sudden illumination' (4) and 'revelation' (6), throughout his stormy life, in which he persistently defended his radical model against the dominance of Enlightenment progressivism, while retaining his modesty and integrity to the end.

Jacotot is also characterized as someone who was born to a poor family (11) yet managed to overcome his social condition and become an outstanding and famous intellectual. The character of Jacotot thus intertextualizes with those workers recounted in *The Nights of Labour*, demonstrating a clear, live example of Rancière's concept of the political subject whom he would present in his later publications: someone who has realized his own model of universal teaching/learning and who, from the moment of his intellectual breakthrough on, has never stopped claiming and verifying his own equality of intelligence through expressive-poetic speech. Moreover, the portrayal of Jacotot as of working-class origin enables Rancière to adopt a melodramatic storyline in which the hero moves from misfortune to fortune and back again to misfortune. The high-spirited, promising tone of the storyteller thus gradually converts into a somewhat disappointed and elegiac tone, only to end in the dramatic irony of the final words of the text.

Humour and Irony

Alongside the 'larger than life' empathetic and admiring characterization, Rancière also creates humoristic and ironic comic-relief punches. Humour and irony, as Mackenzie and Porter indicate, are forms of repetition by which humour 'dramatizes the contingency and absurdity of the concept' and irony 'ridicule[s] and usurp[s] the tendency to speak about it [the concept] in rather lofty terms' (Mackenzie and Porter 2011a, 486). 'Humour', as they add, is 'a form of artistic political intervention' (Mackenzie and Porter 2011b, 6), which 'has a significant philosophical function' (76) as an art of 'sabotage' (76) that 'creates an important felt sense' (76) of the argument. Rancière follows this line several times: It appears that Jacotot was not satisfied with the already incredible number of subjects that he had taught, and thereby decided to 'add Hebrew [...] . He believed, God knows why, that that language had a future' (12). Furthermore, his enthusiasm for his intellectual invention was so high that 'he began to teach two [more] subjects at which he was notably incompetent, painting and the piano [...], but he still didn't know Flemish' (14–15). Later on, the storyteller discloses that Jacotot managed to teach his printer's retarded son Hebrew and, surprisingly enough, he 'became an excellent lithographer. It goes without saying that he never used Hebrew for anything – except to know what more gifted and learned minds never knew: *it wasn't Hebrew*' (18, emphasis in original). Shortly after, the humoristic characterization continues when Jacotot is presented as 'a learned man, a renowned man of science and a virtuous family man [that] had gone crazy for not knowing Flemish' (18). From that point on Jacotot is presented not only as 'the Founder' but also as 'the madman' (22, 134).

The gloomy speech in the last section of the book continues to the very end, containing an ironic layer. The storyteller recounts the sad fate of Jacotot, whose journal was closed a short time after his death, and even the inscription on his tomb, which Rancière writes in capital letters, 'I BELIEVE THAT GOD CREATED THE HUMAN SOUL CAPABLE OF TEACHING ITSELF BY ITSELF, AND WITHOUT A MASTER', was unfortunately vandalized. However, even this melodramatic tone contains dramatic irony too, enabling Rancière to dramatize, for the last time, his theory as the slogan of all the other slogans in the book, insinuating that even if he himself will arrive at the same misfortune as Jacotot, it will not be that bad, since Jacotot himself was eventually saved from oblivion by the storyteller (Rancière). Thus, even if the radical idea conceptualized in his book 'wouldn't take [...] it would not perish' (139) ...

Self-Characterization

This multi-layered characterization that alternates between legendary, melodramatic, ironic and humoristic styles enhances the appearance of Jacotot as an invented, fictitious, character (based on a real person) of a magnitude that fits the grand mission of bringing his/Rancière's theory to life. Additionally, and no less important, the characterization of Jacotot also implies the self-characterization of Rancière as the storyteller who alternates between identification and distance regarding his story and its hero. Thus, this rich and skilled characterization offers the reader/s an active role in solving the riddle: Who is who, when and where, and what is the moral lesson of the parable (book)? At the same time, the characterization also signals the process of the political subjectivization of Rancière himself, which in this book is still in-between dependence on and detachment from Jacotot, all the way to his full autonomy and emancipation, which would manifest only in his subsequent texts.

The self-characterization of and by Rancière is also intended to present himself as a gifted storyteller and theatre facilitator. The political implication of storytelling as a mode of the theatrical as-if has already been discussed. However, the self-characterization of Rancière as a storyteller rather than a philosopher who explicates his theory bears another, additional, political meaning, since explication is strongly denounced from the beginning of the book to its end as the main principle of the accepted, hierarchical, stultifying educational model in Western societies. Consequently, Rancière reinforces his self-characterization as a storyteller and theatre facilitator through direct speech, questions and stage directions by which he seeks not only to retain the attentiveness and involvement of the audience/readers but also to reinforce his own engagement, belief and enthusiasm with his evolving new theory. For example, when he directs changes of tone, mood and intensity of speech: 'For if you think about it a little [...]. Let's call this way of learning "universal learning"' (16). 'Who would want to begin?' (17). 'Don't try to fool me or yourself. Is that really what you saw?' (23). This is then followed by a louder tone: *'What do you think about it?'* (23, emphasis in original). 'Let's look at the facts' (25). 'Slow down' (46). 'So, be it!' (49). 'Man is *a will served by intelligence*' (51–52, emphasis in original). *'An individual can do anything he wants'* (56, emphasis in original). Sometimes this direct speech is developed into guided affective imagery: for example, when the storyteller facilitates the audience/readers to imagine a moment from the book by Fénelon: 'Let's go ashore, then, with Telemachus onto Calypso's island' (19). Later, the storyteller facilitates a stressed moment when Jacotot receives bad news: 'Someone knocking at the door. It's the envoy from the Minister of Public Instruction, who has come to call Monsieur Jacotot's attention to a royal decree setting out the conditions for establishing a school in the kingdom. [...] It's the messenger bringing the last issue of [...], containing the *oratio* of our colleague Franciscus Josephus Dumbeck, who sounds the charge against universal teaching, the new corrupter of youth' (75).

The seemingly spontaneous speech of the storyteller is, as previously noticed, more deliberate than it might seem. In addition to the obvious repetition of the basic vocabulary of the pedagogical model, Rancière creates another echoing sound effect by which he circumvents explication: certain words appear first as if casually, but in fact preparing the audience/readers for the moment in the event when these words will become central, and lead to new meanings. Such words, for example, are 'adventure', 'revolution', 'translation', 'distance', 'improvisation', 'poetry' and 'art'. For my purpose here I will refer only to the last four. At the beginning of the story, Rancière emphasizes the word 'distance' in its negative meaning in the traditional, explicative educational model, in which the teaching process begins from a hierarchical difference/distance between the superior educated master and the inferior ignorant teacher. This is the distance of inequality that traditional education has always promised to abolish through explication, but in fact has only managed to perpetuate (5). Later in the story, Rancière returns to this word and appropriates it positively while presenting equality as a practice of any individual or individuals. Here 'distance' is that physical and mental positive separation that preserves self-autonomy through the thing in common that maintains an equal distance between two individuals: 'There is no intelligence where there is aggregation, the *binding* of one mind to another. [...]. The thing in common, placed between two minds, is the gauge of that equality [...], "the only bridge of communication between two minds". The bridge is a passage, but it is also distance maintained. The materiality of the book keeps two minds at an equal distance' (32, emphasis in original) and as autonomous subjects.

When the storyteller cheerfully recounts how Baptiste Froussard had become an excellent pupil of Jacotot, particularly enjoying learning through improvisation, music and poetry, he closes this scene with Jacotot's statement 'that in every human work there is art' (43), leaving it, for the moment, in the form of declaration. Only later are 'improvisation', 'poetry' and 'art' repeated together, this time clearly as the main components of the alternative pedagogical model that directly links education to art, and particularly to theatre. Thus, for Rancière aesthetics, art or theatre are not external to education but, rather, education is a theatrical event that inherently comprises 'canonical exercises of universal teaching' (64) by which any individual, regardless of his extent of knowledge or talent, can verify his mental equality through artistic expressivity. 'In the act of speaking, man doesn't transmit his knowledge, he makes poetry. [...] He communicates as a *poet*: as a being who believes his thoughts communicable, his emotions sharable' (65, emphasis in original). 'All that *improvisation* in short – is this not the most eloquent of poems?' (68).

This leads the story to one of its pivotal moments, when the focus on education explicitly turns to politics through the idea of 'a society of artists' (71). Here it becomes apparent that the entire theatrical event has been intended to offer the alternative educational model as a way of life, a political, creative practice that posits the individual as an equal autonomous human before being first a citizen, as the accepted premise claims: 'One must first be a man before being a citizen' (138). The political way to reach this is through art, which can thwart any deprived economic, social, cultural or political circumstances. The premise of the society of artists is that everyone can become an emancipated subject by acting like an artist, who consistently translates his feelings and thoughts by means of art into a communicable expression that can be 'shared with others' (66).

Being aware that this idea might sound superficial and unconvincing, the storyteller asks straightforwardly, 'What good is triumphing in the forum if one already knows that nothing can change the social order?' (Rancière 1991, 96). The answer, which is also given straightforwardly, is the seed that germinates all Rancière's subsequent texts on politics: Human beings are indeed equal by their intelligence. However, what inevitably divides them are the external conditions determined by any and every social order whose basic necessity was, is, and always will be hierarchy/inequality (88). Therefore, instead of political revolutions it is better to develop societies of artists as a way of living freely within and alongside the inevitable confines of the political order. The poetic/artistic methods thus constitute not only an educational pedagogy but much more than that: they constitute a pedagogy of and for life.

Role-Playing and Audience Participation

Rancière, as the leader of the theatrical event, appears not only as a gifted storyteller who knows how to tell a good story but also as an actor who plays the role of Jacotot and the other secondary characters in a virtuoso way by quoting from numerous excerpts that he had found in the archive as if they were texts to be acted out. Role-playing is an additional device by which Rancière replaces explication with artistic operation. In the first lesson he only takes on the role of Jacotot (and does not yet act it out). Thereby, although being very sympathetic to him, the storyteller continues to speak in the third person, even when expressing Jacotot's thoughts: 'He expected horrendous barbarisms. […] No matter! And how surprised he was to discover that the students, left to themselves, managed this difficult step' (2). Very soon, however, the storyteller begins to act like an actor when he plays the role of the traditional, stultified teacher by moving smoothly from third person to first person: 'The more he knows, the more evident to him is the distance between his knowledge and the ignorance of the ignorant ones. […], he will say, the student must understand, and for that we must explain even better. […]. I will find new ways to explain it to him […] and I will verify that he has understood' (7–8). He then also starts to act as a facilitator, approaching his audience/readers, directing them to act like a chorus in order to repeat and memorize the important part of the story up to that moment:

Let's call this way of learning 'universal teaching' and say of it:

'In reality, universal teaching has existed since the beginning of the world, alongside all the explicative methods. This teaching, by oneself, has, in reality, been what has formed all great man.' But this is the strange part: 'Everyone has done this experiment a thousand times in his life, and yet it has never occurred to someone to say to someone else: I've learned many things without explanation, I think that you can too. ... Neither I nor anyone in the world has ventured to draw on this fact to teach others.' (16)

From this interactive, participatory scene on, the distance between the storyteller and Jacotot diminishes, and the difference between the style of the storyteller's speech and that of Jacotot is obliterated.

In the next lessons/chapters role-playing and audience participation are increased. In order to build up the difference between the prevalent Old Master's educational model and that of Jacotot, the storyteller directs two scenes in which he plays all the roles. In the first, the storyteller plays the Old Master and his student:

but the Old Master would say: such and such a thing must be learned and then this other thing and after that, this other. Selection, progression, incompletion [...] . I understood that, says the satisfied student. You think so, corrects the master. [...]. What does this mean? Asks the curious student. I could tell you, responds the master, but it would be premature: you wouldn't understand at all. (21)

In the next scene the storyteller plays the good teacher and his student, gradually guiding the audience to participate in the role-playing, demonstrating together an exemplary lesson in Jacotot's enabling and encouraging pedagogy:

Take it [the book] and read it, he says to the poor person. I don't know how to read, answers the poor person. [...]. As you have understood all things up until now: by comparing two facts. Here is that fact that I will tell you, the first sentence of the book [...]. Repeat: 'Calypso', 'Calypso could' ... Now, here is a second fact: the words are written there. The first word I said to you was Calypso. [...] Tell me 'the story of the adventures, that is, the comings and goings, the detours – in a word [...]'. Don't say you can't. You know how to see, how to speak, you know how to show [...]. What more is needed? An absolute attention for seeing and seeing again, saying and repeating. [...] You have a soul like me. (23)

Following these scenes of collaborative role-playing stimulates the storyteller to relate to himself and to his audience as to one intimate group of 'we' and 'us', and also to act and talk exactly as Jacotot:

We know that a justification of the equality of intelligence would be equally tautological. We will therefore try a different path: we will talk only about what we see; we will name facts without pretending to assign them causes. [...] 'I explain nothing, I give a name to what I see.' [...] I will not say that the one's faculties are inferior to the other's. I will only suppose that the two faculties haven't been equally exercised. [...] I will say that he has brought less attention to his work. (50)

All these forms of role-playing and audience participation are repeated until the end of the book, encouraging the readers through experimental and experiential reading to become from that moment on Rancière's partners and followers in his radical thinking.

CONCLUSION

Considering the exceptional theatre-like literariness of the philosophical text *The Ignorant Schoolmaster* by Jacques Rancière, I have read it here from the viewpoint of a theatre scholar and practitioner. To undertake such an approach, I have followed the detailed analytical model of Mackenzie and Porter, 'Dramatization as Method in Political Theory', which advocates that 'in order to know the political, political theorists must change it – dramatically' – (Mackenzie and Porter 2011b, 2) by means of an explicitly artistic intervention engaging both with writing and reading texts of political theory. Accordingly, my intention has been to present my 'translation' to the book through 'the method of dramatization' and to show how this extends and deepens the perception of this text. By 'translation' I follow Rancière's conceptualization in his book, which ignores the usual sense of translation as an expertise, and suggests it rather as the basic activity of anyone's thinking as being expressed through speech and its counter-translation by any addressee. Any translation is consequently already a counter-translation (Rancière 1991, 68–69). My reading here should therefore be accepted as a counter-translation of Rancière's own translation (or counter-translation of Joseph Jacotot's books).

The focus here has been on the discussion of the central ideas of *The Ignorant Schoolmaster* through the devices by which they are introduced. Reading the book through the lens of theatre has revealed Rancière's skilful artistry in constructing an intensive, multi-layered philosophical written text that appears as an oral and performed philosophy. It has also revealed the book not only as a core text of Rancière but, more than that, as the highly ambitious and passionate project of a philosopher at the crucial moment of an intellectual breakthrough. The theatre-likeness of this book discloses a special transitional moment in Rancière's intellectual trajectory, from criticism to activism – from ignoring his Old Master's political premise of inequality (in his previous publications) to formulating the anchors of his alternative, novel idea of equality. Thus, the process of dramatization became for Rancière an intellectual adventure and initiation ritual towards intellectual maturity.

Tyson indicates that Rancière's philosophy offers in general a 'type of thinking that replaces critique with performance' (Tyson 2012b, 11). Such a type of thinking emerges most clearly in *The Ignorant Schoolmaster*, in which Rancière 'posits the artist [the teacher and the student] as the true embodiment of universal teaching' (Tyson 2012a, 38). As an educational philosopher, Tyson argues that 'the relation between theatrical performance and education remains under-theorized in his [Rancière's] work' (Tyson 2012b, 9). *The Ignorant Schoolmaster*, however, indeed presents 'the vital roles that acting and staging have in the educational relationship' (9).

Through scripting, staging and performing a storytelling theatrical event, Rancière manages to present his theory in the process of its coming into being. The gradual growth of the theory, as-if, spontaneously and lightly is intended to facilitate its secure delivery and reception. The book, as I have demonstrated, implies not only a scripted play to be acted out by the reader/s but also and mostly a collaborative educational theatre directed and performed by Rancière as storyteller, actor and theatre facilitator, with the readers in the role of audience as participants. Rancière seeks first to approach as much of a heterogeneous readership as possible, through the indirect, sensuous affective power of theatre; second, to encourage this readership to dare to think differently, against the grain of their axiomatic thinking; and third, to accept the pedagogical-political model as intelligible by experimenting and experiencing it. This dramatization has enabled Rancière to offer Jacotot's radical educational model not only as if it were his own but also in and through the model's own practice, as an artistic experiment/experience of a model that is itself based on artistic experiment/experience.

The central radical idea of the book is encapsulated, as discussed here, already in the title, especially in the term *The Ignorant Schoolmaster*. The optional meaning or meanings of this term are embedded throughout the book, like a riddle to be solved by the reader. By the end of the book it becomes clear that the ignorant schoolmaster refers to that someone who does not necessarily need to be an expert in any field in order to be an emancipated teacher, who ignores the traditional progressive pedagogy, and also, and no less important, ignores his own mastery by dissociating teaching from knowledge and concomitantly knowledge from intelligence and knowledge from emancipation/equality. Consequently, the identity of the ignorant schoolmaster is also deliberately manifold: he might be the ignorant student, Jacotot, Rancière, or any reader who chooses to follow the alternative pedagogy and act as an emancipated and emancipating person. Above all, the ignorant schoolmaster encapsulates Rancière's chosen self-identity as it was to appear in his subsequent texts, in which he portrays himself as 'in the first instance, a student' (Rancière 2003, 194), and an amateur intellectual who opposes and ignores the authority of specialists, preferring instead to be a maverick wanderer who discovers new passages and paths that enable him to reconfigure the accepted intellectual domains (Rancière 2006, 2011).

REFERENCES

Althusser, Louis. 1976. 'A Reply to John Lewis'. In *Essays in Self Criticism*, edited by Louis Althusser, 33–100. London: NLB.
Citton, Yves. [2010] 2014. 'The Ignorant Schoolmaster: Knowledge and Authority'. In *Jacques Rancière: Key Concepts*, edited by Jean-Philippe Deranty, 25–37. New York, NY: Routledge.
Deleuze, Gilles. 1994. *Difference and Repetition*. New York, NY: Columbia University Press.
Deleuze, Gilles. 2004. *Desert Islands and Other Texts 1953–1974*. Los Angeles, CA: Semiotext(e).
Hallward, Peter. 2006. 'Staging Equality: On Rancière's Theatrocracy'. *New Left Review* 37: 109–129.
Kear, Adrian. 2013. *Theatre and Event: Staging the European Century*. London and New York, NY: Palgrave Macmillan.
Mackenzie, Iain, and Robert Porter. 2011a. 'Dramatization as Method in Political Theory'. *Contemporary Political Theory* 10 (4): 482–501.
Mackenzie, Iain, and Robert Porter. 2011b. *Dramatizing the Political: Deleuze and Guattari*. London and New York, NY: Palgrave Macmillan.
Rancière, Jacques. 1991. *The Ignorant Schoolmaster: Five Lessons in Intellectual Emancipation*. Stanford, CA: Stanford University Press.
Rancière, Jacques. [1981] 1989. *The Night of Labour: The Worker's Dream in the Nineteenth Century France*. Philadelphia, PA: Temple University Press.
Rancière, Jacques. 2003. 'Politics and Aesthetics'. Interview by Peter Hallward. *Angelaki* 6 (2): 191–211.
Rancière, Jacques. [1983] 2003. *The Philosopher and His Poor*. London: Duke University Press.
Rancière, Jacques. 2006. *Film Fables*. Oxford: Berg Publishers.
Rancière, Jacques. 2011. 'The Gay Science of Bertold Brecht'. In *The Politics of Literature*, edited by Jacques Rancière, 99–127. Malden, MA: Polity Press.
Rancière, Jacques. [1974] 2011. *Althusser's Lesson*. London: Continuum.
Ross, Kristin. 1991. 'Introduction'. In *The Ignorant Schoolmaster: Five Lessons in Intellectual Emancipation*, edited by J. Rancière, vii–xxiii. Stanford, CA: Stanford University Press.
Schechner, Richard. 1969. *Public Domain*. New York, NY: Bobbs-Merrill.
Schechner, Richard. 1971. 'Actuals: Primitive Ritual and Performance Theory'. *Theatre Quarterly* 1 (2): 49–65.

Schechner, Richard. 1982. *The End of Humanism*. New York, NY: Performing Art Journal Publications

Simons, Maarten, and Jan Masschelein. 2011. 'Introduction: Hatred of Democracy ... and of the Public Role of Education?' In *Rancière, Public Education and the Taming of Democracy*, edited by Maarten Simons and Jan Masschelein, 1–14. Chichester: Wiley-Blackwell.

Tyson, E. Lewis. 2012a. 'Teaching with Pensive Images: Rethinking Curiosity. In Paulo Freire's Pedagogy of the Oppressed'. *Journal of Aesthetic Education* 46 (1): 27–45.

Tyson, E. Lewis. 2012b. *The Aesthetics of Education: Theatre, Curiosity, and Politics in the Works of Jacques Rancière and Paulo Freire*. London and New York, NY: Bloomsbury

Tyson, E. Lewis. 2013. 'Jacques Rancière's Aesthetic Regime and Democratic Education'. *Journal of Aesthetic Education* 57 (2): 49–70.

Chapter 4

Staging the People

Performance, Presence and Representation

Adrian Kear

> A 'people' ... is not an assemblage of social groups and identities. It is the polemical form of subjectification that is drawn along particular lines of fracture, where the distribution of leaders and led, learned and ignorant, possessors and dispossessed, is decided (Rancière 2011, 15).

> Because 'the people' does not exist. What exists are diverse or even antagonistic figures of the people, figures constructed by privileging certain modes of assembling, certain distinctive traits, certain capacities or incapacities (Rancière 2016, 102).

THE PLAY OF PRESENCE AND REPRESENTATION

This chapter aims to explore a question at the heart of Rancière's conception of the interrelation between politics and aesthetics: the demonstration of the inevitable gap and recurrent tension between presence and representation made manifest in the internal contradictions of the 'distribution of the sensible' (2004, 12) and the 'division of the perceptible' (2011, 14). It maintains that the relationship between presence and representation is primarily a *theatrical* question, with the theatre operating as a site for investigating the politics of their co-appearance. This is because theatre relies upon the constant modulation and inter-animation of presence and representation for both its material condition and formal operation, with the interplay between them co-determining not only what it might mean but who is there and how they are seen. Specifically, this chapter seeks to examine how the aesthetic practice of 'staging the people' – a title drawn from two volumes of Rancière's writings investigating the post-revolutionary aesthetic regime of representation and political apparatus of subjectification (2011, 2012) – is central to imaging the political figure of 'the people' in representative democracy and to managing their 'political claim' (Rancière 1999, 87–88). The chapter investigates how the consensus logic of democratic representation – and the representational regime – is dependent upon the exercise of an imaginary political claim to represent 'the people', and, coextensively, how aesthetic practices of 'staging the people' might open up its normative operation to dissensual intervention and reimagining the 'sphere of appearance' of 'the people' as the site of a political invention. Accordingly, the performative construct of 'the people' is shown to be reliant on the aesthetic logic of representation and its capacity to frame, codify and remediate the presence of people per se.

And yet, in this representational configuration the people are also precisely what is missing, rendered absent by their very invocation as a figure. The figure of 'the people' at once seems to open up a space in which the people appear as significant, and at the same time closes down the possibility of their actual irruption or intrusion into the representational system which necessarily displaces their presence as its trace. In this way, 'the people' are necessarily *theatricalized*: staged as a figure whose very staging articulates material presence to representational practice and empties out its manifest content. The more 'the people' are spoken of, named and claimed by the machinations of 'representative democracy', the more the 'post-democratic' apparatus appears to render obsolete actual people as such. They become an image, and image material, tied to the political imaginary as if always already representation (Didi-Huberman 2016, 68). The people are missing from this political operation because, as Deleuze contends, the people 'no longer exist' and never did as any unified totality but only as a diverse, coexisting plurality. Accordingly, there is no majoritarian conception of the people that isn't predicated on their erasure, 'because the people exist only in the condition of minority, which is why they are missing' (2013, 215–17). The figure of 'the people' is never coextensive with the material reality of actual people, and the inevitable non-equivalence between presence and representation remains the recurrent ground of political and aesthetic tension. However much managerialist accounting or populist rhetoric attempts to close the gap between them – covering over the construction of the people and their missingness as the contested site of politics as such – the practice of 'staging the people' continues to operate as the locus for articulating competing representational claims, including that of bringing the people into being. Enacted through representation – recalling Marx's dictum in the *Eighteenth Brumaire of Louis Napoleon* that 'they cannot represent themselves, they must be represented' – 'the people' remain different from any particular representation or mode of representation, acting as its constitutive exclusion or ontological excess. As Rancière insists, 'the people' are 'always more or less than the people': the locus of an 'internal division' and index of the unbridgeable gap between presence and representation that constitutes politics' primary condition and site of operation (1999, 22, 87).

This gap, the chapter argues, appears and *reappears* in the current conjunction as a tear in the very fabric of the visible; as a crisis of representation 'in representation' (Frank 2010, 35) that exceeds and undermines the normalizing effects of politics as either a post-democratic show or populist theatrical spectacle. It investigates aesthetic practices of 'staging the people' that serve to question the rhetorical and imaginary privileging of the figure of 'the people' and point towards the people's missingness from the aesthetic-political regime. Further, the chapter examines performance's reopening of the gap between presence and representation as the ground of *the political* as such, and as the site of its reappearance within the otherwise bounded theatricality of the representational regime.

STAGING THE PEOPLE

Staging the People is the title of Rancière's two volume exploration of the relationship between 'the overly broad words of people, worker and proletarian', concerned with examining the differences within and between them as a 'space of dissenting invention' and a creative resource for reanimating their political potential (18). Throughout this project, Rancière seeks to demonstrate the non-equivalence between the discursive construction of 'the people' and the quotidian practices and historically lived experiences of actual ordinary people, thereby pointing towards and making manifest the gap between reality and its representation *in* representation. His detailed analysis of the scenes and conventions of French working-class historical cultures serves to illustrate the reality *of* representation and its constitutive role in the construction of 'the visible and the expressible' (15). By contrasting the falsely homogenizing and vacuously totalizing discourse of representing 'the people' to more nuanced investigations of 'fragments of experience and forms of symbolization' (14), Rancière draws attention to the plurality of persons and modes of existence. He stresses that 'there are always several kinds of workers in the factory, several forms of movement in the street, several audiences in the theatre' (15). This is not to create a set of social sub-categories or cross-cutting identities but to argue that 'the people' are neither uniform nor unified but rather appear as the site of a 'division of the perceptible' and the ground for the articulation of competing political claims. Further, as Rancière insists, there are always 'several ways of occupying the site and symbolizing its 'normal' functioning' (15), recognizing the plurality of aesthetic-political practices that serve to contest the normalizing function of the regime of representation.

Staging the People meticulously exposes the gap between presence and representation, but at the same time explicates the constant interplay between them. Rancière repeatedly demonstrates how the 'dominant fiction' of the social formation – the construction of 'an image of social consensus' – is dependent on a 'privileged mode of representation' which attenuates the presence of real people to a national-popular 'unamist fiction' whose dramaturgy stages 'the people' in order to characterize them as such and to invite identification with the image created (2017, 5). The representational regime is thereby sustained through a repertoire of representations and repository of images which serve to construct 'the people' as their aesthetic-political effect. The material reality of the stage as offering an apparatus of appearance in which the embodied presence of real people is attenuated to and codified within both the fictional framework of the dramatic narrative and the social situation of the face-to-face theatrical encounter would seem essential in this respect. In the first essay of the second volume of *Staging the People*, Rancière traces to Michelet the national-popular project of constructing a 'people's theatre' in which 'the people would perform their own grandeur for themselves' by enacting 'their own legend'. For Michelet, 'the people's theatre' enables the representational function to 'feed the people from the people', transubstantiating presence into theatrical representation and incarnating embodied actorly presence as a seemingly 'democratic' representative form (2012, 9). To do this meant adopting the egalitarian principle, 'abolishing class division' to ensure the unity of the people would be enacted and enshrined in the very structure of the theatrical event. Only then would there be 'a theatre that is truly that of the people', with the actors appearing on stage also being representatives of the community they represent. In this respect, the theatre would act as a homology for democracy, suggesting a formal correlation between theatrical and political apparatuses of representation. Rancière calls this condensation a 'theatrocracy', repurposing the term used pejoratively in Plato's *Laws* to redesignate democracy as a political structure dependent on spectatorial enthrallment to display, deception and dramatization (10). For Rancière, the 'theatrocratic' operates as a principle of equality in producing a community of thought and action 'based on a spectacle that was fundamentally a self-representation' (10). Accordingly, the arrangement of the people's theatre envisaged by Michelet would instantiate a formal configuration of 'representation without separation' so that 'the people could view their own actions' on stage and in the auditorium. Its political aspiration was to ensure 'each half of the people was alternately a representation of the other' (10), thereby erasing the boundary between presence and representation through the logic and practice of participation.

Staging the People situates this proto-modernist aesthetic desire to transcend the separation between stage and audience as a synecdoche of an egalitarian political objective to redress the foundational division constituting the social. In this respect, the theatre operates as 'the sphere of appearance of the people' by making manifest the gap between 'the people as community and the people as division' which constitutes the 'fundamental grievance' of *democracy* as an aesthetic regime and political distribution (Rancière 1995, 96–97). As Rancière elaborates, the modes of appearance of 'the people' under these conditions are dependent on the non-coextensiveness but inter-animation of presence and representation, in which 'it is not the king but the people who have a double embodiment' (97). Presence and representation are only ever partially conjoined in this performative suturing, producing a necessarily 'provisional and polemical' configuration which reiterates the 'division of the perceptible' and its attendant 'ways of acting, ways of seeing and ways of speaking' (Rancière 2011, 14). Forms of representation – political and aesthetic – draw upon the material presence of actual people to produce 'the people' as a discursive effect, retroactively constituted, at the same time as mobilizing its performative operation to normalize and regulate popular presence through the attribution and occupation of specific social roles and cultural identities. Hence, according to Rancière, 'the people' is not an ontological foundation to be given a seemingly 'natural' political expression but rather 'a polemical form of subjectification' – a mode of production of individual people as well as 'the people' as a discursive formation – 'that is drawn along particular lines of fracture, where the distribution of leaders and led, learned and ignorant, possessors and dispossessed, is decided' (15).

The performative operation of this 'double embodiment' is evident in the material arrangement of 'the people's theatre' as a space in which the people are supposed to appear to themselves as a people, and yet the condition of their appearance is contingent upon the theatrical apparatus and frame of representation separating actors from spectators, action from political agency. The representational effect of the staging itself appears as 'the setting up of a part of those that have no part' (Rancière 1999, 14). This 'setting up' is both an aesthetic-political apparatus of staging and the installation of a distributed ensemble of power relations across the social formation. As such, the theatrical relation supports and sustains as a mode of appearance which re-inscribes the 'imparity' between actors and onlookers: a structural division of the perceptible which remains evident even in forms of theatrical practice that seek to draw attention to its operation or celebrate its inversion. For Rancière, this optical bifurcation is integral to the theatre's role in revealing yet maintaining a certain 'distribution of the sensible' that partitions political roles and attributes these 'parts' to discrete social 'parties' (2004, 12), with the gap between stage and audience serving as an 'allegory of inequality' imbricated in the play of 'domination and subjection' (1993, 277). In developing his theory of emancipated spectatorship, he proposes a model of aesthetic experience that 'starts from the opposite principle, the principle of equality' (277). This entails rejecting the association of looking with passivity and the hierarchical organization of knowledge implicit in the apparatus of staging, while 'embracing the unreality of representation' as part of a 'poetic' capacity that enables us to see and imagine things otherwise. It also enables the recognition that spectatorship is a critical activity that confirms, contests and changes the 'hierarchy of intelligences' with which it is presented. In 'starting from the point of view of equality, asserting equality, assuming equality as a given' (1995, 52), Rancière suggests that the theatrical relation may be reconfigured as a mode of *dissensual* engagement and *democratic* political potential.

Theatrical attempts to think through 'staging the people' might be reapproached as critical attempts to rethink the very logic of staging as that which 'determines the conditions for a constitutive rethinking' of aesthetic-political relations. This might entail acknowledging their 'restaging' of the very dynamics of representation in different forms and modes of representation, enabling a critical-poetic re-investigation of foundational aesthetic-political 'moments of thinking' and social formation (Rancière 2017, 91). In this context, the work of Quarantine (Manchester, UK) can be seen as providing a sustained interrogation of the staging of the people under the 'democratic' political regime and a series of theatrical attempts to re-balance the aesthetic priority of representation over presentation. Their first work, *See-Saw* (Tramway, Glasgow, 2000), offered something of an adumbration and re-examination of the principles of a 'people's theatre' outlined by Michelet. The show began with the audience seated in an auditorium facing a red velvet theatre curtain consistent with a conventional proscenium end-on stage configuration. However, as the curtain opened it revealed not a boxed stage 'in which the people could view their own actions' but an even more concrete illustration of the theatre as a 'mirror' of the people: another audience, facing its own image. Neither side of the traverse was performing, and nothing was being performed 'for' them. Nothing happened 'on stage' for at least five minutes, during which time the two audiences watched each other watching, simultaneously seeing and being-seen. Here in the theatre (where else?), a highly theatrical conception of democratic theatricality was being both advanced and exposed. With 'each half of the people' acting as 'a representation of the other' (Rancière 2012, 10) – without either 'acting' or 'representing' – the theatrical 'set-up' served to concretize the Enlightenment idea of the theatre of the people in the construction of a decidedly post-dramatic theatrical space. The theatrical image created of the theatre operating as a space of the people appearing to themselves and as themselves could not be clearer. Accordingly, when the 'action' as such began, it compromised people within the audience presenting themselves to the other members of the audience rather than 'acting' in any demonstrably representational sense. The only directly imitative or characterological performance offered was that of an Elvis impersonator, and even so we see the impersonator over and above the impersonation in this frame. While the audience and the actors might appear indistinguishable they are not in fact indivisible as their entry into the field of representation codifies their presence in differential ways. Although the people in *See-Saw* were directly drawn from the city in which it was performed, and in this respect could be regarded as being representative of it, it is not this that primarily matters in the *mise-en-scène*. It is rather the mechanism of staging itself – the apparatus of representation – that conditions their appearance in the field of the visible and reproduces the division between actor and spectator as both its effect and ground.

Interestingly, Quarantine's director, Richard Gregory, regards *See-Saw* as both setting in train the arc of the company's artistic enquiry and offering a point of potential return. He notes on the company's website, 'One day, knowing what we do now, I hope that we'll do *See-Saw* again, and see what happens.' Arguably, though, the questions the work raises and the modes of practice it sets in play have never really gone away. For example, in the opening work of the 2017 Manchester International Festival, *What Is the City but the People?*, Gregory and Quarantine co-founder and scenographer, Simon Banham, worked on a conceptual proposition by artist Jeremy Deller to enable some of the people who live in the city to take to the stage and present themselves and their stories in order to represent the city rather than the city's people being represented by actors within a dramatic representational form (figure 4.1).

Figure 4.1 'What is the city but the people?' Piccadilly Gardens, Manchester. Manchester International Festival, 2017. Photo: © Adrian Lambert / Adrian Lambert Photography Ltd.

That the title, *What Is the City but the People?*, is a direct quotation from Shakespeare's great drama of political discord and division, *Coriolanus*, suggests that the question of the people's presence and representation in the body politic still sounds and resounds not only in the mouth of an actor playing Sicinius but across the cacophony of voices in contemporary democracy. The question asserts both the ontological existence of ordinary people and their right to be counted not just as material presence but as mattering socially and politically, as having a political voice. Its eponymous repetition appears to ask how, in a contemporary aesthetic-political frame, is this presence to be represented? How are the people to be staged, figuratively and materially? *What Is the City but the People?* offers a subtle but significant reversal of the aesthetic priority of representation over presentation implicit in the apparatus of the drama itself. Its focus on ordinary people simply presenting themselves on stage obviates against the theatrical event taking the form of what Rancière calls 'the modern visit to the people' (2017, 28) – that is, a touristic encounter with the lives of others of the kind facilitated through conventional narrative practices of dramatic fiction and filmic documentary. In contrast to these tendentiously 'political' modes of imaging the lives of 'the people' critiqued by Rancière for their representational construction of imaginary worlds and fabulated figures, the presentational mode of the performance seeks to ensure that the people appear as themselves rather than as they have been represented. The seemingly simple dramaturgical configuration of their ontological presence on stage enables them to occupy the space of appearance as individual subjects and not simply the embodiment of a claim to name a collective subject, 'the people'.

The scenographic set-up of *What Is the City but the People?* demonstrates that there is a very conscious *staging* involved in this presentational aesthetic. A large yellow runway constructed across Manchester's Piccadilly Gardens operated as a theatrical stage supporting the performers' appearance in the public domain, enabling this diverse group of people to simply move across the stage without the presumption of either artifice or absorption. Here they were, simply people: people aware of themselves 'performing', people aware of themselves being looked at in an explicitly theatrical relation of viewing that nonetheless sought to resist their default theatricalization as 'other' than those doing the spectating. Small biographical details and fragments of personal stories were projected on large screens behind the people on stage, enabling the audience to imagine as well as see the performer's lived experience as well as live presence. Here they were, simply people: people aware of their own personhood, people aware of themselves being looked at and inviting others to recognize them as such. Not 'the people', just people. People enacting their own presence, presenting themselves as existing; existing prior to, and in excess of, the deployment of their name as 'a claim to the political' (Butler 2015, 18). Judith Butler suggests that gathering together, the simple act of assembly, should be seen as in itself 'an embodied form of calling into question the inchoate and powerful dimensions of reigning notions of the political' (9). In stressing that 'forms of assembly already signify prior to, and apart from, any particular demands they make', Butler draws upon the logic of the Occupy movement to argue the primacy of presence over representation (8). In asserting that 'gathering signifies in excess of what is said', she foregrounds 'bodily enactment' as a constitutive mode of political signification indexing the foundational premise of representative democracy as a form of delegated authority (8). This material presence acts as a reminder of the 'constitutive outside' upon which the figure of 'the people' relies for its performative force and legitimating ground. The persistence of this presence would seem to insist that those assembled 'do something other than represent themselves; they constitute themselves as the people' being represented (2016, 51). While Butler contends that 'this act of self-making or self-constitution is not the same as any form of representation', and is 'separate from the very representative regime it legitimates' (62), it is difficult to see how it is either foundational or refoundational in anything other than a narrowly constitutional frame. Butler's focus on embodied enactment seems to neglect the retroactive and recursive subjectivating effects of the apparatus subtending the actors' appearance on the political stage as such. As Rancière demonstrates, the act of staging itself serves the apparatus of representation, putting presence into play in a *theatrical* space of 'visibility and speech' which conditions and codifies its forms and modes of signification (2007, 88). The material reality of the stage thereby appropriates the materiality of the people it presents, fusing 'the drama of the ordinary life' to the 'sensible reality' embodied in the theatrical scene (Rancière 2013, 115). The theatre, then, continues its work *as theatre* by rethinking and reworking the relation and interpenetration of presence and representation that constitutes its operation and modifies the heterogeneous network of its effects.

RE-THINKING THEATRE'S REPRESENTATIONAL CLAIM

At the same time, it is important to recognize the limits of the apparent homology between theatrical and sociopolitical discourses of representation. As Tony Fisher has argued, it would be something of a category error to conflate aesthetic and democratic representation as this misrecognizes theatre's 'power of ventriloquism' and actorly surrogation that '"clones" the space of politics without thereby reproducing its effects' (2017, 8–9). This misrecognizes the force of what Rancière calls the 'aesthetic cut' separating aesthetics from politics and preventing the crossover and conflation of their domains of intention and effect (2010, 151). It risks overextending theatre's 'representative claim' – the role it plays in the dynamic of representational practices which political theorist Michael Saward characterizes as integral to the operation of democratic culture – by equating this mode of representation with the structural determinants of representative democracy (2010). In Rancière's terms, representative or representational claims can be seen to contribute to the lived experience and material practice of democracy as not simply a 'form of government' but 'a style of life that is opposed to any well-ordered government of the community' (2006, 36). Democracy thereby 'implies a practice of dissensus', not simply a mode of governmentality, erupting as a disruptive energy 'that keeps reopening' the gaps and contingencies 'that the practice of ruling relentlessly plugs' (2010, 54).

Quarantine's critical-aesthetic enquiry into the ways in which the theatrical frame conditions and mediates the modes of appearance of the people who appear within it should therefore be placed in this context. Their theatre might be seen to not only re-stage and rethink the representative claim to 'the people' it otherwise appears to enact but to open up the gap between presence and representation as a dissensual practice of democracy. Two important lessons from Rancière are worth recalling here: first, that 'the people' are 'always more and less than the people' (1999, 22), and as such cannot be simply 'counted' or rendered equivalent to their representation, and second, that 'the people' are only ever enacted through representation even though, constitutionally and politically, they remain 'in excess of any particular representation' or representational regime (Frank 210, 3). As the political historian Jason Frank succinctly puts it, 'The people require representation in order to be enacted, yet this authorizing entity also – and by definition – resists the closure of representation. The voice of the people is a figure of impossible presence' (2010, 10). According to Rancière, it is because of this 'magnitude that escapes measurement' that 'politics exists' (1999, 15). As such, for Rancière, 'politics is the sphere of activity of a common that can only ever be contentious, the relationship between parts that are only parties and credentials or entitlements whose sum never equals the whole' (14). The ineluctable tension between presence and representation is thus evident in the very forms and practices of representation itself. As Frank puts it, 'democratic representation is always in part a crisis in representation' (2010, 35), a crisis of representation made manifest in representational forms. How, then, is theatrical representation implicated in rethinking the grounds of its formalization?

Rimini Protokoll's *100% City* series of performance works might be regarded as an investigation of a crisis of democratic representation conducted through a rethinking of the seemingly homologous form of theatrical representation. Running since 2008, the *100% City* series follows a basic representational premise in order to show the people of each city in which it takes place a stage picture of the city's population. The set-up of the work is simple: one hundred people appear on stage, their presence corresponding to, and thereby seemingly directly 'representing', one hundred per cent of the city's population according to the demographic categories of the official census information through which the people are counted and made sense of statistically. The people who appear on stage are not actors – or at least, not professional actors endowed with the responsibility of representing – but amateurs – or, rather, ordinary people selected for their 'representativeness' rather than their capacity to represent. The theatre is thereby reanimated as a 'community' event, with ordinary people appearing on stage both as themselves and as the section of the community they represent, enabling the city to appear to be showing itself to itself as a 'self-representation ... a representation without separation' (Rancière 2012, 10).

As the title of the work suggests, *100%* both utilizes and appears to question the logic of 'representativeness' as a political operation. It seeks to investigate theatre's 'representative claim' by interrogating who and what is considered to be 'representative' and how a seemingly 'democratic' representational form might be seen to function. In so doing, it opens up the question of the relationship between presence and representation, on stage and in the social formation, and seeks to examine how the logic of staging is implicated in the politically subjectivating apparatus of democratic representation.

In *100% City*, the democratic, or perhaps more explicitly, 'theatrocratic', logic of the work appears to situate presence and representation as always already existing in dialectical tension within normative systems and forms of representation, and so self-presentation necessarily takes place within the existing frame of representation. This is perhaps most directly evident in the economic division and labour relations underlying the work's mode of production and operation. While the name of the company, Rimini Protokoll, accompanies the work in each city in which it appears, the work of organizing and orchestrating the performers within in the pre-established *mise-en-scène* is subcontracted to local theatre professionals. The claim to geo-locational specificity is thereby cross-cut by the pre-determination of the dramaturgy, and the desire to enable community self-presentation is limited by the theatrical mode of appearance as 'a limit of the theatre itself' (Rancière 2012, 34). Likewise, while those appearing on stage, simultaneously presenting themselves and representing the people of city of which they are part, do so 'voluntarily', without pay, as citizen-amateurs, those orchestrating the theatrical event are paid professionals engaged by the absent theatre artists to deliver their work and realize their vision. A highly stratified 'hierarchy of intelligences' and socio-economic partitions thereby underpins and undermines the claim to totality and inclusivity implied by *100% City*.

The division of socio-economic labour in *100% City* indexes a division in the distribution of power in the geopolitical formation it represents. The theatres of the thirty-five cities in which it has been performed are not, however, simply franchised factories producing goods to a set blueprint as the people who appear within them differ between as well as within themselves. Their presence is not simply material for representation; it is representation's constitutive ground and domain of performative effects, demonstrating the retroactive production of the very things it appears to 'represent'. In this respect, the act of 'staging the people' in *100% City* – putting ordinary people on stage and on show as the embodiment of abstract or even arbitrary demographic categories – has to be understood as connected to the political-aesthetic process of staging the people in order to constitute them as such. These people, as much as 'the people', might therefore be regarded as a representational construct, and representation might be seen to lay claim to and 'produce' the very people it represents. 'The people' are thereby not only the locus of a 'representational claim' (Saward 2010); they are the product of an apparatus of representation that presumes to speak in their name. Representing 'the people', as the aesthetic-political form espoused by *100% City* attests, is therefore a way of counting, and accounting for, people as units of social organization and attenuating their public appearance to their role in the political 'distribution of the sensible'. It is part of a political apparatus that turns people into 'the people', re-subjectivating political subjects as inevitably subject to politics and its inexorable counting – and miscounting – of the community's parts (Rancière 1999, 10).

In exposing who is counted and what is made to count, *100% City* might be regarded as a theatrical elaboration of those forms of 'post-democratic' representation which appear to eliminate political differences precisely by accommodating and aestheticizing them. According to Rancière, this is consistent with 'a democracy that has eliminated the appearance, miscount, and dispute of the people' by expanding its appropriative mechanisms and anticipatory practices of inclusion, thereby 'making the subject and democracy's own specific action disappear' (102). The logic of *100% City* would seem consistent with this neutralization of the demos as the site of the political, as it presents everything and everyone as not only already counted but as infinitely countable. The process of accounting for presence through representation thereby appears as a totalizing field, enabling people to be aligned with 'the people' by simply rendering them visible *as people* in this seemingly self-presentational post-democratic form. *100% City* does this by deploying an already partially deconstructed and seemingly non-representational post-dramatic theatrical aesthetic which allows the people on stage to appear as 'ordinary people' rather than actors explicitly inhabiting a space of representation. This appears as something of a conjuring trick, inviting the audience to look away from the mechanism and simply focus on the image created. The question concerning the role of the apparatus of representation in producing the appearance of self-presentation persists despite this sleight of hand. The people presenting themselves and representing 'the people' on stage remain subjectivated by the apparatus of representation that stages them, their conditions of appearance determined in advance by a prestidigitation (look away now) that would otherwise enable the apparatus of appearance itself to appear.

Despite the work's apparent adoption of the post-democratic 'consensus' correlating demonstrable 'identities and alterities' with the political apparatus' capacity to identify and produce the 'modes of subjectification' which support and sustain it, how presence is rendered as representation – how representation *represents* – remains at the heart of the aesthetic and political questions raised by *100% City*. Through investigating what Rancière calls 'the set of relationships that the *we* and its *name* maintain with the set of "persons"' – the representative configuration through which certain people are designated as embodying 'the people' – the performance becomes 'implicated in the demonstration' of the practices through which these relations are constructed and 'defined' (1999, 59, emphasis in original). Its very operation as performance reminds us, above all, that 'politics is a question of aesthetics, a matter of appearances' (74). In this respect, its deployment of 'amateur' performers, whose 'ordinary' status appears to provide the very ground of the claim to their representativeness, raises the question of the extent of their apparent non-knowingness about how the theatrical machinery of representation operates – how it produces them as subjects (subjects of representation and subject to representation), rather than simply serving transparently to enable their self-presentation and its extension to representing 'the people'. The mechanisms through which the apparatus of staging itself stages and subjectivates the people within it becomes increasingly visible as the theatre's representational dynamics – explicitly conjoined in *100% City* with the dynamics of 'representative' politics – performatively produces people as 'the people' through the constitutive mode of performance itself. Their very *theatrical* presence in the aesthetic-political apparatus of representation allows for this double valence, producing the 'double embodiment' of material presence and the materiality of representation.

The labour conditions and professional divisions in *100% City* repeat and reinforce the expropriative mechanisms which instrumentalize politics into a set of class relations, with professional politicians claiming to represent 'the people' whose enunciation both escapes and exceeds their own enactment. Marx's coruscating critique of representative politics – its insistence that the people 'cannot represent themselves, they must be represented' – seems to persist even as the performers of *100% City* appear to be representing themselves, as their mode of appearance is not itself made to appear. Their action, even their 'acting', is over-determined by the apparatus that makes it visible and allows them to be seen. This was evident in some of the performances in *100% Salford* (The Lowry, 7 May 2016). The performers' seemingly naive (or perhaps resistive) relation to the apparatus of representation was made manifest in a lack of awareness (or perhaps hyper-awareness) of their own being-on-stage. This assumption of an unmediated presence (or perhaps the recognition of the ascription of an impossible presence) seemingly misrecognizes the theatrical relation made manifest in the divide between stage and audience. Their performance is, of course, structured by the frame of representation and its role in maintaining and supporting the existing aesthetic-political regime. In this respect, the theatrical frame already operates both aesthetically and politically as the key modality through which presence is attenuated to, and turned into, representation. The theatrical relation constantly mediates presence, continually producing and circulating representations and their constitutive relations. In other words, it serves to construct the 'we' who are there, on either side of the divide, through our very being-there. Its material is both presence and representation: never exactly coextensive, never precisely coterminous, but also never entirely distinguishable.

In short, the question for a dissensual theatre practice emerging from the analysis of *100% City* is whether its post-dramatic presentational form sufficiently explicates the theatrical apparatus as being intrinsically imbricated in the political apparatus of 'democratic' representation. To what extent does the post-dramatic aesthetic dovetail with a post-democratic fantasy of 'democracy *after* the demos' (Rancière 1999, 102, emphasis in original) in which the people appear not as the site of political division or dispute but as the sociological legitimation of a consensus operation? And to what extent does the concomitant post-democratic evacuation of politics see it return in the space the post-dramatic aesthetic leaves open between performer presence and the apparatus of representation?

RE-POPULATING THE STAGE

In contrast to Rimini Protokoll's *100% City*, Quarantine's *Quartet* (*Summer, Autumn, Winter, Spring*; 26 March 2016, Old Granada Studios, Salford, UK) offers a post-dramatic event that constantly accentuates the material presence of the theatrical apparatus as the very machinery producing the appearance of people both on stage and in the audience. It begins and ends with the recognition of audience presence, and with an insistence on the singularity of both performers and audience as people. Any sense that these people – the people assembled here, gathered together onstage, in front of the other people assembled here, as audience – are somehow 'the people' is rendered primarily as representational *effect* rather than content. That is, as an effect of a representational practice that is foregrounded rather than denied.

In *Summer*, performer presence is always shown as mediated, 'performed'. From the outset, the task-based dramaturgy of instruction and interview is made visible, and rendered explicit, as constructing and conditioning the mode of appearance of the people on stage. As the side-lighting bar goes up to signal the start of the show, ELO's *Mr Blue Sky* is played over the sound system, a visual theatrical joke signalling the indexical presence of the theatrical mode of representation throughout. Over the course of the first 'scene', forty or so people come on stage and follow the explicit 'First instruction: Look at us while we look at you' which is there in the 'surtitles' for all to see. The basic materiality of the theatrical relation is thereby drawn attention to, and through it we see the self-awareness of the performers' knowledge of themselves as *performing*. Accordingly, the presence of ordinary people here on stage, as themselves, is rendered as a *co-presence* with the audience and presented as *constructed through the material fabric of the stage apparatus*. To put it slightly differently, the ontological presence of the people on stage is articulated to, and through, the specific ontology of 'staging' as such. 'Staging the people' thus appears as an aesthetic practice as well as political operation. Presence and representation appear here in close relation, so that the lives presented onstage are framed and staged through the material conditions of live performance. In other words, *Summer* – and the rest of the works in the *Quartet* – is as much about interrogating and articulating the specific conditions of theatrical appearance as it is about examining the everyday lives of the performers who appear as its manifest 'content'. Take, for example, the predomination of the interview mode in *Summer*: performers are asked primarily about what they do. ... Any sense of who they are is articulated through activity, action, dramaturgy. The 'who' always appears as a performative construct, an effect of performance, always performed and performing, always framed through the theatrical mode of seeing. As, for that matter, are the objects assembled on stage. Initially primarily personal – these things appear as being significant to these people – they are 'rearranged' in the space of the theatre under the instruction 'try to make sense of it all'. Sense-making is of course what theatre – as an apparatus of representation – does, and we do, as audience, while watching.

The situating of co-presence as the condition of the theatrical relation and the foregrounding of the co-construction of both the *mise-en-scène* and narrative meaning as an integral part of the activity of spectating is continued in *Autumn* as the explicit ground of the theatrical encounter. Here, the scenography reconfigures the audience as participants in the event rather than simply onlookers (or, rather, draws attention to spectating as a mode of aesthetic participation and sense-making rather than a 'passive' relation). The task-based dramaturgy of *Summer* is extended and explicated as a set of tasks audience members are invited to undertake: making samosas for the next performance, retelling the history of the world, discussing the nature of identity, exploring books significant to the company, engaging in tarot reading/fortune-telling, playing table tennis, placing yourself on a pinboard of degrees of separation. Through these activities, the audience become the event, appearing to ourselves through occupying the space of appearance and being explicitly staged as co-present along with the performers, technicians and company members. While apparently avoiding the 'theatrical' division between action and audience by making the audience the action, *Autumn* in fact demonstrates that the audience is effectively divided within itself – simultaneously doing and watching, seeing and being-seen – much as the performers themselves were staged in *Summer*'s opening scene. In other words, the logic of participation – much like the logic of presence – remains framed and mediated by the theatrical relation rather than simply appearing to 'overcome' it through some empty gesture of emancipation. Here, the intrusive, recursive nature of representation makes its presence felt again – enabling the set-up of *Autumn* to be read not as the overcoming of a division but as the ground of its re-inscription. Perhaps my own decision to retreat to the raked seating of the auditorium, resuming the 'spectator position', was testimony to that effect? Perhaps this move simply reflected the reassertion of what Rancière calls the 'theatrocratic' organization of democratic participation, installing 'a community of thought based on a spectacle that was essentially a self-representation' (2012, 10).

In *Winter*, the directly spectatorial relation is re-established through a film portrait of a woman with a terminal diagnosis. A large screen is wheeled onto the stage and set centrally. We watch as the stage space is framed as the site of a temporal encounter between the time of the filming (the presentation of live 'presence'), its direction towards the time of the future (the 'will have been' of time's passing, and her passing too), and the time of viewing (the audience's awareness of their own looking, looking back retrospectively though in sync with the narrative time of the viewing). The woman the film portrays is the aunt of a member of the company. The film provides a portrait of her presence in the world – a testimony to the future of her having been. It records her actions, her thoughts, her presence, and, of course, mediates them through the aesthetic frame of the film itself, and through the representational encounter with the theatre audience. The film draws attention to the singularity of presence – the uniqueness of this woman, her non-reproducibility – within the apparatus of representation and its technology of reproduction. It therefore seems to be drawing attention to the way representation appropriates and expropriates presence, and especially the 'live presence' of people as such. Here the liveness of performance, its 'life', is tied to the aliveness – however temporary, however fragile – of the people who appear within it.

In *Spring*, the intrinsic 'doubling' of presence and representation, ontology and the apparatus of sense-making, is itself redoubled. The work is performed by a group of nine pregnant women, whose own double-presence (as pregnant) mirrors their theatrical double-presence (as performing).

The women respond to questions posed as questions to, for and about their as yet unborn children, covering and uncovering their hopes, fears, expectations and future imaginings. The dramaturgy of questions is unrelenting. The questions appear to come from the outside – from the theatrical apparatus – remediating the performers' ontological presence as the ground of the representation (and its affects). Should these questions be answered? And whose labour is at stake in answering them? The visual pun here is doubtless intentional: the theatrical labour of performing redoubles the anticipated future labour of giving birth to, and bringing up, these children. The tension between the text, the task and the 'person' performing them is palpable – it appears as the exacting work of performance itself. The work of performance becomes evident as that which takes place *between* presence and representation, *between* being-on-stage and the mediation of what that being-there amounts to *being*.

To what extent are the performers in *Spring* aware of how their ontology as pregnant women inflects their representation as performers? To what extent does their mode of appearance objectify them as women, as already doubled? How does the doubled body of the performer – both present and representing – become redoubled when the performer is a pregnant woman, performing her own being-pregnant? Does this constrain and over-determine the mode of performing? Can they *only* appear, in other words, as pregnant women? Does this overly *ontologize* them as pregnant women (rather than as *working* performers, for example, who happen to be pregnant)? Are they simply being objectified, or does their 'double embodiment' draw attention to how 'the people' are continually de-/re-subjectivated by the frame of representation and mode of appearance that stages them as such? And what are the boundaries between the theatrical frame of representation and the political modes of representation conditioning and constraining their appearance?

The specific ontology of these performers and the construction of a specific dramaturgy conditioning their mode of performing further draws attention to tension between presence and representation – appearance and the frame of appearance – at the heart of the representational regime. In this respect, the 'ordinary people' appearing on stage seemingly presenting themselves 'as themselves' – which appears to characterize a significant strand of post-dramatic theatre – serves to foreground a crisis of representation 'in representation' (Frank 2010, 35). The tension between the theatrical representation of performer presence and the presence of the performer through their self-presentation is a tension at the core of the political apparatus as well as the aesthetic regime. Rather than seek to 'overcome' it, the Quarantine works studied here serve to explicate, examine and situate this 'crisis of representation' within the sphere of theatrical representation rather than outside of it, thereby reiterating the interpenetration of politics and aesthetics in the 'distribution of the sensible' (Rancière 2004, 12).

CONCLUSION

This chapter has sought to provide a comparative analysis of contemporary theatre works explicitly concerned with 'staging the people', performed in the British post-industrial cities of Manchester and Salford: Quarantine's *Quartet* and Rimini Protokoll's *100% Salford*. Both works examine how the lived experience of everyday lives might be brought to the stage through an apparent logic of presentation rather than representation: by ordinary people occupying the space of theatrical performance rather than seeing themselves and their lives represented by others. In so doing, they reanimate the questions Rancière investigates in *Staging the People* by situating the theatre as a site for the investigation of the political configuration of 'ways of acting, ways of seeing and ways of speaking' that seek to produce 'the people' as both their ground and effect. In particular, they revisit and rethink what Rancière calls the 'theatrocratic' organization of democracy and the structures of democratic representation as the people's mode of appearance to themselves while recognizing that 'the people' remain always more or less than 'the people', always different from a particular representation or form of representation, always the locus of the 'internal division' constituting the site of politics as such and never a totalization (1999, 87). This is because '"the people" does not exist. What exists are diverse or even antagonistic figures of the people, figures constructed by privileging certain modes of assembling, certain distinctive traits, certain capacities or incapacities' (2016, 102). In short, figures constructed through a certain apparatus of staging and the theatrical configurations of presence and representation. And yet, the people remain what is fundamentally missing from the scene of representation. In this context, the task of a dissensual post-dramatic theatre practice is not to elide their missingness with the evacuated political territory of the post-democratic but to draw attention to the apparatus of representation as that which produces absence even as it claims presence as its effect.

REFERENCES

Butler, Judith. 2015. *Notes Toward a Performative Theory of Assembly*. Cambridge, MA: Harvard University Press.

Butler, Judith. 2016. '"We, the People" - Thoughts on Freedom of Assembly'. In *What is a People?*, edited by Alain Badiou et al. Translated by Jody Gladding. New York, NY: Columbia University Press.

Deleuze, Gilles. 2103 (1989). *Cinema II: The Time-Image*. Translated by Hugh Tomlinson and Roberta Galetta. London: Bloomsbury Academic.

Didi-Huberman, Georges. 2016. 'To Render Sensible'. In *What is a People?*, edited by Alain Badiou et al. Translated by Jody Gladding. New York, NY: Columbia University Press.

Frank, Jason. 2010. *Constituent Moments: Enacting the People in Postrevolutionary America*. Durham, NC: Duke University Press.

Rancière, Jacques. 1995. *On the Shores of Politics*. Translated by Liz Heron. London: Verso.

Rancière, Jacques. 1999. *Disagreement*. Translated by Julie Rose. Minneapolis, MN: University of Minnesota Press.

Rancière, Jacques. 2004. *The Politics of Aesthetics*. Translated by Gabriel Rockhill. New York, NY and London: Continuum.

Rancière, Jacques. 2006. *Hatred of Democracy*. Translated by Steve Corcoran. London: Verso.

Rancière, Jacques. 2007. *The Future of the Image*. Translated by Gregory Elliott. London: Verso.

Rancière, Jacques. 2010. *Dissensus: On Politics and Aesthetics*. Translated by Steven Corcoran. London and New York, NY: Continuum.

Rancière, Jacques. 2011. *Staging the People: The Proletarian and his Double*. Translated by David Fernbach. London: Verso.

Rancière, Jacques. 2012. *The Intellectual and his People: Staging the People*, Vol. 2. Translated by David Fernbach. London: Verso.

Rancière, Jacques. 2013. *Aisthesis: Scenes from the Aesthetic Regime of Art*. Translated by Zakir Paul. London: Verso.

Rancière, Jacques. 2016. 'The Populism That is Not To Be Found'. In *What is a People?*, edited by Alain Badiou et al. Translated by Jody Gladding. New York, NY: Columbia University Press.

Rancière, Jacques. 2017. *Dissenting Worlds: Interviews with Jacques Rancière*, edited by Emiliano Battista. London: Bloomsbury.

Saward, Michael. 2010. *The Representative Claim*. Oxford: Oxford University Press.

Chapter 5

'Apart, We Are Together. Together, We Are Apart'

Rancière's Community of Translators in Theory and Theatre

Nic Fryer

'Apart, we are together.' This quotation from Mallarmé is cited by Rancière in his essay 'Aesthetic Separation, Aesthetic Community', first published in 2008 and subsequently in *The Emancipated Spectator* collection in 2009 (Rancière 2009a, 51). In coming together as distinct disparate elements around an artwork which is itself an entity comprised of distinct separate elements, Rancière sees the aesthetic community as being together while apart. In this chapter I want to explore Rancière's outlining of this paradox as a desire to identify divisions and ruptures within a notion of community. I will outline ways in which some critics have seen Rancière's writing on community as being unduly pessimistic and as failing to articulate a clear programme for how a community might realize and sustain political change. However, I will suggest that a notion of community underpins his understanding of theatre and art, and that it is here that he offers a vision of community as a creative activity and political act where individual spectators translate performances in their own way, but within a community of other translators and signs. For me, a vivid example of this is my own experience of watching the play *People, Places and Things* by Duncan Macmillan, where the desire to be part of a community and to break out of it existed within the narrative itself and was mirrored in my own experience as a spectator. I want to argue that this tension created a productive space for the characters in the play and agency for me as a viewer, as I negotiated a complex set of relationships between the characters and between myself and the protagonist.

RANCIÈRE – AGAINST PLATO, AGAINST ARISTOTLE

When exploring Rancière's relationship to theatre and community it is easier to begin by outlining what he is most passionately against rather than what he is for. For Rancière, Plato's *Republic* outlines a society in which everyone's role in the community is predetermined, with differing roles being ultimately unified to form a coherent social whole. The form of this society becomes normalized and ultimately becomes invisible. Such invisibility can be seen as what Rancière calls the 'distribution of the sensible', which is a key idea in Rancière's thought. According to Gabriel Rockhill in his glossary of Rancièrian terms in *The Politics of Aesthetics*, Rancière sees many such distributions. These function as 'an implicit law governing the sensible order that parcels out places and forms of participation in a common world by first establishing the modes of perception within which these are inscribed' (Rockhill 2004, 85). The 'implicit' nature of the distribution of the sensible structures the ways that people see and understand the world around them, without them being aware of it.

For Rancière, Plato's fear of theatre is based on its possibility to make this visible. It does this in at least two ways. First, the dual nature of the actor challenges the stability of one's identity. Writing about the relationship between theatre and politics, Joe Kelleher notes that for Plato, playing a role beyond yourself and your prescribed role in the community 'involves the actor in a division between himself and the character he is imitating or inventing, is a sign of human weakness. It is also a means of provoking weakness in others, and hence a threat to or an infection of the body politic' (Kelleher 2009, 48). There are behavioural ideals to maintain, and the aim for the citizen is to adhere to these ideals. The aim, in a Platonic society, is to know yourself and your identity, not to question it. However, according to Rancière,

> The mimetician is, by definition, a double being. He does two things at once, whereas the principle of a well-organised community is that each person only does the one thing that they were destined to do by their 'nature'. [...] He sets up a stage for what is common to the community with what should determine the confinement of each person to his or her place. (Rancière 2004, 42–43)

The stage thus becomes a place where the community loses the coherence and certainty of its constituent parts, and its attendant 'invisibility', through the indeterminacy of acting. Acting means that people's identities become disturbed, since 'those who speak on the stage do not speak in their own name and do not identify with or authenticate what they say' (Hallward 2006, 116). They move beyond the confinement of their predetermined identity.

Second, for Rancière, the act of performing challenges the distribution of the sensible because it challenges the limitations of one's social role. Rancière asserts that the 'distribution of the sensible both excludes artisans from the political scene where they might do *something other* than their work *and* prohibits poets from getting on the artistic stage where they might assume a character *other* than their own' (Rancière 2009b, 26, emphasis in original).

In the act of going on the stage, the artisan would be revealed as more than an artisan. She would become a citizen with other skills. And by going on the stage, the poet or actor is able to 'become' other than herself. Both disrupt the stable identity presumed by the distribution of the sensible.

Despite this suggestion that theatre can unsettle the subject's 'parcelled out' place within the community, Rancière supposes that there is often a contrasting 'presupposition that theatre is in and of itself communitarian' (Rancière 2009a, 16). In the public nature of the audience coming together and furthermore doing so in a shared space with performers, with clearly defined roles, there can be a notion of theatre as being an 'exemplary community form'. Theatre is a unique place 'where the audience confronts itself as a collective' (ibid., 5) as it comes together as a unified community of spectators to witness a community on stage. This is exemplified for him in the classical stage of Molière and Voltaire. He states that here 'the stage was thought of as a magnifying mirror where spectators could see the virtues and vices of their fellow human beings in fictional form' (ibid., 60). Here, '"[b]eing apart" of the stage was enveloped in a continuity between the "being together" of the signs displayed by the representation, the being together of the community addressed by it, and the universality of human nature. The stage, the audience and the world were comprised in one and the same continuum' (ibid., 61). In this vision, while the stage is separated from the community, the community is unified in its presence. The stage reflects the agreed social order it is separated from, and the actors and the spectators agree about what is being represented. Within its narrative space the different elements of the story cohere, and common understanding is concretized through the performance.

Despite this imitative construct, Rancière states that it 'was supposed to prompt specific changes in their minds: Molière's *Tartuffe* supposedly taught spectators to recognize hypocrites; Voltaire's *Mahomet* to fight for tolerance against fanaticism, and so on' (ibid., 60). Similarly, the classical stage's Aristotelian model of tragedy both simultaneously reflects and tries to dissipate Plato's fear of the subversive power of theatre by ensuring that while subversive behaviour may be represented, it must have consequences, ensuring that the moral qualities of the man are reflected in his destiny:

> It follows plainly, in the first place, that the change of fortune presented must not be the spectacle of a virtuous man brought from prosperity to adversity: for this

moves neither pity nor fear; it merely shocks us. Nor again, that of a bad man passing from adversity to prosperity: for nothing can be more alien to the spirit of Tragedy; it possesses no single tragic quality; it neither satisfies the moral sense nor calls forth pity or fear. (quoted in O'Toole et al, p.17)

For Aristotle, maintaining the status quo and universalizing the intended response is the aim. To invoke Rancière, theatre is a distribution of the 'sensible' supporting the social order, but this process is invisible. This process is not only politically and aesthetically limiting but limits the heterogeneous possibilities of how a community can be conceived.

RANCIÈRE, ETHICS AND COMMUNITY

Rancière's ambivalence about a homogenous conception of community extends beyond theatre. Writing about Plato's *Republic* in the chapter 'Aesthetics and Politics', he states that 'Plato simultaneously excludes both democracy and theatre so that he can construct an ethical community, a community without politics' (Rancière 2009b, 26). The term 'ethical' is used by Rancière to reflect a place where democratic debate is stifled in favour of universal morality; a place where political dissent or even negotiation is suppressed in favour of the security of the distribution of the sensible. For Rancière such a stifling is viewed as necessary because of horrific events such as the Holocaust, the horror of which brings a desire to avoid 'anything that threatens the social bond holding the community together' (ibid., 114). There may be a sense of security in the consensus of such an ethical community, but it disavows the possibility of political change. Furthermore, the anxiety to preserve the ethical community can be mapped on to the political sphere with lethal consequences. For example, in his essay 'The Ethical Turn of Aesthetics and Politics', Rancière sees George W. Bush's controversial desire for 'infinite justice' as a connected universalizing term 'occasioned by a preventative justice which attacks anything that is sure, or at least likely, to trigger terror, anything that threatens the social bond holding the community together' (ibid., 114).

Rancière sees just such an attraction to ethics as also rearing its head in contemporary artistic practice, where the 'ethical turn' springs from the desire to 'restore lost meaning to a common world or repair the cracks in the social bond' (ibid., 122). In opposition, Rancière posits the notion of dissensus. For him dissensus is not merely an argument between two points of view. Rather, it is a political 'demonstration (*manifestation*) of a gap in the sensible itself' (Rancière 2010, 38). Acts of dissensus reveal the arbitrary nature of what usually appears unchangeable, and thus from an 'ethical' perspective become associated with the criminal or deviant. By creating a space of contingency, a sense that things could be 'other' than how they usually are, they shatter the stability of Plato's 'community without politics' which needs to be preserved at all costs.

In terms of community, dissensus can be seen in Rancière's description of the 'political community', a 'community of interruptions, fractures, irregular and local, through which egalitarian logic comes' (Rancière 1999, 137–8). This logic is based on the ability of all to disrupt the political order, however temporarily. It exists 'in the often short-lived moment when those who are excluded from the political order or included in it in a subordinate way, stand up and speak for themselves' (Corcoran 2010, 6). These individuals collectivize on a strategic and temporary basis, knowing their differences. Such collectivization lies in the assembling of disparate identities who share a common ground but who are not collapsed into each other. According to Steven Corcoran, citing Rancière, such collectivization happened with nineteenth-century workers and women. Corcoran states that 'through the fact of their speech they showed that they had the rights that they had not, and did not have the rights that they had' (ibid., 6). It is notable that Corcoran's apparently paradoxical statement here echoes Rancière's own writing, where he often sets up apparently contradictory statements that need unpicking, and which resist a simple 'sensible' interpretation. Corcoran also reflects here Rancière's argument regarding universal intelligence outlined in *The Ignorant Schoolmaster* (first published in French in 1987). Such speech asserts the speaker's innate intelligence, but it also introduces what Corcoran calls 'supplementary speech that is irreducible to the constraints of social space' (6). Through the 'instituting of a dispute' (Rancière 2010, 37) over the distribution of the sensible, they created a new 'political' community. Their speech articulated what they as a group did not have, but did so through them insisting and demonstrating that resistance *was* possible. In this 'staging' of a dissensual moment lies the possibility of agency for the subject, and the revelation of the possibility of contingency through social (re)organization.

It is this 'separat[ion] of the community from itself' (Rancière 2010, 16) that most interests Rancière, and for him theatre can function as a model of this. Rancière's interest in theatre challenging the distribution of the sensible is evident in his early essay 'Good Times, or Pleasure at the Barriers'. In it, he discusses culture in nineteenth-century France. Rancière argues that in this period, across art forms, there was initially a controlling dynamic reminiscent of the Aristotelian model: a provision of a regulated leisure activity which attempted to limit audience response and functioned as social control.

As he puts it, 'The passions and energies of the working classes [were given] the means, the forms and the outlets for a regulated satisfaction and optimal use of their leisure' (Rancière 1988, 46). However, Rancière sees a number of more subversive political elements developing over time. The social mix in the theatre, where 'passageways between classes proliferated' (Rancière, quoted in Lewis 2012, 41), meant that the attempt to address the working class became diffused. Artists did not know how to address across the social mix. For example, Rancière states that 'a play which established the dire consequences of working-class immorality in a completely unambiguous way would bring few benefits for public order if by encouraging applause from the stalls it were to provoke 'collisions' with the 'cheap seats'' (Rancière 1988, 56). In this theatre, as Rancière sees it (according to Lewis), three things happened: workers saw things that were normally prohibited, workers took an active interest in areas normally denied them and the theatre itself 'promoted a habit of being where you're not supposed to be, in "uncertain spaces"' (Lewis 2012, 41). Through theatre, dissensus was possible. Therefore, although he opposes the authoritarian basis of Plato's argument, for Rancière, Plato is right in recognizing the subversive power of theatre to unsettle the community. This means, to quote Hallward, that 'it is Aristotle, rather than Plato, who is Rancière's most significant adversary' (Hallward 2006, 124). For Rancière, Aristotle's attempt to prescribe what theatre should be is doomed to fail and ignores its inevitable dissensual potential. Plato on the other hand recognizes that theatre can provide a dissensual challenge to the distribution of the sensible, including unsettling 'sensible' notions of communities and individuals' places within them as they currently exist.

The view of theatre reflects Rancière's writing elsewhere on community. According to him 'community' can be conceptualized in different ways. He states, 'There are two major ways of symbolising the community: one represents it as the sum of its parts, the other defines it as the division of the whole. [...] I call the first police, the second politics' (Rancière 2010, 100). The term 'police' here is aligned with the sensible, the institution that institutes the order of things brought together as an indivisible whole. The term 'politics' conversely articulates disruption and the possibility of change. Lewis describes Rancière's (di)vision of the political community as a 'contingent, sporadic encounter between sense and sense that divides the community against itself' (Lewis 2012, 34). Rancière's ultimate preference is for the 'division of the whole' and 'dissensus' in a short-lived 'political community', as people come together to create a 'staging of a "we" that separates the community from itself' (Rancière 2010, 16). A creation of community is thus simultaneously a disavowal of a larger community, and it is the latter that particularly interests Rancière.

IF THE COMMUNITY ISN'T 'ETHICAL', WHAT IS IT?

Such an emphasis means that Rancière has been criticized for failing to present a coherent or long term vision of community. I noted above that with Rancière's views on community in relation to theatre it is often easier to see what he is against than what he is for, and this criticism has been taken up by recent theatre scholars writing from a left perspective. As Janelle Reinelt puts it, 'It is possible that the applauded theatrical and political disruption is just a gesture – a momentary redistribution of the sensible without a follow-up move to consolidate gains' (Reinelt 2015, 246). Such a view of community, for Liz Tomlin, is also visible both in contemporary theatre and contemporary society. It is part of 'a critique of the desirability of co-ordinated mass resistance emerging from a coherent and organised community' (Tomlin 2016, 29). For Tomlin, there is a shift towards 'seemingly leaderless mass movements such as Occupy that have been inspired by and, in turn, have continued to invoke a leaning in radical political philosophy that tends towards a networking of disparate acts of multifarious resistance as opposed to organised and ideologically-coherent revolt or political opposition' (ibid., 29). (For Tomlin such a philosophy can be seen not only in Rancière's work but also in the work of Michael Hardt, Antonio Negri and Jean-Luc Nancy.)

For Tomlin and Reinelt, Rancière prioritizes the individual over the communal. There is, for them, little clarity on how to cohere individuals into a movement that can sustain itself. Instead, for some of Rancière's critics he ultimately promotes what Reinelt calls 'neo-liberal individualism' (Reinelt 2015, 247). Reinelt cites Andy Lavender in her article, who states that in Rancière's writing, and in its conception of theatre, 'communities are not so much defined by their *togetherness* as by their facilitation of *difference*, the fact that they enable individual expression' (Lavender 2012, 310, emphasis in original). Furthermore, as Hallward put it in 2006, writing about Rancière's work more broadly, the 'emphasis on division and interruption makes it difficult to account for qualities that are just as fundamental to any sustainable political sequence: organisation, simplification, mobilisation, decision, polarisation, to name a few. [...] Rancière neglects many of the more intractable problems of organising and sustaining such a sequence' (Hallward 2006, 128). Reinelt similarly suggests that for Rancière 'the distribution of the sensible cannot be modified or improved; it can only be ruptured so a new possibility can appear' (Reinelt 2015, 246).

Looking through Rancière's writing it is indeed difficult to find clear articulations of a sustainable political community. However, I want to suggest that it is in his writing on art, and perhaps on theatre particularly, that one can find a vision of community that is more tangible. In art, he argues, the community is coming together to try to understand from a range of perspectives, with each person translating the artwork in relation to their experience. In the experience of art itself, the subject is trying to understand how they relate to others …

INTERLUDE 1 – RUPTURING THE SENSIBLE: EMMA, DISSENSUS AND THE COMMUNITY IN *PEOPLE, PLACES AND THINGS*

Watching Duncan Macmillan's 2015 play *People, Places and Things*, I see the main character Emma (who variously also calls herself Nina and Sarah, and who is called Lucy by her mother) in rehab. As part of this she is invited to participate in group therapy. Emma resists the community of 'The Group' for some time, particularly the rules which it requires of its members. Foster tells her, 'You have to take part in the Group. I'm afraid we're pretty strict about this. You can't just pick and choose what you take part in. You have to do everything' (Macmillan 2016, 46–47).

Part of what she is expected to take part in is role play:

FOSTER: One of the ways we prepare for life in recovery is to practice certain interactions, important conversations,
EMMA: what, like, *role-play?*
THERAPIST: Would you like to practice Emma?
EMMA: God no. (72, emphasis in original).

As she is an actor, performing does not even allow her to move beyond her artisanal role; it reinforces it. She feels it offers no agency for her. But although I also work in theatre, I can't form a community with her. I find her refusal to engage arrogant and irritating. I want her to let her guard down and allow herself to be not a professional but a citizen finding an alternative social role through performing.

Instead, she stages an attempt to 'overthrow' the rules established by the group. One way in which she does this is by supporting a suicidal patient who is told they must leave the clinic after breaking its rules. She attempts to institute a democratic debate about his right to stay by reframing the debate about his potential future: 'Who thinks he should stay and get well and who thinks he should be sent to his death?' (65). This dissensual interruption of the rules of the clinic and introduction of an alternative perspective leads the Therapist to accuse her of 'attempt[ing] to demolish it from within' (67). My previous antipathy to her is now challenged. I want to join her community, and challenge the inflexible orthodoxy of the clinic's rules. I am torn between allegiance and antipathy.

Her challenge to the sensible behaviour of the Group is also evident in her lying about her life story by appropriating the plot of Ibsen's *Hedda Gabler*, and when she is asked to play a sister of another character she refuses. This behaviour disrupts the community and the agreed ethical position it has adopted of curing its participants through role-play. Indeed, she suggests that the Aristotelian model of acting is something that might hinder progress in her real life. She outlines how 'I played Antigone and every night my heart broke about her dead brother. Then my own brother died and I didn't feel anything. I missed the funeral because I had a matinee' (90). The Aristotelian frame of catharsis, via *Antigone*, provided closure and returned her to her emotionally limited state, rather than offering her a vision of a more fulfilled or at least alternative life. Again, my response is complex. I empathize with her grief, while finding her disruptive behaviour destructive to the well-being of herself and the others in the group.

The community of the clinic is disturbed by Emma's behaviour, which questions the function of role-play and acting. However Emma's outbursts give her a sense of autonomy within the community, and she is able to connect with people within it through her dissensual behaviour, even when destructive. Mark states, 'Emma's refusal to engage with the process is compromising everyone's recovery' (86). She responds, 'If your progress here can be jeopardised by me being a cunt then you truly are a lost cause' (88) and calls him a 'cunt' in return. He tells her, 'I might also be your best friend in the world' (88). Despite their sparring, her dissensual act has created a moment of engagement, a frisson with someone she might otherwise have been in thoughtless 'ethical' consensus with.

Watching Emma, I find her intelligent; her outbursts and attempts to subvert thrilling to watch. I am simultaneously attracted to her, yet irritated by her refusal to want to find solutions to her issues. No clear articulation of how she might employ her intelligence to move forward, rather than just disrupt, is yet visible for either me or her. I can't see how she is moving forward into any kind of community where she can engage constructively with others in a sustainable way.

ART AS COMMUNITY

At first Rancière's writings on artistic communities might appear to sound similar to his writings on political communities; for example, his assertion that 'the aesthetic community is a community of dis-identified persons' (Rancière 2009a, 73). But I will contend that in his writing on art a more complex picture begins to emerge. One such complexity is illustrated by Oliver Davis, who asks how Rancière's insistence 'on the *dissensual* character of the community [...] coheres with his own broadly Kantian vision' (Davis 2010, 157, emphasis in original). Looking at Kant's definition of the universality of aesthetic judgements, one can see a consensual rather than dissensual community being articulated; indeed for him 'a person who can feel neither the solemnity nor the awesomeness of nature lacks [...] the necessary sense of his own limitations' (Scruton 2001, 110). Apart from the arguably consensual nature of 'necessary limitations' and of knowing one's place, there is also a sense of Rancière's 'ethical' in Kant's aesthetic judgements: such judgements are rooted in a judgement all should feel. The Kantian attempt to define 'judgements of taste' (Kant 2007, 35–74) is thus ultimately an attempt to define *'universal'* (Kant 2007, 25, emphasis mine) judgements of taste, which would appear a long way from the celebration of dissensus favoured by Rancière.

However Kant also states a paradox about this universality: 'In all judgements by which we describe anything as beautiful we tolerate no one else being of a different opinion, and yet we do not rest our judgement upon concepts, but only on our feeling' (Kant 2007, 70). Kant uses the term 'subjective universality' to define this paradox (ibid., 43). As Rancière points out, '"Subjective" doesn't mean "individual", and isn't opposed to "universal". The opposite of subjective is "objective"' (quoted in Battista 2017, 247). In other words, the moment of subjective processing can be seen not so much as an individual moment but rather as a moment based on feeling. In grasping the importance of feeling in the moment of the subject processing the beautiful object, according to Rancière, Kant allows for the possibility of the aesthetic to 'suspend [...] the power relations which usually structure the experience of the knowing, acting and desiring subject' (Rancière 2009b, 97). Such 'suspension' might reveal the arbitrary nature of the distribution of the sensible, and can find common ground with Rancière's own notion of the aesthetic regime of art, which 'strictly identifies art in the singular and frees it from any specific rule, from any hierarchy of the arts, subject matter, and genres' (Rancière 2004, 23). In this ambiguous world, as in Kant's contemplation of indescribable beauty, there is a tension between the subject and what they encounter. The moment of Kantian aesthetic experience supersedes interpretation. For both Rancière and Kant, albeit in very different ways, such a moment is potentially open to everyone. Kant's sense of the aesthetic being rooted in a universal sense of what is beautiful is overturned by Rancière into a vision of an egalitarian and communal space where all are able to contemplate the thing presented.

In *Aesthetics and Its Discontents*, Rancière sees this aesthetic contemplation as exemplified in the notion of the statue outlined by Schiller in *Letters on the Aesthetic Education of Man*, which is 'closed on itself' (Rancière 2009b, 34), meaning that it has a 'free appearance' (ibid., 29). The spectator is given space by the autonomy of the work to contemplate it. The artwork is a 'resistant volume' (ibid., 34) from which the viewer will always remain at a distance. Because it exists as a bounded entity that is by definition outside the sensible it is resistant (though perhaps not immune) to its influence. This singular volume is combined of a range of elements. Similarly, he says in 'Aesthetic Separation, Aesthetic Community' that in an aesthetic community 'the assemblage of data and the intertwining of contradictory relations are intended to produce a new sense of community' (2009a, 58). This 'new sense' is crucial and is another place where Kant and Rancière can be seen to differ. Kant's notion of the aesthetic is about unity, the singularity of the artwork and therefore it as a reflection of the transcendence of God. Rancière's however is about the multiplicity of elements it contains. As a heterogeneous experience outside the everyday, the artwork offers disparate elements presented in a frame beyond life. This offers an opportunity for the individual to translate it in their own way, relating it to their own experiences but without it being reducible to those experiences.

ART AS A PROCESS OF COMMUNITY

I want to now foreground here the ways in which this sense of the individual apprehension of art might be understood in relation to others and to a sense of community. Like Rancière, Jean-Luc Nancy suggests that the emergence of art 'is the effect of a general transformation of our commonality, of the conditions for possibility of our being together, and thus of the conditions for the manifestation of this "being together"' (Nancy 2009, 91), a 'means [...] of understanding our communal existence and the very modes of being-in-common' (ibid., 92). I mentioned earlier that Nancy, like Rancière, has been criticized for his refusal to articulate a clear vision for community. However, in Nancy's idea of 'being-in-common', an individual being exists independently from others but also shares a common being with other individuals through the transformative possibilities of art. For Rancière too, art can hold in tension both independence and collectivity. He writes, 'The solitude of the artwork is a false solitude: it is an intertwining or twisting together of sensations, like the cry of a human body. And a human collective is an intertwining and twisting together of sensations in the same way' (Rancière 2009a, 56). In both his notion of art and his notion of community, then, there is an attempt to value both the fragments and the whole that the fragments constitute.

What Rancière identifies as happening in communities of audiences and art makers is not only a vision of art as something which can dissolve what currently exists but also a vision of it as constitutive; it is the power of the aesthetic community to forge new communities, made up of people coming together outside their normal social identity, which for him suggests the possibility and crucially the *process* of change through dissensus. In 'The Misadventures of Critical Thought', Rancière emphasizes the way in which the 'emancipation' of the individual links with the notion of community. He states that a 'collective understanding of emancipation is not the comprehension of a total process of subjection. It is the collectivization of capacities invested in scenes of dissensus' (Rancière 2009a, 49). The process of freeing up, or 'emancipating' the spectator, is not just about returning the spectator to a state of individualism. Rather, by freeing the individual from the ethical community, she is able to collectivize with others in her own way at specific moments.

Drawing on *The Ignorant Schoolmaster*, in the 2007 essay 'The Emancipated Spectator' (also published in the collection of the same name), Rancière outlined a notion of art as an active process. He states, 'In the logic of emancipation, between the ignorant schoolmaster and the emancipated novice there is always a *third thing* – a book or some other piece of writing – alien to both and to which they can refer to verify in common what the pupil has seen, what she says about it and what she thinks of it' (Rancière 2009a, 14–15, emphasis mine). He states further, 'It is not the transmission of the artist's knowledge or inspiration to the spectator. It is the third thing that is owned by no one, whose meaning is owned by no one, but which subsists between them' (ibid., 15). This 'third thing' is unknowable, and has the aesthetic power to open up a space for the individual. This third thing is open to all. This third thing *creates a community* through the process of individuals apprehending it; it 'subsists between them'. I note, for example, the emphasis on *making* the community in a comment by Rancière that might at first appear to emphasize division: 'There is a political agency when there is the *construction* of a *we* that splits up the community and the *invention* of names for that *we*' (Rancière 2009c, 284, emphasis mine). Like his depiction of politics as 'a *process*, not a sphere' (Rancière 2010, 70, emphasis mine), Rancière emphasizes not a desire to abolish community but to rather see it as being constantly in process and shifting through time and in different social contexts. It is not a boundaried, fixed entity but a dynamic one.

I see Rancière's thinking on art in the essays in *The Emancipated Spectator* (published in 2009) as being a development from those in *Aesthetics and Its Discontents* (first published in French in 2004 and in English also in 2009). In the first book, Rancière's vision of dissensual aesthetics is seen in the shape of the 'resistant volume' (Rancière 2009b, 34) of the artwork, whereas *The Emancipated Spectator* brings in a processual element (what Davis calls 'a critical reflection on what it means to be a spectator') (Davis 2010, 153). This extra layer means that for Davis '*The Emancipated Spectator* presents a far more persuasive and more coherently theorised account of political art' (153).

Yet I would argue that there is also some recognition of the importance of process in Rancière's earlier book.

Discussing a Mallarmé poem in *Aesthetics and Its Discontents*, Rancière states that it has 'the inconsistency of a gesture which dissipates in the very act of instituting a common space' (Rancière 2009b, 34). In its articulation, the poem brings people together as it is simultaneously experienced. However, its indeterminacy and inconsistency means that as it does so it emphasizes its inability to provide certainty. A shift can be seen here from art as an aesthetic 'thing' to be contemplated in itself, to an awareness of the importance (as within a Kantian appreciation of aesthetics) of the aesthetic existing in the spectator's process. Its existence is both a material thing and something that instigates a process in human beings. By noting this, it is possible to see Rancière as emphasizing not only the artwork itself but also the importance of how the spectator comes into contact with the artwork. Therefore the book can be seen not just as a 'bourgeois survey of some recent works and exhibitions', as Oliver Davis rather belittlingly describes *Aesthetics and Its Discontents* (Davis 2010, 153), but of the process of the perception of art. This process of engaging with the work, of translating it, is what interests Rancière.

A shift towards the apprehension of art as a process of translation between subjectivities can be seen in Rancière's term 'sensus communis', outlined in 'Aesthetic Separation, Aesthetic Community'. According to Rancière this term can be broken down into three elements. The first is the individual elements that are presented in the artwork itself: 'sense data: forms, words, spaces, rhythms and so on' (Rancière 2009a, 57). The second is the 'dissensual figure' (ibid., 58) of the presentation of this data within the entity of the artwork, so the 'sensorium' of the elements of data being 'superimposed [by] another sensorium' creates a 'tension between two sensory worlds' (ibid., 58). (Although Rancière does not define the term clearly, 'sensorium' can be understood here as an amalgamation of the ways different things that are sensed interact to develop an overall way of perceiving.) In addition to this, however, as already stated, Rancière suggests something more is involved: the 'assemblage of data [first level] and the intertwining of contradictory relations [second level] also creates "a new sense of community"' (ibid., 58) that is the third level. Artistic practice takes elements of data and reconfigures them, and a similar thing happens within the aesthetic community where people are brought together but as individual constituent elements engaging with the practice in subjective ways. For him such 'aesthetic experience allows for new modes of political construction of common objects and new possibilities of collective enunciation' (Rancière 2009a, 72). While the critiques mentioned previously suggest that Rancière does not clearly articulate politics in a programmatic way, he does see artistic practice as offering an ongoing process of dissensus, as people connect and disconnect to communities as they are formed and reformed.

INTERLUDE 2 – *PEOPLE, PLACES AND THINGS*: CONSTRUCTING COMMUNITY

For me:

I dip in and out of connecting and disconnecting to the 'third thing' of the performance and the character Emma, as I watch her journey through recovery and slip back into addiction. I imagine myself as an addict going through rehab, and think of the difficulty of sustaining the willpower to not slip back into taking drugs. I watch and admire her struggle but find her irritatingly flippant and wish she could form more sustainable connections with people to enable her to feel more part of a community where she can be in a relationship of listening and being listened to. I discuss her behaviour with the person I am watching the performance with, and we discuss the 'third thing' of this ambiguous, not always likeable character. Our community is disrupted by the 'third thing' but is also created by it. Emma makes us rethink the ways that therapy and theatre work and how they might work together.

For Emma:

Her resistance to the group has given her confidence. She begins to work with the group while challenging it from within when she wants to. She allows herself to be vulnerable and asks the doctor how she can trust the process: 'I really want to know. I want to try' (Macmillan 2016, 100). This is not a succumbing to the ethical community, just seeing what in that community she might draw on. She wants to see how she might engage in a process of change, rather than just fit in with her predetermined role. She uses the rehearsal space of the Group to construct a role-play of a potential reconciliation with her parents that could be seen to be partially determined by a sensible notion of a happy family structure but could also be seen as her exploring how she might move beyond what has become her socially agreed role as an addict. The role-play might function not just as a distribution of the sensible but as a 'third thing' that will enable her to reflect on her life and to consider how she will create her possible future self.

ART AND THEATRE AS TRANSLATION

In *The Ignorant Schoolmaster*, Rancière articulates a pedagogical process characterized by a non-hierarchical teacher–student relationship. In this, he suggests that 'what brings people together, what unites them, is nonaggregation' (Rancière 1991, 58). They retain their individuality as they come together. Similarly, when discussing politics in *Disagreement*, Rancière suggests that 'political being-together is a being-between: between identities, between worlds ... between several names, several identities' (Rancière 1999, 137–8). Rancière calls for people who come together, whether in politics or pedagogy, to retain distinct elements and refuse to 'aggregate'. For Hallward, this ultimately means a lack of power as 'crowds come together to stage the process of their own disaggregation' (Hallward 2006, 117). However, I want to suggest the possibility for this 'nonaggregation' of people to be reimagined in a more positive way: as an articulation of what Yves Citton has identified in Rancière's theory as 'a collection of singularities, a *chaotic aggregation*' (Citton 2009, 131, emphasis mine), as distinct, 'apart' people come together and negotiate their differences.

In *The Ignorant Schoolmaster* Rancière asserts, 'People are united because they are people, that is to say, *distant* beings. Language doesn't unite them. On the contrary, it is the arbitrariness of language that makes them try to communicate by forcing them to *translate* – but also puts them in a community of intelligence' (Rancière 1991, 58, emphasis mine). For Rancière, such distance is not to be feared. In 'The Emancipated Spectator', which takes the idea of a radical equality in the relationship between teacher and student and applies it to the relationship between performer and spectator, he claims that distance 'is not an evil to be abolished, but the normal condition of any communication' (Rancière 2009a, 10). In fact, the separation implied by this notion of distance simultaneously implies a sense of people coming together as they try to translate through their mutual intelligence. Rancière states further that 'an emancipated community is a community of narrators and translators' (ibid., 22).

This notion of distance seems to me to be particularly well illustrated in Rancière's metaphorical use of the term 'translation'. By choosing the term 'translation' to describe the communication process, Rancière foregrounds a notion of the complexity of the activity of being understood, with different people who are ostensibly speaking the same language system actually thinking, decoding and understanding through their speaking of different 'languages'. If translation is something that people do as communicating social beings, it is nonetheless intrinsically difficult. Rancière's choice of the word 'translation' to refer to the ambiguity inherent in communication is reflected in other writers' views on translation. For example, Umberto Eco states that 'a perfect translation is an impossible dream. In spite of this, people translate' (Eco 2001, ix). By using the word 'translation', Rancière also invokes a concept of communication as taking place within wider cultural structures of language, and not just from individual interpretation. This significance is reflected in Susan Melrose's statement that translation always activates a complex relation between complex systems (including systems of values, ethos and attitude) which make up 'one culture' and the material real of that culture on the one hand, and *similar* systems (but not necessarily 'the same') in their relation to the material real, in the target culture. (Melrose 1994, 26, emphasis in original).

By working with another to understand in a context of translation, then, not just individual but also cultural differences are explored and negotiated.

From such a perspective of difference, grasping what someone is trying to say or trying to communicate is universal, and everyone is able to engage in the process of conception. On the other hand, everyone's ability to communicate experience is partial, and the quality of communication bears no inherent relation to the quality of the ideas or the depth of feelings the communication springs from. Indeed, in *The Ignorant Schoolmaster* Rancière gives the example of a mother whose son returns from a war, whose complexity and depth of emotion is exactly what makes the experience difficult to communicate (Rancière 1991, 68). It is in such situations that one is most present to both the richness of human experience and the equality of intelligence implicit in the universal impossibility of full comprehension of another. As Lewis puts it, the notion of translation 'is essential to Rancière because it operates under the principal axiom of the equality of intelligences' (Lewis 2012, 103). There is a 'polemical verification of equality' (Rockhill 2004, 86) as all involved in the process encode and decode across the distance between their subjectivities, and the universal nature of translation of human beings overrides or at least challenges any educational or social limitation.

In *The Ignorant Schoolmaster* Rancière explores what becomes possible under the assertion of this equality in an educational context, suggesting that 'conceiving well is a resource of any reasonable person' (Rancière 1991, 67). And 'conceiving well' might not necessarily mean 'conceiving accurately' but might rather emphasize the active, communal and ambiguous nature of translation. In 'The Emancipated Spectator', he similarly states that from the 'ignoramus, spelling out signs, to the scientist who constructs hypotheses, the same intelligence is always at work – an intelligence that translates signs into other signs and proceeds by comparisons and illustrations in order to communicate its intellectual adventures and understand what another intelligence is endeavouring to communicate to it' (Rancière 2009a, 10). Rancière is asserting here not a polemic but rather an ontology premised on the ability of all human beings to think as they engage in communication. In his words, 'Man does not think because he speaks. [...] Man thinks because he exists' (Rancière 1991, 62).

Reflecting the kinds of journeys and gaps that the translation of the communication process entails, Rancière states that 'one must learn near those who have worked in the gap between feeling and expression' (ibid., 68). He sees the artist as his example of someone from whom the reader can best learn about such 'gaps', and he specifically uses the example of Racine. For Rancière, what Racine knows is not skill but rather impotence: 'He knew the limits of translation and the powers of counter-translation. He knew that the poem, in a sense, is always the absence of another poem' (ibid., 69). (In their book on Rancière and education Bingham and Biesta put this as 'knowing that language is never up to the task of such a translation' [Bingham and Biesta 2010, 119].) What becomes important is the creation possible through translation, or what Rancière elsewhere calls the human 'poetic capacity for translation' (Lewis 2012, 89). 'The book', or the artwork, is the central 'third thing' here, since it provides a stimulus for activity that is distant and distinct from the speaker and the listener, a focal point. For Rancière 'the relation between two ignorant people confronting the book they don't know how to read is simply a radical form of the effort one brings every minute to translating and counter-translating thoughts into words and words into thoughts' (Rancière 1991, 63). In this sense it might be possible to argue that in art the process of translation is foregrounded, with even the creator trying to translate the work as it declares itself distant from and independent of her. This would be particularly evident in the aesthetic regime of art that Rancière argues for, which 'asserts the absolute singularity of art and at the same time destroys any pragmatic criterion for isolating this singularity' (Rancière 2004, 23).

Across *The Ignorant Schoolmaster* and subsequently 'The Emancipated Spectator', pedagogy and theatre are reimagined. Rather than being premised on a hierarchical relationship, where it is the job of the student/spectator to directly decode what the teacher/performer is trying to communicate, a relationship is instigated where the student/spectator finds agency through their individual process of translation. For Rancière, theatre is a communal activity not because spectators come together as a singular entity but rather because they interpret what they see and hear as individuals, relating it to other experiences of their own and to those of other spectators. Rancière states that

> the collective power shared by spectators does not stem from the fact that they are members of a collective body or from some specific form of interactivity. It is the power each of them has to translate what she perceives in her own way. [...] This capacity is exercised through irreducible distances. (Rancière 2009a, 16–17)

If for Rancière, art, including theatre, can be a particularly effective vehicle for the ambiguity of communication and expression, it is important to preserve its autonomy from a claim for efficacy in any simplistic sense. Indeed, it is because the artwork stands independently in its own right, retaining its autonomy, that it can ignite a contingent process where the viewer has power to translate it in a model that reinforces their agency. Davis puts it thus:

> The community which the artwork under the aesthetic regime envisages is one of individuals whose autonomous capacity to interpret the world in which they find themselves as spectators is recognised; this will necessarily be a 'dissensual' community, whose members reinterpret the works they encounter in the light of their own experiences and their knowledge of other works. (Davis 2010, 156)

Crucially, I would emphasize here the co-presence of both autonomous interpretation (or translation) and other translators. This translation happens in a relationship with other translators, and is a democratic understanding which allows people to see new possibilities, and in principle (even if there are social limitations or issues around access that Rancière avoids) it 'includes those who are not included by revealing a mode of existence of sense experience that has eluded the allocation of parties and lots' (Rancière 1999, 58). It is open to everyone because everyone is a translator. It lies beyond what has been socially allocated through the distribution of the sensible.

In this uncertain space, this uncertain community, there are many layers of translation. As Rancière's notion of 'the third thing' suggests, the self is made to encounter the 'other' of the artwork. In theatre specifically, however, there is also the performing body that contains the performer him/herself translating his/her role. And this performer/role is in a community of performers, whether present on stage or present through the ghosts of previous performances. In the ambiguous world of Rancière's aesthetic, when we are together, we are apart, trying to translate across subjectivities. The frequency with which Rancière mentions the term 'community', particularly in his more recent writing, emphasizes its centrality to his thought. While the criticisms mentioned in this chapter regarding his refusal to articulate a specific strategy for moving forward may be understandable, in his invocation of translation, it is possible to see a view of community which resists a purely neoliberal individualistic world view. Translation is only possible through a process of consideration of and engagement with other languages and other subjectivities. So while it may be true that Rancière's view of community emphasizes the individual as well as the communal, that when we are together we are apart, the converse is also true. It is also impossible to be apart without being together with others in a translating relationship, and this has profound consequences for the individualistic world of the twenty first century.

CODA – *PEOPLE, PLACES AND THINGS*: A COMMUNITY OF TRANSLATORS

Emma is nervous about having to engage with her family again, and how they will translate the apology she will make to them that she rehearses in the group. And her nervousness is well founded. The performance doesn't match the rehearsal; the translation and response of her parents doesn't match Emma's intention. Her father interrupts her and tells her 'thank you for your little speech but it doesn't mean anything' (Macmillan 2016, 127). And her mother, in anger, tells Emma, 'Drink and drugs were the only things that made you any fun. [...] This family is broken. Forever. [...] Don't expect a fucking trophy for trying your best. That's the bare minimum you should be doing' (131). Worse, her mother has brought Emma's collection of drugs into her bedroom in what could be variously perceived as an act of anger, a challenge to her commitment or following Emma's wishes when she went into rehab. There is no consensus in the community of this family. The mother's act and speech, in particular, disrupts any expectation of her maternal or social role. What is left for the characters is to translate each other's feelings, actions and words, and to negotiate with each other. This community of difference is not resolved, and may never be resolved, but it is a community where all are forced to confront each other. For me watching it, I can sympathize with Emma when her attempt at reconciliation is thwarted, but I also hear how she stole from her mother and broke her fingers. I am negotiating my own translation of what I have seen in this 'third thing'.

In itself, it's an example focused around one person and their small network of relationships, which doesn't play out around any particular explicit political issue or in a large community. But in this piece Emma can be seen to dynamically engage in processes of translation with the communities she is involved in, and these processes shift dynamically the nature of those communities and the relationships within them. And she is also involved in negotiating possible versions of herself, an entity composed of different elements. This is concretized in several fantasy sequences during the play where other performers who look like her appear on stage and create a multiplication of 'Emmas'. And in watching the process of translation set up through this production, for me meaning and certainty have loosened a little, my own thoughts and expectations have been challenged, and I have seen, connected to and sometimes felt distanced from the translations across distances shown in the production.

Such translation is also evident in an essay by Jennifer Parker-Starbuck, who draws on Rancière as she outlines a history of watching theatre with her daughter. She relates going to the theatre with learning, quoting Michel Serres's 'No learning can avoid the voyage' (Serres 1997, 8). The voyage of translating, of discussing, of thinking, can indeed also be seen as teaching – a teaching in line with the work on 'will' Rancière outlines in *The Ignorant Schoolmaster* that ongoingly creates an openness to learning, rather than a hierarchical passing down of knowledge. The will to keep voyaging and learning is possible because of the multiple distances theatre sets up: quoting Jill Dolan, Parker-Starbuck describes sitting 'bolt upright, caught in the *density* of a *communal* epiphany' (Parker-Starbuck 2014, 130, emphasis mine). This density is multiple, but crucially it is also something that is *communal*, it happens with others as people engage with translating across the distances around them. It happens as people try to understand themselves, their world and the relationship between them.

REFERENCES

Battista, Emiliano, ed. 2017. *Dissenting Words: Interviews with Jacques Rancière*. Translated by Emiliano Battista. London/New York, NY: Bloomsbury.

Bingham, Charles, and Gert Biesta. 2010. *Jacques Rancière: Education, Truth, Emancipation*. London/New York, NY: Continuum.

Citton, Yves. 2009. 'Political Agency and the Ambivalence of the Sensible'. In *Jacques Rancière: History, Politics, Aesthetics*, edited by Gabriel Rockhill and Philip Watts, 120–139. London: Duke University Press.

Corcoran, Steven. 2010. 'Introduction to Jacques Rancière'. In *Dissensus: On Politics and Aesthetics*, 1–24. Cambridge/Malden: Polity.

Eco, Umberto. 2001. *Experiences in Translation*. Translated by Alistair McEwen. Toronto/Buffalo/London: University of Toronto Press.

Hallward, Peter. 2006. 'Staging Equality: On Rancière's Theatrocracy'. *New Left Review* 37 (January/February), 109–129.

Kant, Immanuel. 2007. *Critique of Judgement*. Translated by James Creed Meredith. Oxford: University Press.

Kelleher, Joe. 2009. *Theatre & Politics*. Basingstoke: Palgrave Macmillan.

Lavender, Andy. 2012. 'Viewing and Acting (and Points in Between): The Trouble with Spectating after Rancière'. *Contemporary Theatre Review* 22(3), 307–326.

Lewis, Tyson E. 2012. *The Aesthetics of Education: Theatre, Curiosity and Politics in the Work of Jacques Rancière and Paulo Freire*. London/New York, NY: Bloomsbury.

Macmillan, Duncan. 2016. *People, Places and Things*. London: Oberon.

Melrose, Susan. 1994. *A Semiotics of the Dramatic Text*. Basingstoke: Macmillan.

Nancy, Jean-Luc. 2009. 'Rancière and Metaphysics'. In *Jacques Rancière: History, Politics, Aesthetics*, edited by Gabriel Rockhill and Philip Watts, 83–92. Durham, NC/London: Duke University Press.

O'Toole, John, Madonna Stinson, and Tiina Moore. 2009. *Drama and Curriculum: A Giant at the Door*. Australia/Singapore: Springer.

Parker-Starbuck, Jennifer. 2014. 'The Spectator and Her Double: Seeing Performance through the Eyes of Another'. *Theatre Topics* 24(2), 125–136.

Rancière, Jacques. 1988. 'Good Times, or Pleasure at the Barriers'. In *Voices of the People: The Social Life of 'La Sociale' At the End of the Second Empire*, edited by Adrian Rifkin and Roger Thomas, 45–94. Translated by John Moore. London/New York, NY: Routledge and Kegan Paul.

Rancière, Jacques. 1991. *The Ignorant Schoolmaster: Five Lessons in Intellectual Emancipation*. Translated by Kristin Ross. Stanford, CA: Stanford University Press.

Rancière, Jacques. 1999. *Disagreement*. Translated by Julie Rose. Minneapolis, MN: University of Minnesota Press.

Rancière, Jacques. 2004. *The Politics of Aesthetics: The Distribution of the Sensible*. Translated by Gabriel Rockhill. London/New York, NY: Continuum.

Rancière, Jacques. 2009a. *The Emancipated Spectator*. Translated by Gregory Elliott. London/New York, NY: Verso.

Rancière, Jacques. 2009b. *Aesthetics and Its Discontents*. Translated by Steven Corcoran. Cambridge/Malden: Polity.

Rancière, Jacques. 2009c. 'Afterword: The Method of Equality: An Answer to Some Questions'. In *Jacques Rancière: History, Politics, Aesthetics*, edited by Gabriel Rockhill and Philip Watts, 273–288. Durham, NC/London: Duke University Press.

Rancière, Jacques. 2010. *Dissensus: On Politics and Aesthetics*. Translated by Steven Corcoran. Cambridge/Malden: Polity.

Reinelt, Janelle. 2015. 'What I Came to Say: Raymond Williams, the Sociology of Culture and the Politics of (Performance) Scholarship'. *Theatre Research International* 40(3), 235–249.

Rockhill, Gabriel. 2004. 'Glossary of Technical Terms'. In *The Politics of Aesthetics: The Distribution of the Sensible*, edited by Gabriel Rockhill. London/New York, NY: Continuum.

Scruton, Roger. 2001. *Kant: A Very Short Introduction*. Oxford: University Press.

Tomlin, Liz. 2016. '"Constellations of Singularities": The Rejection of Representative Democracy in Coney's Early Days (of a Better Nation)'. *Studies in Theatre and Performance* 36(1), 27–34.

Part III

SPECTATORSHIP AND PARTICIPATION

Chapter 6

Nights of Theatrical Labour in the Victorian Workhouse

Jenny Hughes

The writings of Jacques Rancière offer a valuable set of provocations for theatre and performance studies. In particular, his explorations of aesthetics and politics, often cited by theatre and performance researchers, have challenged a number of orthodoxies relating to the educational and political efficacy of theatre. While only rarely turning his attention directly to theatre as a practice, Rancière frequently draws on an abstract idea of theatre and theatricality to describe the terrain of politics. Concerned with how representational practices across the domains of philosophy and formal politics work to reproduce inequality, Rancière turns to theatre as a figurative site to narrate an idea of politics that embraces heterogeneity and is virtual rather than representational. The political terrain appears, for Rancière, when the subjects of history elude their predetermined role and function in any order of representation, challenging the limits of visibility and legibility, and creating space for new kinds of experience to take shape in the public realm. As part of this, Rancière notices how, in accounts of history, an association with theatre and theatricality can accrue to those subjects and objects that refuse their assigned place in the order of things. Writing, for example, about the description of Percennius, leader of a revolt in ancient Rome (in the *Annals* of Tacitus), Rancière notes how Percinnius is depicted a 'man of the theatre' and that, hidden in the folds of this account, 'the one who had no place to speak' comes to express 'the roar of urban theatrocracy' (1994, 25). As Peter Hallward shows, Rancière's concept of 'theatrocracy' refers to the disruption of systems of emplacement and verification, in favour of a terrain in which 'every political subject is first and foremost "a sort of local and provisional theatrical configuration"' engaged in 'performing or playing, in the theatrical sense of the word, the gap between a place where the *demos* exists and a place where it does not' (Hallward 2006, 111, citing Rancière, emphasis in original).

In this chapter, I examine Rancière's writings on history and historiography, as well as his discussions of theatre and politics more broadly, for what they might offer to the critical project of theatre history. I explore a theatrical entertainment given by a company of music hall performers from Collins' Music Hall to an audience of paupers in Islington workhouse in London in 1891. Taking place on a specially erected stage in the large dining hall of the workhouse, the performance was one of a series of annual New Year entertainments at the workhouse arranged by Herbert Sprake, proprietor of Collins' Music Hall on Islington Green from 1881 to 1898. It consisted of a series of turns by the company, and here I focus on three acts in particular: 'sensation of the season', Tom White and his Street Arabs; renowned 'change-artists', the Pylades, with an act that was 'as good as a visit to Madame Tussaud's exhibition'; and finally, music hall celebrity Charles Coborn 'who, of course, obliged with the perennially popular "Two Lovely Black Eyes"', which had 'the male portion of the audience' joining 'heartily in the chorus'.[1] Turning to Rancière's writings on labour and social history, relatively neglected by theatre and performance scholars and providing the foundations for his later work on aesthetics and politics, my aim is to respond to the methodological challenge of attending to the out-of-place, anonymous figures of social history via a close analysis of a theatrical event that has left little trace. While there is a body of evidence that might be brought to bear in its analysis, the performers and audience members at the entertainment left no account of their experience. The silent figures of this event of performance, in Rancière's terms, have 'no place to speak', however, it is possible, by carefully tracing the figures of speech and gesture in the extant record, to speculate on how the performance created a disturbance of order in the workhouse. The performance provided a counter to the repressive context in which it occurred, while also subjecting both performers and audience to disciplining forms of performative social work.

The title of a review of the entertainment in *The Era*, 'Paupers and Professionals', evokes its eccentric quality for contemporaneous observers. Victorian workhouses were authoritarian institutions that operated according to a principle of rigid classification and spatial segregation of the poor (Driver 1993, 65). The aim was to deter all but the most desperate from seeking social support. On the one hand, workhouses provided care and education for the frail, ill and abandoned, and on the other hand, they aimed to instil habits of work into the idle, able-bodied poor. The entertainment reviewed here interrupted the daily order of the workhouse by bringing pauper inmates together (still segregated in the hall, however), with a contingent of Guardians and local gentry, to witness a spectacle of philanthropy that, as will become clear, comprised of a series of disciplined exhibitions of virtuosic labour. If inequality is created by social, economic and cultural practices that support a consensus about who and what is permitted visibility and legibility in the representative order, then for Rancière '*[t]he essence of politics is the manifestation of dissensus as the presence of two worlds in one*' (2010, 37, emphasis in original). 'Dissensus', a Rancièrean term related to his 'theatrocracy', describes aesthetic and political processes that create fractures in the sensible world, 'a conflict between a sensory presentation and a way of making sense of it' (ibid., 139), which reveal 'a new fabric of common experience, a new scenery of the visible and a new dramaturgy of the intelligible' (ibid., 141). As such, and drawing on Peter Bailey's description of British music hall at this time, it becomes possible to argue that this multi-layered performance communicated a 'knowingness' (Bailey 1994) between performer and pauper, revealing hidden, and shared, worlds of experience and meaning.

Alongside a consideration of the potential contribution Rancière's work makes to the writing of theatre history, the analysis of the workhouse entertainment provides an opportunity to probe this notion of dissensus. In the material contexts of theatre as a practice, and of nineteenth-century music hall as part of an emergent culture industry, the breaks in order created by the performance are produced by the labour of the performers. While this work occurred as part of a performance given by a group of out-of-place performers ostensibly not-at-work and expending their leisure time engaging in an act of charity, it is clear that the dissensual energies of the performance were complementary, as much as a counter to, the disciplinary regimes of music hall and workhouse. A repeated feature of the workhouse entertainment was the revelation of a profoundly *un*equal world of economic struggle of working performers inside its sensible fabric, drawing attention to a disavowed economic relation in the operations of dissensus and critical potencies of a theatre event. As such, the workhouse entertainment, created by and for the economically precarious, casts a critical perspective on Rancière's propositions about the forms of equality that may be afforded by the time and place of theatre.

THEATRE HISTORY AND ITS POOR

Rancière's historical work, *Proletarian Nights*, explores writings of workers from nineteenth-century France, focusing on moments when the worker's occupation by the socio-economic conditions of poverty and the task of work is interrupted or suspended.[2] The text represents Rancière's radical break with classical Marxism and is one of several works on history produced during his period of disillusionment with programmatic left politics following the May 1968 uprisings. *Proletarian Nights* contests the placement of the worker, by contemporary labour and social historians, in an order of representation that denotes their subjective lives as wholly determined by productive labour and concomitant experiences of exploitation and degradation. 'It seems to me that I have not found my vocation in hammering iron' (2012, 3), writes itinerant worker, 'J. P. Gilland', knowing all the time that poverty limits his choice of work: 'I would have liked to have been a painter. But poverty enjoys no privileges, not even that of choosing this or that fatigue for a living' (ibid., 8). Through the book, Rancière traces the ways in which labourers, 'secretly in love with useless things' (ibid., 8), break with their preordained orientation to the task of work and 'appropriate to themselves the night of those who can stay awake' (ibid., 22).

In a historical essay exploring other kinds of nights of labour, Rancière describes how nineteenth-century workers attending popular theatres in Paris became a focus of concern for authorities by enacting a similar appropriation, and in a way that echoes concerns of authorities in nineteenth-century Britain about music hall audiences. Interestingly, the problem for Parisian authorities arose not from these places of entertainment as sites of immorality but in the challenge constituted by the very act of appropriation: 'in the cross-cutting between circuits of work and circuits of leisure, in the proliferation of those trajectories, real or ideal, by which workers moved in the space of the bourgeois and let their dreams wander there' (2011, 178). The opportunity to be something other than a worker, via the mimesis of habits of bourgeois leisure, represents a political gesture, for Rancière, as it challenges the idea of the worker as wholly occupied by a world of alienating and exploitative work. Broader recognition of the critical force of such appropriations by labour activists and historians has been delayed by the resilience of a representative schema that denies the worker the capacity to be something other than a worker, or, in Rancière's terms, to be more than one thing at a time.

This is comprehensively explored in the book that followed *Proletarian Nights*, entitled *The Philosopher and His Poor*, originally published in French in 1983. Here, Rancière draws attention to the way economic and political philosophy and sociology, from Plato's account of the perfect republic, Marx's narrative of the capitalist economy, to Bourdieu's sociology of class, are each founded on a kind of 'exclusion by homage' of the 'poor' – a part of the demos, comprised of the working class as well as the economically unproductive lumpenproletariat so hated by Marx, allocated a singular and silent place in the order of representation, denied the capacity of thought (2004, xxvi). The 'poor' here become a stand-in cipher that provides a securing foundation for scholarly accounts of the world. While being subject to analytical capture in this way, the 'poor' also figure as a dissensual presence in those schemas, as carefully traced in Rancière's book. Rancière's figuring of the poor calls for careful attention to the means by which we categorize, organize and fix the difficult-to-discern subjects and objects of theatre analysis.

The audience, for example, the silent figures that provide the conditions for the existence of debates about theatre's efficacy, tend to disappear with the event itself, leaving little account of their experience. Theatre analysis and theatre history thus proceeds via analysis of the absence as much as existence of (often partial and fragmentary) empirical evidence, supported by critical or methodological frameworks borrowed from aesthetics, cultural theory or the social sciences that perform their own exclusions.

Such critical interrogation of the frames by which we come to know something about theatre and its audiences can be productive, as is evident in contemporary scholarship on music hall. Jacky Bratton, for example, in her reading of histories of theatre in England, has shown how theatre historians from the early nineteenth century onwards have excluded popular theatre and its audiences, constructing a binary between theatre as art and theatre as popular entertainment that continues to define theatre history to a degree (Bratton 2003). Citing the work of Bratton, alongside Dagmar Kift and Peter Bailey, Paul Maloney reflects on 'a new appreciation of the depth and complexity of the cultural negotiation afforded by music hall' (2016, 7). He provides a useful summary of the way scholars have, in their consideration of music hall performance, the diverse make-up of its audiences, and via specific case studies, challenged the hegemonic project of theatre history that Bratton draws attention to. Music hall, in its diversity of form, offers a representative realm open to appropriation and exploitation in ways that are dynamic and multi-directional. Bratton, for example, comments that 'the kaleidoscopic, self-reflexive, endlessly slippery surfaces of a world thickly polished with comic conventions' are 'so unyielding to investigation' (1986, xiii). She also draws attention to how the move to establish popular performance as a respectable focus of scholarly study was delimited, in its early phases, by a combination of anti-theatricalism and the 'ideological smoke' of left-oriented, class-based analysis (Bratton 2003, 10). Classifications of music hall in earlier studies as politically 'conservative', for example, on the grounds of its progressive embrace of commercialism and search for respectability, are too quickly dismissive of the critical potency of music hall performance and the intelligence of its audiences.

That said, the workhouse entertainment in Islington certainly was part of Herbert Sprake's effort to secure a respectable place for Collins' Music Hall in the new socio-economic order of this London borough, and in the crowded leisure marketplace of London, via a series of moves common to music hall proprietors at this time. By the latter half of the nineteenth century, there is evidence of long-term relationships between several London music halls and workhouses, with many music hall proprietors seeking respectability via a construction of their own 'poor' – including the Middlesex and St. Giles workhouse through the 1890s, and Foresters and Bethnal Green workhouse through the 1870s, among others.³ Sprake's respectability was affirmed by regular participation in networks of philanthropy and civic administration in Islington, including via the annual spectacle at the workhouse, conducted at his own expense, and place on the workhouse school board, with this participation frequently reported in both local and industry press. By the middle of the nineteenth century, Islington, between east and west and slightly north of Central London, was a district finding a new footing in the socio-economic order of the city, and it housed a mixed population, with poorer classes living alongside an established genteel class (Porter 2000, 253). By means of his philanthropic activity, Sprake created a narrative of a socially responsive, confident business – like other music hall proprietors of his time, forging a new kind of 'capitalism with a beaming human face' (Bailey 1986, 49). Sprake's legibility in this new order was made doubly tenable by a familial connection to poverty. He was second cousin by birth and uncle by marriage of one of the first proprietors of the Collins's, Sam Collins, a comic singer who had an inauspicious start in life and 'never forgot that at one period of his life he was inmate of a workhouse school' (*The Islington Gazette*, 31 December 1864). It was Sam Collins who initiated the tradition of annual entertainment at the workhouse, and these are the earliest examples of entertainments in Victorian workhouses that I have found to date.

To cement his place among the local elite, Sprake was anxious to maintain the appearance of propriety in the hall. The Collins's, known as the 'Chapel on the green', included in every printed programme an encouragement to audiences to report any impropriety (*The Islington Gazette*, 7 November 1893). These efforts, although occasionally mocked in the press, helped to secure the favour of his mixed customer base but also reveal the precarity of Sprake's place in the socio-economic hierarchy. This was emphasized by an incident occurring a few months before the workhouse entertainment in 1891, when a music hall inspector identified the side lounges of the bar area as the 'hunting grounds' for prostitutes ('a goodly number of unfortunates of the better clad sort'), threatening the renewal of the annual licence (London County Council 1890). The incident demonstrates the well-documented illegibility of women's appearances in music hall (and indeed the contested nature of women's presence in public space in Victorian London), and it is difficult to ascertain what was in fact observed by the inspector, with at least one report suggesting that the women were in fact the wives of friends of Sprake (*The Islington Gazette*, 6 November 1890). *The Era* was supportive, describing this incident as a 'calumnity' created by an overzealous local authority, and also noting the vehemence of local support for Sprake: 'How that calumny was disposed of, and how friends and neighbours of the popular Islington proprietor rallied round him and showered upon him their sympathy, are now matters of music hall history' (*The Era*, 13 December 1890).

Here, the policing of those deemed out-of-place at the theatre is attempted, although not necessarily achieved.

In his book of essays on historiography, *Names of History* (1994), Rancière emphasizes that the task of the historian is to attend to the multitude of silent voices of revolt that generate the conditions for those who speak and write history:

> It is, then, this world of silent witnesses that the historian brings into signifiance without lies, that history in our century will reclaim as its realm – in place of ambassadors' letters or of the paperwork of the poor, the multiplicity of spoken words that do not speak, of messages inscribed in things. (1994, 58)

These silent witnesses are not to be found in administrative records but in the dissensual study of such records to locate: 'phrases and arrangements of phrases that transform, into something visible and utterable, what had no place to be distinguished and was heard only as inarticulate noise' (ibid., 93). A dissensual practice of theatre history, open to tracing the mute chatter that provides the conditions of existence for the historical account, is perhaps most important to pursue when researching the experiences of audiences. A long-time source of anxiety for the theatre scholar, the audience, as inferred previously, is the 'poor' of theatre analysis – a repository of silent voices creating the conditions for critical arguments about theatre's potencies, and often only via the methodologically reductive schematics of empiricism or ideologically framed readings. These approaches, while illustrating important features of the context of reception have, arguably, revealed little about the significance of a performance for an audience. Rancière explores this in his critique of the orthodoxies of political theatre which, in privileging the notion of educating and activating an audience politically, are founded on a presumption of the audience's poverty of intellect. Rancière counters this by insisting on the emancipated nature of spectatorship:

> We also learn and teach, act and know as spectators who all the time link what we see to what we have seen and said, done and dreamed. ... We do not have to transform spectators into actors, and ignoramuses into scholars. We have to recognise the knowledge at work in the ignoramus and the activity peculiar to the spectator. (2011a, 17)

Following Rancière's suggestions, the workhouse audience might be enlisted as a critical agent in the creation of an account of this event via a translation of features of the extant evidence to reveal what is *not* represented there. This necessitates openness to speculation and an appreciation of the audience as exhibiting provisional forms of presence arising from the role they play in the broader environs of the workhouse. The reviews of the entertainment record the audience's appreciation, expressed via small gestural responses that, when considered in relation to other accounts of workhouse entertainments at this time, reveal appreciation alongside other kinds of response. Newspaper reviews of workhouse entertainments describe audiences' laughter, singing along, cheering, tears and shining eyes, and occasional speeches of thanks or renditions of a song in response. There are references to coughing, a sign of ill health to be expected in this context but perhaps also an expression of boredom, disgruntlement or disapproval. There are references, in minute-books that record the day-to-day operation of workhouses, to entertainments in workhouses that go on too long and exhaust the patience of their audiences. The illustration of a New Year's entertainment organized by veteran performer John Maclean in 1881 at St. Giles's workhouse in the West End (see figure 6.1) offers a rare opportunity to consider the 'games of social theatricality' that might have been in play between performer and pauper during such events (Rancière 2011, 228). The illustration shows rows of men and women with bowed heads, accompanied by coughing, and some evident enjoyment. The voice of the audience member who is speaking is dismissed by the caption, 'an old naval hero, much

Figure 6.1 **'New Year's Eve at St Giles's Workhouse'.** *Source: The Illustrated London News,* 12 January 1881.

given to spinning long yarns', echoing Rancière's point that the voices of the poor, when they speak, accrue associations with theatricality. The postural deference of the man in the left-hand corner, and on the right, the back of an elderly woman being helped to make an exit because she has 'had enough of it', indicates something of the discomfort felt by some of those participating in such spectacles (figure 6.1).

In the remainder of the chapter, I consider three acts that contributed to the entertainment at Islington workhouse in 1891, and as part of this, continue to trace the silence of the poor as a condition of the historical record of this event. My aim is to weave a critical appreciation of this silence into an analysis of the dissensual and disciplinary characteristics of the performance in its particular context.

DYING IN HARNESS: TOM WHITE'S STREET ARABS

Tom White and his Street Arabs, an act repeatedly remarked on for its cleverness, humour and novelty, is variously named in contemporaneous reports, with each naming carrying Orientalist and racist overtones – 'Wild Arabs', 'Buffalo Tom White with his Egyptian Dervishes', 'City Arabs', 'Wild West Arabs'. The Arabs were a group of street children selected and trained as a juvenile performance troupe by White, a blackface minstrel clown. The narrative of the troupe, likely related by White himself during the act, is that while touring a poor area of London, he noticed a group of children at a street barrel organ, earning money entertaining a crowd. White selected five boys from this group and trained them himself (*The Stage*, 17 January 1890; *Bristol Mercury*, 28 August 1900). The troupe's sketches consisted of burlesques, led by White, played out via verbal play and patter, physical tricks, chases, tumbles, dances, and song. It is not possible to be sure what precisely was performed at the workhouse but at the time of the entertainment, which coincided with the early phase of their career, there were at least two sketches in their repertoire. Both sketches comprised of a failure of the Street Arabs to fully obey the instructions the master, with this failure expressed, paradoxically, via a skilful expenditure of labour. The first was a burlesque of a mesmerism act, where White 'affects to mesmerise [the boys], and whilst in that condition to put them through several curious antics' (*The Stage*, 17 January 1890). Second, there was an acrobat sketch called 'Wild Worst Arabs'. The detailed report of this sketch, performed a few weeks following the workhouse entertainment, is worth considering in full:

> They are now giving a very amusing burlesque of the feats of a company of acrobats, each of them having first been introduced to the audience by some fantastic title. This travesty of what one of the performers calls 'acrobating'

provokes roars of laughter. A trio consisting of Tom White and two of his Arabs next make an attempt to sing 'Sweet Violets' but their rendering is horribly out of tune, which causes the leader of the band and his merry men to expostulate in loud tones. 'We *will* sing it if we die for it' shouts Mr White, making a third attempt. 'Then you'll have to die,' replies the exasperated *chef d'orchestre*, suddenly levelling a revolver and firing at the unmelodious trio, in which murderous action he is joined by other members of the band. All this is very good fun, and is heartily enjoyed by the audience, who also loudly applaud the youngest member of the troupe for his capital rendering of 'Rocked in the cradle of the deep'. (*The Era*, 24 January 1891, emphasis in original)

The themes of the sketches are, despite the fun, disturbing – power inequalities, forced labour, abuse and threat – echoing the concerns of campaigners against child labour in the theatre at this time (see Colclough 2016). In the mesmerism sketch, for example, a group of poor children act out their subjection to an adult with charismatic power in pursuit of a profitable act, and the acrobatic sketch ends in the murder of White and two of the boys. The virtuosity – smartness, agility, comic skill and timing – of the performers testify to a punishing rehearsal regime. But, in turn, the power of the master is undermined by the humour created by the boys, which principally arises from their skilfully performed failure to fully realize their instructions. In these master-servant sketches, the blackface clown-master appears to be in charge, but the poor boys get the better of him, and as one reviewer suggests, the part White played in the act was as a 'butt for their comic impudence' (*The Islington Gazette*, 19 September 1900). This is not a sketch which dupes its performers or audience, however, but rather one in which both performers and audience share a joke at the expense of those who might be duped; a parody of mesmerism spectacles popular in late Victorian performance. In the 'acrobating' sketch, the involvement of the conductor of the music hall band opens up the game of knowingness to the audience. This extension of playfulness to include the audience as equal partner in the rule of disorder is a moment which, arguably, reveals that all that is visible and legible, from the charitable disposition of the Guardians of the poor to the postural deference of the pauper audience, is open to contamination by shared pretence and play.

Child performers on the Victorian stage, as pointed out by Tracy C. Davis, made significant contributions to the economic well-being of their families and were also subjected to punishing training regimes and exploitative and dangerous working conditions (Davis 1986). Caroline Steedman, in her exploration of street children, draws on Arthur Symons's representation, in a poem about a child dancing with abandon on stage, of his experience of seeing a poor street child too tired to dance. Steedman comments that such conceptualizations of the poor performing child express 'an adult desire ... embodied in many visions of the child dancing: *that the child be itself*, in all its "earnestness of purpose"' (1995, 128, emphasis in original). Citing John Lucás's analysis of the poem, she argues that Symons gives the reader a 'briefest vision' of the possibility of 'a life not entirely determined by circumstances' (ibid., 129). Drawing on this suggestion, it becomes possible to argue that the disciplined labour of the poor performing boys in the workhouse present an illusion to the pauper audience of successfully overcoming their circumstances, with a little effort on their part. Reviews at the time frequently comment on the economic success of the act: 'It says much for Mr White's gifts as a coach to have whittled his material into such capital form, and to have framed so good an entertainment from what at first sight would seem to be unlikely expedients. Capitally does this "show" succeed' (*London and Provincial Entr'acte*, 31 May 1890). It is possible, however, that for a pauper audience watching White's Street Arabs, a more layered transaction was in play. The disorder created by the street child-turned-performer inflects the legible order with a sense of theatricality. Not only does the audience know that the boys are not mesmerized and/or not failing in their performance, but both performer and pauper share an experience of play-acting within a managed regime of surveillance. Here, evocation of feeling for the poor and affirmation of the effort of labour is played out alongside an acknowledgement that nothing is as it seems.

This celebration of the disturbance of appearances is also evident in the way that the act draws on conventions of blackface minstrel performance. There is no evidence of the boys themselves performing in blackface but White certainly did. As master and butt of the jokes, the act trades on racist stereotypes of the black character as stupid, common in minstrel performance. But White, called 'clever darkey' in one newspaper review, was also the acknowledged intellect behind this novel and profitable act, and a skilful comic in his own right (*The Era*, 24 May 1890). Michael Pickering offers a complex reading of the blackface mask, arguing that 'what was symbolically worked out in minstrelsy, at a metalevel of commentary, were questions about the status of white Victorian society in the whole human social and biological order', with an affirmation of the superiority of whiteness underpinning many of the acts (Pickering in Bratton 1986, 84). Minstrel troupes adopted and exploited racist tropes to generate new commercial opportunities. This affirmation of white superiority, however, also worked to invert a Protestant work ethic, representing 'a *mundus inversus* of the white world' (ibid., 89). The theatricalization of self, and of racist hierarchies of white self and black other, as features of this act, create a place in the sensible fabric of the world for recognition of the intellectual and entrepreneurial capacities of the white parts of the poor population, as well as a place for White and Sprake, as music hall proprietor, to exploit theatrical labour for profitable return.

The troupe's success lasted into the early 1900s, and the act, arguably, secured a place in the socio-economic order for a group of poor boys, at least one of whom may have been physically disabled. The 'youngest member of the troupe' giving the rendition of the hymn at the end of the acrobat sketch was a boy 'whom the audience playfully denominate 'Pimple,' a probable reference to the abnormal size of his head' (*The Era*, 1 March 1890). Pimple is frequently referred to as a favourite of audiences, with his unusual appearance as well as his comic and singing ability marking him out for particular attention. His real name was John Hipple, and his relationship with Tom White reveals the worlds of care, exploitation and exhaustion enfolded within the dissensus of this performance. White apprenticed Hipple for his act following the recommendation of a local councillor engaged in charitable work in Hartlepool, who had noticed the boy earning a living as a ballad singer (*The Era*, 5 May 1894). John Hipple, along with his brother (also a member of the troupe), appeared in police court in late 1890, after being arrested for 'wandering about without visible means of subsistence' in London. In the same year that the act achieved notable success on the stages of London music halls, Hipple, nine years old according to the court record, had run away from White's home, alleging that Mrs. White 'knocked him about'. In court, Hipple's mother testified that White regularly sent a portion of the boys' wages to her, and that, as she did not have means to support her children, she wished them to stay with the Whites (*The Era*, 22 November 1890). Following this inauspicious start, Hipple worked with White for the next ten years and, after White's premature death aged forty-two years in 1900, took on the management of the troupe. An obituary in *The Era* relates how White was taken ill following a Saturday performance and died of pneumonia a few days later, and that 'a striking proof of the sustained popularity of the entertainment is that with the exception of one week during his lengthy career he has not had even a few days rest'. The reporter notes that White 'may be said to have died in harness', having worked himself to death (*The Era*, 18 August 1900). Whatever the circumstances of their relationship, the longevity of Pimple's affection for his master was remarkable. On the anniversary of White's death, and for at least thirty consecutive years following, Pimple placed in *The Era* an 'in memoriam' notice: 'In ever loving remembrance of Tom White. Founder of the famous Tom White's "Arabs", who died Aug. 17th, 1900. Gone but never forgotten.'

EPIC FEATS OF LABOUR AND REPOSE: THE PYLADES

In a mock-ethnography of the music hall published a year before the entertainment in Islington workhouse, critic Percy Fitzgerald provided a description of the Pylades:

The most clever and amusing of these 'change artists' were certainly two young Germans, who presented in quick succession every public character known to Europe, in judiciously selected pairs. ... To effect the changes these adroit beings merely turned their backs to the audience; by skilful manipulation of face, wigs, &c., and a change of clothes, revealed themselves in a few seconds completely transformed, or almost 'transmogrified'. Appropriate music heralded each character. ... The last coup was most effective. A small tree was carried on, and in an instant we had before us the Grand Old Woodcutter, feverishly wielding his axe to tumultuous applause and hissing, mingled in equal proportions. (1890, 54)

A review of the Pylades a few years previous to this account described the act as offering 'a Liberal education', with representation of 'historical celebrities' from music, poetry, the stage, military history and royalty in the form of Mozart, Beethoven, Shakespeare, Hugo, Wellington, Nelson, the emperor Frederick and Prince of Wales (*The Era*, 28 April 1888). Two years later, a reviewer noted that the performance offered 'an excellent entertainment; one that answers the expectations of the sternest ascetic who ever turned aside from the paths of frivolity' (*The Era*, 4 January 1890). The figure of the Grand Old Woodcutter, described by Fitzgerald, was former Liberal prime minister William Gladstone, who developed a much-mocked hobby of cutting down trees, and the revelation of this personage in the act, as Fitzgerald points out, provided an opportunity for audiences to express their political sympathies. In other reports, a figure representing 'Lord Beaconsfield', former Conservative prime minister Benjamin Disraeli (referred to as 'Dizzy'), solemnly looks on the woodcutting scene, with the duo provoking 'a political demonstration, which combined cheers and counter-cheers' at the Oxford Music Hall in 1888 (*The Era*, 23 June 1888). In the year before the entertainment at the workhouse, a humorous element of the act was added with the appearance of common soldier figure, Tommy Atkins, who has the temerity to indulge in smoking a cigarette in front of his commander, the Duke of Cambridge, with the sketch that followed satirizing military leadership. The culmination of the act comprised of 'a most effective tableau of Wellington and Nelson, the latter in the act of dying, and supported by Britannia holding the Union Jack. Enthusiastic cheers greeted the two men who did so much to uphold the honour of old England, the patriotic pulse of the audience being evidently stirred' (*The Era*, 13 December 1890).

The grandly named 'Pylades' – evoking the classical culture of ancient Greece – lends the act an aura of respectability, and it was frequently commended for offering an encounter with edifying culture, in which patriotic impulses are affirmed. The inclusion of a 'liberal education', generally extended only to the upper classes, in the realms of music hall exemplifies what Fitzgerald disparagingly describes as the 'spurious gentility' of music hall (Fitzgerald 1890, 7). Frequent references to the educative potencies of the Pylades in the press are infused with mockery at times, but they also reflect the search for respectability by music hall proprietors by means of the offer of 'rational' forms of recreation (Kift 1996, 97). As Bailey (1978) highlights, concerns about the ways in which the masses were using their newly won leisure time in the latter third of the nineteenth century led to a series of elite-sponsored cultural programmes to promote respectable forms of cultural engagement. And so, it is possible to view the Pylades as paying a subversive kind of homage to respectable culture, with their mimicry of the great and good, and skilful control over the realm of appearances comprising a playful appeal to common sensibilities. The Pylades offer an exhibition of skill in bizarre transformations, by two performers who can bend appearances to their will, and the impropriety of impersonating the elite may have been provocative for elements of the audience, as Laurence Senelick notes of representations of 'Dizzy' in music hall song (Senelick 1975, 161).

The Pylades sketch at the workhouse, like the Street Arabs, affords the pauper audience a mock opportunity to participate in a representational regime where they become legible as music hall spectators as well as citizens in the formal environs of politics and education. The realm of respectability is stretched here to include both the music hall and pauper as a legible part. Notably, this happens by the depiction of breaks, of moments of repose – images of leisure and idleness – of the personages mimicked and, again like the Street Arabs' misfiring performances, the exhibition of these moments of repose are underpinned by a skilled and disciplined expenditure of labour on the part of the performers. The personages depicted are either not at work, because they are engaged in a leisure time occupation of wood-cutting, having a cigarette break, or they are artists engaged in the expenditure of high status but materially non-productive work, as with the depiction of the cultural celebrities in the act. A subversive kind of pleasure is generated by an encounter with these personages in states of repose, and this echoes the way the entertainment as a whole creates of a moment of suspension in the operations of the workhouse. Rancière, notably, was fascinated by the dissensual potency of bodily forms freed from their 'proper' function, an idea that emerges in a different form in his argument that the efficacy of art is always in excess of designations of educational, social or political function. For Rancière, the interrupted form is a reminder that there is no stable relationship between a representation and what it represents and affects. Instead, a gap between a bodily form and its designated function, expressed, for example, in the statue of the Torso de Belvedere – 'the mutilated statue of an idle hero, unable to propose anything to imitate' – signifies the insecurity that underpins any attempt to fix the function or purpose of a subject (2010,

138). In these breaks and interruptions, it is not that something is identified that replaces those representations. Rather, what emerges is a renewed sensibility of the provisional and multitudinous nature of the world, and of its forms and relations.

If there is dissensus in the Pylades' act at the workhouse, it is in part in its redistribution of a sense of who might be afforded the right to idleness. At the workhouse, the Pylades' celebration of moments of repose, and of the production of illusions rather than useful artefacts, signal the co-presence of bodies and forms that do and that do not work, that do and do not fit into the socio-economic order. The search for respectability by music hall performer and proprietor is staged, but what is also inferred is that the securing of an *equal* place in the socio-economic order is concomitant with access to a time and place of not-work, a time and place of leisure. But, and once again drawing attention to the complementarity between the dissensus of performance and the workhouse and music hall as sites of inequality, it is important to note that this depiction of idleness is an output of the virtuosic labour of the performer.

SINGING A WORLD OF INJURY: CHARLES COBORN

The star turn in the workhouse entertainment was Charles Coborn, music hall celebrity, singing 'Two Lovely Black Eyes', a song that became a hit of this period and stayed in Coborn's repertoire throughout his fifty-year-long career.[4] The singer is a man 'strolling so happily down Bethnal Green' with 'Tompkins' and Tompkins's 'girl', who is handed 'two lovely black eyes' by Tompkins after praising the Conservatives. Learning his lesson, when next in company 'the merits of Gladstone I freely pressed', with the same result, leading to a final verse relaying the moral 'Never on politics rave and shout, Leave it to others to fight it out'. Performing the song in character, Coborn wore faded black frock coat, with charcoaled smudges around both eyes, wearily wielding a ragged umbrella and a flat iron, an implement popularly thought to reduce the swelling of bruises. The song, then, tells a drama of a common man, an awkward and unwelcome third with Tompkins and his girl, whose attempt at achieving social acceptance by reproducing the political chatter of the day ends in physical injury. He appears as poor Everyman, battered and bruised by both sides of formal politics, Conservatives and Liberals – a humorous but also powerfully empathic character.

The significance of this song in Coborn's career is signalled by the fact that he devotes a chapter of his autobiography to it, and the story told there echoes the song's themes in uncanny ways. A reportedly outspoken character, and 'much mixed up in what may be called the politics of my profession', Coborn was a key player in establishing the Music Hall Artistes Association (MHAA) in 1886 (Coborn 1928, 168). Music hall performers at this time were subject to poor pay and employment conditions, reliant on the shifting tastes of audiences as well as interests of proprietors, in need of the next popular turn to keep themselves solvent, and often subjecting themselves to working lives characterized by exhaustion and premature death (Bailey 1986, 39–40; Kift 1996, 49). It is important to note that Coborn's unionization work did not reflect a politically left orientation but rather a lifelong Conservativism and associated commitment to free trade that he felt was undermined by protectionist pay, contracting and management practices in the music hall industry. The initial moves to establish a union led, in Coborn's own account, to a particularly lean period, and with a young family, he concluded that he needed a reliably marketable song – 'a song which the boys in the gutter would sing' (Coborn 1928, 173). A parody of a song imported from America, 'My Nellie's Blue Eyes', which apparently had lyrics so trivial that they invited parody, 'Two Lovely Black Eyes' was an immediate success. 'Two Lovely Black Eyes', a song about injury sustained by entry into the realm of formal politics, afforded Coborn an opportunity to successfully navigate a precarious economic context while campaigning for improved rights and conditions for performing artists.

The unpredictability of social interaction and the challenging nature of finding a voice in the social realm constitute the overarching themes of 'Two Lovely Black Eyes'. The refrain of the song (also its title) promises a romantic encounter, but the song turns out to tell a story of injury incurred by the risky nature of political discourse for the common person. As with the Street Arabs, the representation of failure is countered by the control over the realm of appearance evidenced by the virtuosity of this popular artist. Coborn's linguistic expertise is a feature of the historical life of the song. Over the years, Coborn sang the chorus in various languages, including French, German, Italian, Spanish, Greek, Hebrew and Welsh (Coborn 1928, 180–81). But his virtuosity was quintessentially theatrical – in his autobiography he confesses that he learned these versions of the chorus without ever understanding the words. There is appreciation of the performers' skill in controlling appearances here, but this control over appearance is also an illusion. The linguistic expertise on display is spurious, but the performer's virtuosity is appreciated nonetheless, and the 'knowingness' shared by music hall performer and spectator in these moments of performance is at one and the same time bogus and emboldening. Here, performers 'were applauded not just for their naturalistic re-creation of a shared world but for their authority in the actual business of living in that world, an authority perhaps most potently demonstrated in songs of its many fallible inhabitants' (Bailey 1994, 153). The diverse languages of the chorus that Coborn sang, without linguistic expertise, also affirmed that the appearance (rather than reality) of a genteel education were quite enough to achieve artistic and economic success. Reflecting on the use an audience might make of the dissensual qualities of speech in popular performance, Rancière states that 'shifts in the relationship of words to the "real" that they represent define fragile productions of meaning and moveable plays of identification' (2011, 14). Here, the dissensual qualities of the performance promise, if only for a moment, an expanded repertoire of possibility for the common person.

The challenge of finding a voice and a place in the social realm is key to another song Coborn sang in the workhouse entertainment. 'English as she is spoke' was a song inspired by a Portuguese guide to speaking English published in 1855 that featured many comical errors. The song celebrates the improper and unregulated use of speech in England, including the improvised and exaggerated expressions used by costermonger, soldier, barrister and railway porter. It also includes, in the third verse, some mockery of the formal and obscure speech of the stage actor:

The mission of the Drama is to educate and teach,
And every actor in his time plays many 'parts' of speech,
If you would shine upon the boards don't speak as mortals would,
You'll die an 'understudy' if you're always understood ...
PATTER (Parody some well-known actor) To be or not to be, &c

(Coborn and Dance, n.d.)

Due to the non-arrival of one of the acts at the workhouse (a ventriloquist act, fittingly), Coborn gave one more than the traditional two-act music-hall turn, and 'English as she is spoke' may have been this third song. It is interesting that this break in the planned programme mocks the 'Art' of theatre by drawing attention to obscure and exclusive uses of speech, at the same time as performing a kind of mock-education in and sharing of know-how about the informal speech patterns of the audience. Over the course of this night of labour in the workhouse, the diverse forms of speech on display are notable, reflecting the aural traditions of folk song, glee, ballad, and the improvised patter and dialogue of sketches and novelty songs associated with music hall. In an article in the MHAA Gazette, a writer who may well have been Coborn himself, undermines the potential value of this sharing of know-how, by disparagingly describing the way that comic songs play a role in helping the uneducated navigate the difficulties of finding a voice:

> A very curious idea emanated from a gentleman the other day who was discussing with us the Music Halls. He said that he looked upon comic singers as real benefactors because they supply by their songs conversational sparks for the

> lower classes, whom he averred have no capacity for sustained conversation, or ease of language at all, and are positively dependent on the 'gags' given from the stage, which they can and do apply in a thousand difficulties of speech otherwise insurmountable. ... Every man knows the self-satisfaction of saying something that *fits* or seems to ... but what about the those who are denied the brains to attempt so much! To them comes, like an Angel of Mercy, the gracious form of the comic singer. Their imagination is impressed; they retain his 'gags' which do so conveniently fit a multitude of occasions. ('Notes and Notions'. *MHAA Gazette*, 23 February 1887, 3, emphasis in original)

This note, regardless of its dismissive tone and content, conveys a tangible sense of the chatter of silent voices that provide the conditions for its iteration, and the conditions that lead to the production of comic songs more generally – the diverse and multi-layered aural landscapes of a common social world. While the speaker – perhaps Coborn himself, as noted – appropriates to himself, the comic singer, the capacity for speech-making here, the relationship between the song and a common discursive realm hints at the 'roar of urban theatrocracy' contained in the mute chatter of the people in revolt, discussed in the opening paragraph of this chapter. As such, it becomes possible to read this fragment of evidence dissensually, for the hidden worlds of experience concealed within its inferences, and in doing so appreciate the openness of a common discursive realm, sung and spoken, to the many voices seeking a place in its environs.

CONCLUSION

Theatre, in its doubling and multiple forms, expenditure of effort without material production, and troubling of borders between reality and fiction is, for Rancière, a mobilizer of theatrocracy and its promises of equality. As Peter Hallward, in his discussion of Rancière's theatrocracy, points out, 'Peopled by multiple voices, the theatre is likewise the privileged site of a more general displacement – a place for the out-of-place' (2006, 118). But the songs in the workhouse entertainment, including 'Two Lovely Black Eyes' and 'English as she is spoke', are not quite captured by this idea, because what is voiced here is not so much a multitudinous roar as a series of improvised attempts to find a place in the sensible fabric of the world, while also disrupting the limits of visibility and legibility that would close down the life of a thing to playing only one role in a representative order. The aural landscapes of comic songs, like the physical antics of the Street Arabs and the illusions of the Pylades, share a know-how conscious of its closeness to collapse, and at the same time celebrate a theatrics of self and social realm that is both mimetic of and a useful counter to economic precarity. These performances generate affect via their navigation of an unpredictable and injurious sensible world, creating a temporary pause, a moment of repose, wherein those who do not fit might encounter subjective and social life in all of its complexity and intelligibility. The entertainment, then, created a moment of suspension in the workhouse regime, but also, an uncanny expression of its punitive practices and reproduction of the race and and class inequalities of its broader historical context.

This suggestion of a disavowed relation of exploitation in the operations of dissensus in performance indicates that Rancière's propositions about the forms of equality afforded by the time and place of theatre should be engaged with critically and contingently – that is, with a healthy degree of scepticism and with reference to the specificities of a performance's time and place, its materiality and theatricality. The virtuosic labour of the precariously employed performer is a staple of a commercialized and alienating theatre industry. The motifs of repose and suspension in the acts were released into the atmosphere of this particular performance via the energies of play, exuberance, risk, novelty, enterprise, exhaustion, sacrifice, and themes of mesmerism, betrayal and death that, in turn, reveal the discriminating economic conditions configuring the working lives of the performers and the pauper inmates in the workhouse. The social games of theatricality being played here carry inferences, in their discriminatory potencies, of forms of social violence and social death, with the poor an ever-abundant, fertile terrain to be mined for its value. Rancière is interested in a point of tension between bodies assigned to a singular place and function, and bodies in excess of those designations. This is the point of tension that theatrical labour works in and on – and it is one that is also important to the precarious ways in which opportunities for survival in the socio-economic order are assigned and struggled for.

Rancière's years in archives of workers' writing in nineteenth-century France provided multiple encounters with the discursive realm that ordinary labourers used to describe their worlds. In theatre studies, there is no comprehensive body of writing left behind by the performers and audiences in the theatre, but even so Rancière's provocations provide a useful avenue for learning how to credit the coded speech, skilful control over appearances and gestural language of performers, and the silence of audiences, in the meaning-making effort. The methodological challenge here is as pertinent to the researcher of contemporary theatre as for the theatre historian, and it invites attention to absences in the record, and openness to imaginative speculation. If the project of this chapter was to consider how a dissensual historiographical practice for theatre studies might be conducted, then the response has drawn attention to the importance of the mute chatter of a multitude of figures that provide the conditions of existence for a performance's archive. In other words, it has drawn attention to the importance of what is not there in an account, and to consider how this has provided the conditions of existence for what is left behind.

NOTES

1. The citations are taken from two newspaper reports on the entertainment: 'Paupers and Professionals', *The Era*, 10 January 1891; 'Mr. H. Sprake's entertainment at St. John's Road Workhouse' *The Islington Gazette*, 12 January 1891.

2. *Proletarian Nights* was originally published in French in 1981, translated into English as *Nights of Labour* in 1989 and re-published as *Proletarian Nights* in 2012.

3. Casting the net nationally, many workhouses, right through to the official end of the workhouse system in the 1930s, had vibrant cultural lives, featuring a programme of popular entertainments by visiting performers, visits to local theatres and music halls, a mass of cultural work with workhouse children as part of temperance and Sunday school activity, and regular input by amateur performance groups and education and cultural associations of all kinds (see Hughes 2016).

4. Readers can view a British Pathé clip of Coborn singing 'Two Lovely Black Eyes' in 1934 here: https://www.youtube.com/watch?v=M2EOvyqZj-4 (accessed 28 December 2017).

REFERENCES

'Amusements in Nottingham'. *The Era*, 24 May 1890.

Bailey, Peter. 1978. *Leisure and Class in Victorian England: Rational Recreation and the Contest for Control, 1830–1885*. London: Routledge and Kegan & Paul.

Bailey, Peter, ed. 1986. *Music Hall: The Business of Pleasure*. Milton Keynes & Philadelphia, PA: Open University Press.

Bailey, Peter. 1994. 'Conspiracies of Meaning: Music-Hall and the Knowingness of Popular Culture'. *Past and Present* 144 (August): 138–170.

Bratton, Jacky. 2003. *New Readings in Theatre History*. Cambridge: Cambridge University Press.

Bratton, J. S., ed. 1986. *Music Hall: Performance and Style*. Milton Keynes & Philadelphia, PA: Open University Press.

Coborn, Charles. 1928. *The Man Who Broke the Bank at Monte Carlo*. London: Hutchinson.

Coborn and Dance. n.d. *English as She is Spoke*. London: Francis Bros & Day. Songbook, available in the British Library.

Colclough, Dyan. 2016. *Child Labour in the British Victorian Entertainment Industry, 1875–1914*. New York, NY: Palgrave Macmillan.

'Collins's Music Hall'. *The Islington Gazette*, 19 September 1900.

'Collins's Music Hall. The 31st Anniversary'. *The Islington Gazette*, 7 November 1893.

Davis, Tracy C. 1986. 'The Employment of Children in the Victorian Theatre'. *New Theatre Quarterly* 2, 6 (May): 117–135.

Driver, Felix. 1993. *Power and Pauperism: The Workhouse System 1834–1884*. Cambridge: Cambridge University Press.

Fitzgerald, Percy. 1890. *Music Hall Land: An Account of the Natives, Male and Female, Pastimes, Songs, Antics, and General Oddities of that Strange Country*. London: Ward and Downey.

Hallward, Peter. 2006. 'Staging Equality: On Rancière's Theatrocracy'. *New Left Review* 37 (January–February): 109–129.

Hughes, Jenny. 2016. 'A Pre-History of Applied Theatre: Work, House, Perform'. In J. Hughes and H. Nicholson, eds. *Critical Perspectives on Applied Theatre*. Cambridge: Cambridge University Press.

Kift, Dagmar. 1996. *The Victorian Music Hall: Culture, Class and Conflict*. Translated by Roy Kift. Cambridge: Cambridge University Press.

London County Council. 25 August 1890. *Inspection of Theatre and Music Halls report: Collins' Music Hall, Islington Green*. London Metropolitan Archive, LCC/MIN/10790.

'London Variety Stage'. *The Stage*, 17 January 1890.

Maloney, Paul. 2016. *The Britannia Panopticon Music Hall and Cosmopolitan Entertainment Culture*. New York, NY: Palgrave Macmillan.

'Music Halls'. *London and Provincial Entr'acte*, 31 May 1890.

'Music Hall Gossip'. *The Era*, 5 May 1894.

'Notes from the Islington Bells'. *The Islington Gazette*, 6 November 1890.

'One of White's Street Arabs'. *The Era*, 22 November 1890.

Rancière, Jacques. 1994. *The Names of History*. Translated by Hassan Melehy. Minneapolis, MN & London: University of Minnesota Press.

Rancière, Jacques. 2003 [1983]. *The Philosopher and His Poor*. Translated by John Drury, Corinne Oster, and Andrew Parker. Durham, NC & London: Duke University Press.

Rancière, Jacques. 2007. *The Future of the Image*. Translated by Gregory Elliott. London & New York, NY: Verso.

Rancière, Jacques. 2010. *Dissensus: On Politics and Aesthetics*. Edited and translated by Steven Corcoran. London & New York, NY: Continuum.

Rancière, Jacques. 2011a. *Staging the People: The Proletarian and his Double*. Translated by David Fernbach. London & New York, NY: Verso.

Rancière, Jacques. 2011b. *The Emancipated Spectator*. Translated by Gregory Elliott. London & New York, NY: Verso.

Rancière, Jacques. 2012. *Proletarian Nights: The Workers' Dream in Nineteenth-Century France*. Translated by John Drury. London & New York, NY: Verso.

Senelick, Laurence. 1975. 'Politics as Entertainment: Victorian Music-Hall Songs'. *Victorian Studies* 19, 2 (December): 149–180.

Steedman, Caroline. 1995. *Strange Dislocations: Childhood and the Idea of Human Interiority, 1780–1930*. London: Virago Press.

'The Cambridge'. *The Era*, 1 March 1890.
'The Canterbury'. *The Era*, 4 January 1890.
'The Collins's'. *The Era*, 13 December 1890.
'The Empire'. *The Era*, 26 December 1891.
'The Foresters'. *The Era*, 24 January 1891.
'The London Music Halls'. *The Era*, 28 April 1888.
'The Oxford'. *The Era*, 23 June 1888.
'The "Sam Collins" Entertainment to the Children at the Infant Poorhouse'. *The Islington Gazette*, 31 December 1864.
'Theatrical Mems'. *Bristol Mercury*, 28 August 1900.

Chapter 7

The Emancipated Educator
Chance, Will and Equality in Higher Education Role-Immersion Pedagogies

Will Shüler

This chapter seeks to interrogate that which Jacques Rancière claims the academy is unwilling to accept: that people can and do learn complex concepts outside of the hierarchical model of institutional education. To get there, I will unpack his theory of universal education outlined in *The Ignorant Schoolmaster* before examining its viability in higher education alongside Caroline Pelletier's counterclaim that there is indeed no use for Rancière's ideas in classrooms today. I then argue that the elements of chance, will and intellectual equality essential to universal education are also at the foundation of a growing higher education initiative: the implementation of complex role-immersion games. This is supported by my practical research building games from the popular U.S.-based role-immersion game series, *Reacting to the Past*, into my syllabuses. In doing so, I seek to demonstrate that performance in role while playing a game is demonstrative of universal education. I also hope to show another performance is a key ingredient to the success of this pedagogy: that of the pedagogue. When the educator's performance of teaching works to subvert or dissolve the classroom and institutional hierarchies which create distance between teachers/students, the elements of chance and will essential to universal education can be cultivated.

THERE IS A TIME

In *The Ignorant Schoolmaster*, Jacques Rancière traces the work of maverick French pedagogue Joseph Jacotot, who put forward a model of education where instructors teach what they themselves do not know. Jacotot discovered this method of *enseignement universel* (universal education) during his tenure at the University of Louvain (1818–1830). When approached by Flemish-speaking students keen to take his course, Jacotot insisted that the pupils first learn French. As Jacotot did not know Flemish, he tasked the students with learning French by comparing the languages with a side-by-side translation of François Fénelon's *Les Aventures de Télémaque*. To Jacotot's surprise, the students returned knowing French.

As Rancière describes, Jacotot had previously believed what all professors of the time believed: 'that the important business of the master is to transmit knowledge to his students so as to bring them, by degrees, to his own level of expertise' (1991, 3). Jacotot saw his students' adventure with *Télémaque* as evidence that all people are of equal intelligence and that a tutor can teach what they themselves do not know.

For Rancière, the work of Jacotot points to an insidious structure within the educational system: the explicative order. Within the explicative order, the act of explication primarily teaches the student that they could not learn without the explicator: 'To explain something to someone is first of all to show him he cannot understand it by himself. Before being the act of the pedagogue, explication is the myth of pedagogy, the parable of the world divided into knowing minds and ignorant ones, ripe minds and immature ones, the capable and the incapable, the intelligent and the stupid' (Rancière 1991, 6). Therefore, to explicate is *abrutir* – to render stupid or treat like a brute – to stultify.

The social implications of the explicative order extend outside of the academy. In 'On Ignorant Schoolmasters', Rancière traces this idea to Bourdieu, claiming that the academy only feigns an equal distribution of knowledge where the gifted may succeed, whereas the social privileges of the children of the elite are what actually allow for this kind of 'success'. In this way, the school and society mirror each other, 'and thus endlessly reproduce the supposition of inequality, precisely by denying it' (Rancière 2010, 14).

In *Jacques Rancière: Education, Truth, Emancipation*, Charles Bingham and Gert Biesta summarize three uses of explication which Rancière problematizes. First, when explication is presented as a means for emancipation, for example, the promise that by going through the explicative order, one is working towards building equality. Second, when it is accepted as a metaphor for society, for example, when the model of the knowing and unknowing persons inculcated within the academy becomes the model of how people understand systems in the world (Bingham and Biesta 2010, 154). In an interview published as 'The Actuality of *The Ignorant Schoolmaster*', Rancière expands on this point, stating, 'Whenever there are social movements in France, or a significant number of votes for the far right, we're told that the reason for this is that "the people are not able to adapt". The framework we're in is one where every social movement can be explained in terms of capacity, or incapacity, to pass one's exams and move on to the next class' (187). The final misunderstanding is when explication is taken for how people actually learn.

For Rancière, universal education works because it foregrounds chance and will; it does not stultify because students are addressed as equals. Universal education is the method employed by children to learn their first language. It involves chance: the experimenting with getting it right and adjusting after getting it wrong – trial and error. It involves will: the drive to accomplish the goal, usually predicated by the external circumstances which demand it. And it involves being treated like someone who, obviously, can learn. Rancière claims that 'this method is practiced of necessity by everyone, but no one wants to recognize it, no one wants to cope with the intellectual revolution it signifies' (1991, 16).

Based upon how *The Ignorant Schoolmaster* has been received in the discipline of education, he may be right about no one wanting to cope with universal education. For example, in *Jacques Rancière and the Contemporary Scene*, Caroline Pelletier, reader at the UCL Institute of Education, was invited by editors Jean-Philippe Deranty and Alison Ross to position Rancière's discourse on education, most specifically that outlined in *The Ignorant Schoolmaster*, in relation to the wider discourse of pedagogic theory. Titled 'No Time or Place for Universal Teaching: *The Ignorant Schoolmaster* and Contemporary Work on Pedagogy', Pelletier's survey of the field finds that pedagogues are far less interested in Rancière's educational treatise than artists. Pelletier justifies this overview, claiming that 'Rancière has nothing to say on how schools might improve their methods of teaching and learning. His work is not an addition or an alternative to disciplines laying claim to pedagogy as their object' (2012a, 99). Furthermore, as Pelletier's title signifies, there is no time or place for universal education, because she (perhaps too simply) elides his theory with the well-known educational theories of constructivism.

Constructivist teaching is based upon the premise of learning as an active process, rather than passive one. A clear articulation of constructivist teaching is Alison King's influential argument for moving from 'sage on the stage' to 'guide on the side'. King argues that 'engaging students in [...] active learning experiences helps them to think for themselves – to move away from the reproduction of knowledge toward the production of knowledge – and helps them become critical thinkers and creative problem solvers so they can deal effectively with the challenges of the twenty-first century' (1993, 35). Rather than lecturing at students in the hopes that what they hear based upon what they have read will become their knowledge, the guide on the side will support students through their 'active' learning.

Pelletier claims that 'the valorisation of constructivism is said to have, for better or worse, removed knowledge from its central position in the classroom and allowed the teacher to become a facilitator of students' self-directed efforts to generate their own understanding' (2012a, 100). Pelletier both equates constructivism with universal education and suggests thereby that Rancière has nothing to add to the 'contemporary work on pedagogy' because constructivism in the classroom is the norm. I find neither claim convincing.

It may be that the current discourse in pedagogic theory disavows the model of teaching where a tutor performs as if they have a container of knowledge and their students are empty vessels waiting to fill their cups. And yet, it appears that this performance is still the predominant one inside university classrooms. To what extent has constructivism actually won the day? Studies, such as those outlined in Derek Bok's *Our Underachieving Colleges* and Ken Bain's *What the Best College Teachers Do*, demonstrate that while some of the most favoured academic instructors in higher education foreground constructivist teaching methods such as group work and experiential learning, these tutors most often are lauded precisely because they stand out in contrast to the majority of academics who do not. So while constructivist teaching is happening in the university, it tends to be the exception rather than the rule.

Furthermore, most U.S. institutions of higher education continue to use tests of rote knowledge such as the SATs, GREs, LSATs and so on as a bellwether of academic success and gatekeeper to programmes of study. Is this constructivism in action? U.S. doctoral programmes within my field of Drama and Theatre Studies currently have oral examinations as part of the PhD process, where candidates are grilled in front of a panel of experts in the field on a broad range of discipline-specific questions.[1] Not only does such a process perform the distance between master and pupil, but it too is a far cry from constructivist teaching methods. The rationale for this assessment technique is not indicated on any of the websites of the institutions which include it. I read this kind of rote-knowledge verification as preparation for when these soon-to-be-experts are themselves teaching within the explicative order, where they will be expected to perform their mastery and exhibit the intellectual gap between themselves and their students.[2] It is precisely this kind of practice which Rancière is denouncing in *The Ignorant Schoolmaster*.

Finally, Pelletier's claim that a substantial shift towards constructivism has rendered Rancière's critique of the explicative order passé does not address the paramount aspect of *The Ignorant Schoolmaster*: that of the pedagogue engaging with the pupil as an intellectual equal and equality being the foundation of the student/teacher relationship. Influential Brazilian pedagogue Paulo Freire, whose seminal work *Pedagogy of the Oppressed* is also critical of the passive 'banking' model of teaching and like Rancière is concerned with the emancipatory potentialities of education, is differentiated from Rancière by Bingham and Biesta. They argue that Freire positions equality as that which one seeks to attain through his 'problem-posing' pedagogy, rather than equality being the essential starting point as with universal education (1970, 68). Equality, for Bingham and Biesta, is a practice (2010, 38–41). From such a perspective, I would argue that equality qua practice must thereby be performed.

Elsewhere Pelletier argues that because Rancière's pedagogy is speaking about equality while simultaneously not offering knowledge, the aim must be 'to dramatise equality at the level of discourse' by making discourse a practical interaction (2009, 146). I agree with the necessary shift in the performance of discourse; however, Pelletier stops short of addressing how that performance might actually play out. Again, in universal education the performance of reason between equals must be the basis of the classroom experience. It may be difficult for tutors to cultivate a sense of classroom equality when having to complete hierarchical tasks such as upholding university regulations on attendance monitoring, policing classroom rules (even when co-determined by students), and administering and marking assessments – perhaps the most overtly hierarchical task from the student perspective. Biesta and Bingham challenge Pelletier's review of their book because 'the very thing that Rancière's critique of explanation does *not* amount to, is an argument for learning, for a "constructivist classroom", or for the abolition of the teacher' (2012, 622, emphasis in original). What if the university lecturer engaged with students in the same way they would with a colleague embarking on a new project which neither had embarked on before? This, I would suggest, is how one performs as an emancipating educator.

One of the biggest concerns in higher education is the increasing commodification of higher education which ends up positioning the university as a business rather than an institute for advanced thought. Books like *Academically Adrift* and *What Are Universities For?*, as well as documentaries like *Ivory Tower*, very convincingly argue and evidence that in most institutions students behave like customers and universities treat them like customers. The relationship of the explainer/explained to is not demonstrative of intellectual equality, and the relationship of provider/customer does not invite intellectual equality to form the foundation of higher education learning experiences. As such, I respectfully disagree with Pelletier's estimation of universal education. There is a place for *The Ignorant Schoolmaster*. There is a time.

PLAY IS THE THING

One day, Mark C. Carnes, professor of History at Barnard College, Columbia, observed that both he and his students found classes 'sorta boring'

(2010, 19). Noticing that some engagement increased during a mock trial of Socrates employed to investigate Plato's *Republic*, Carnes decided to gradually develop the gameful design surrounding the trial into a full-length Greek democracy role-immersion game. Since then, it has expanded with the aid of two classicists to include over twenty unique roles, taking about twelve class hours to set up and play, and including an optional two-class mini pre-game. Carnes co-developed two other games and founded the Reacting Consortium. The Consortium holds two large-scale conferences annually (a Game Development Conference and a Faculty Institute now in its nineteenth year), has an active Facebook faculty lounge and hosts an electronic database which at this time houses twenty-four 'level 4' or completed games, seventeen well-tested 'level 3 games', and over eighty 'level 2' games ready for testing, created by as many academics (*Reacting.Barnard.Edu*).

Carnes did not have an easy time of developing *Reacting* into its current size, largely due to anti-play prejudices he encountered in the academy. He writes, 'From Rousseau to Dewey, and Froebel to Piaget, educational theorists have insisted that one learns best through play. Except in college' (Carnes 2015, 383). I encountered this very objection at an institution where I wanted to implement a *Reacting* game in my class. Twice I asked if I could use the games and was told 'no'. 'Where will the learning happen?' and 'Won't they just be having a bit of fun?' were among the objections. The third time I implemented the game without asking and its success in the classroom observed by my colleagues and attested to by my students led to me being awarded a college-wide innovative teaching commendation. My colleagues were won over after seeing the game in action. Even though play has been demonstrated to serve an educative function, both Carnes and I came across the same anti-play resistance.

Play has variously been related to how one functions and positions oneself within society. In *The Republic*, Plato's character Socrates endorses play as essential to both the world of philosophical inquiry and how one lives one's life generally. Economist Joseph Schumpeter writes in *The Theory of Economic Development* (1932) that play is essential to survival; only through play can an organization create the new combinations it needs to survive. Dutch cultural historian Johan Huizinga argues in *Homo Ludens* (1938) that the human capacity to play is a need and a skill. Play is not real life, it is an 'as-if' life; play creates different orders, excitement, energy and joy. This latter component is paramount. German American psychologist Erik H Erikson suggests that when one plays one 'must feel entertained and free of any fear or hope of serious consequences. [One] is on vacation from social and economic reality' (1950, 191–2). In play worlds, less is at stake and thereby people will make risky choices. This is supported by game theory, a mathematical model of rational decision-making which in part examines the human behaviour to generally make safe choices. And yet, there still seems to be anti-play prejudice in the academy. So, 'Why', Carnes asks 'if play promotes learning, do most professors and administrators know, deep in the marrow of their bones, that playing games in college is wrong?' (2015, 382).

David Cohen in *The Development of Play* suggests that psychologists and theorists tend to not reconcile adult play with pedagogy because, while there is a notion that children's play is to prepare them for adult life, there is also a notion that once one arrives at adulthood there no longer remains a need for this kind of training (1993, 36). Cohen endorses adult play and positions it as 'a step in coping better with the stresses of industrial, post-industrial, post-Freudian life' (ibid). Indeed, the elements of educative play outlined earlier, thought-experimentation, innovative thinking, motivation through joy and risk-taking, are germane to the very echelons of advanced thought which universities lay claim to.

While in favour of the educative value of some adult play, Cohen thinks that players of role-play games and computer games tend to become unhealthily obsessed with gaming (1993, 177 and 186). But this 'obsession' cultivated by performing a role within a gamefully designed scenario indicates precisely how role-immersion learning happens: by activating student drive. Motivation to experiment is also attested by role-play pedagogues in the edited collection *Simulations, Games and Role Play in University Education*. Sandra Wills explains in her chapter 'The Simulation Triad' that 'much of the learning occurs because the learning design requires learners to explore and articulate viewpoints that may not be their own' (2012, 24). By immersing oneself in the role of one's character, students are free to craft and deliver persuasive text as well as design and implement complex gambits intended to achieve desired ends beyond the boundaries of their own impulses.

Carnes posits an alternative theory. The reason why play gets a bad reputation in the academy is because of what he terms 'bad play' in his book *Minds on Fire: Role-Immersion Games Transform College* (2014). Bad play is the distracting play, from social societies to World of Warcraft, and beer pong to humans versus zombies, which has – in some form or other – always been a lodestone for student attention. While Carnes is not against games or non-academic fun, he terms them 'bad play' because of how often undergraduates prioritize these activities over their coursework and because teachers can begrudge these 'bad play' activities when this becomes apparent. I myself am sometimes flummoxed when I see an undergraduate who has not prepared for class (or not even bothered to show up) in that evening's performance of *Oklahoma!*. Whether or not this 'bad play' actually cultivates anti-play prejudice among teaching staff, it is certainly clear that students rarely approach coursework with as much gusto as 'bad play' activities.

So for the professor who already has to battle against the distraction of bad play in order for their pupil to do the serious business of education, co-opting play for a syllabus may be a tough sell. But this is exactly Carnes's invitation: to subvert bad play by bringing playful elements into the classroom. Because 'subversive play worlds do not destroy hierarchy, authority, or order; they depend on it' (Carnes 2014, 64). Historically – from Greek festival, to medieval carnival, to contemporary carnival – 'subversive play did not prefigure social or cultural upheaval' (46). Instead, the temporary relief from social norms allowed for a re-evaluation of orders in productive, liberating ways. This space for re-evaluation lends itself to the exact kind of work the academy requires: critical thinking, creative solutions, collaboration, and cogent and persuasive argumentation.

Role-immersion games entail both the performance in role and the playing of a game. Like all live action role-play games, Carnes's *Reacting* works by immersing players into the world of a character within a fictional scenario. In the case of *Reacting*, students are placed into historical threshold moments or periods of great transition. Each player is given a character dossier with victory objectives to achieve by the end of the game, which usually lasts from six-to-nine class hours (excluding set-up). There is scope for these objectives to be changed by the players, so long as there is justification within the parameters of the game. Players win the game by accomplishing their victory objectives. In 'game mode' students run the classroom and the instructor is not allowed to talk or order the events.

For example, in the game played in my course on Greek tragedy, *Threshold of Democracy: Athens in 403 BCE*, students take on the role of a member of the Athenian assembly picking up the pieces after the ousting of the thirty tyrants imposed by the Spartans after the loss of the Peloponnesian War. One student is cast as the general Thrasybulus, part of the radical democratic faction; another is a shoemaker, Simon, who is one of the followers of Socrates; another is a woman disguised as her dead husband – seeking to make good on the Platonic notion that women are as capable at governance as men. Throughout the game, students prepare speeches to perform in role and deliver them in an attempt to sway the votes of the assembly in their favour. In my version of the game, we read different tragedies alongside relevant assembly topics with the aim of reconciling how a social drama/aesthetic drama continuum may have been at work in ancient Athens. After each assembly session, we discussed the play read and tried sections of it out on its feet. As such, there was a continued relationship between the play world and the world of the play, and vice versa.

I have also built the *Reacting* game *Confucianism and the Succession Crisis of the Wanli Emperor* into my Theatre and Culture 1 course, as a means of examining performance and culture in Ming dynasty China. Over four classes, students perform as members of the Grand Secretariat, advising another student, performing as Wanli himself, on the controversial issue of succession. Having read Ray Huang's *1587: A Year of No Significance*, which positions the succession crisis as the decline of the Ming dynasty, and the *Analects* of Confucius, students practically examined decorum as a form of governance and social control. This is then used as a lens for practically exploring Ming era performance traditions and the fourteenth-century Ssu Fan lyric monologue, *Longing for Worldly Pleasures*. This story of a nun seeking a lover has lyrics which are 'effective for their contrasting of stagnant dogma and enforced ritual with the fact of life as we must live it' (Scott 1969, 16). As such, we juxtapose the social and aesthetic dramas of the grand secretariat and the lyric monologue.

It is one thing to read in an undergraduate course that in 1587, the Wanli Emperor could execute even the most high-ranking state officials. It is another to sit next to an empty chair, because in the previous class, your colleague was executed by His Majesty the Son of Heaven for speaking to him disrespectfully. This is how *Reacting to the Past* students perform and experience history, resulting in deep learning predicated by the multiplicity of learning modalities (aural, visual, bodily/kinaesthetic) which has been shown to be most effective in combination (Moreno and Mayer 2007, 309–26). Furthermore, because gameful design employs a series of 'micro-tests', there are continuous variations which José Antonio Bowen and C. Edward Watson argue contributes to learning (2017, 29).

One teacher commented as they were about to embark on a *Reacting* game for the first time that he was 'worried that a student-run class would turn into "a cringe-worthy night-mare" where "students who knew nothing instructed students who didn't know the difference"' (Carnes 2014, 66). This is precisely the premise of *The Ignorant Schoolmaster*: one has the capacity to learn alongside those who also do not know. Carnes states that many instructors, liberated by the subversive play world of the role-immersion game, teach games outside of their specialization and even discipline (279–80). Like Jacotot, they teach what they themselves do not know, on an intellectual adventure, as an ignorant schoolmaster. And when Carnes claims that *Reacting to the Past* is effective precisely because the subversive nature of classroom play challenges the 'rational, hierarchical, individualistic and well-ordered' model of higher education (13), I hear echoes of Rancière's dismantling of the explicative order in favour of universal education.

In my experience, role-immersion games in the academy are performances of universal education. Playing the game and acting in role invites elements of contingency and chance. The game's framework cultivates will. The erasure of a hierarchy anticipates intellectual emancipation.

CHANCE AND THE ROLE OF THE DICE

For Rancière chance is an essential factor in the success of universal education. Recounting the Flemish-speaking pupils of Jacotot, Rancière writes, 'They moved along in a manner one shouldn't move – the way children move, blindly figuring out riddles' (1991, 10). The students had no set of steps to follow. By necessity, they navigated the adventures of *Télémaque* in their own way. As Bain, Bok, and Arum and Roksa suggest in their works, this is not common practice for university education today. Instead, tutors tend to employ the method of selection and progression: a well-structured syllabus, a primrose path to the desired learning outcomes. For Rancière, this is because 'the advocates of method oppose the nonmethod of chance to that of proceeding by reason' (11). Under this assumption, self-discovery, chance, finding one's way without a map, is not the domain of reason. But when the structure is removed, students must by necessity proceed by employing their reason, developing their own route through the 'forest of ideas'. Rancière invites educators to take a risk as well by allowing the structure of chance a place in pedagogic models. Chance 'is what opens the way to all adventures in the land of knowledge. It is a matter of daring to be adventurous, and not whether one learns more or less quickly' (27).

This breaking of the well-ordered model of education is also championed by Carnes. He states that 'reacting games do not teach history; they constitute an offense against the values of the historical profession' (2014, 249). The act of the historian is called into question because as the students and their characters wade through the tides of the game, they discover the historiographic lesson that events are always more complex and less certain than 'history' can allow for. Students often discover contingency: that events in these threshold moments could very well have gone a differently. And that is what the game invites students to play at. How could this have happened? Why?

Carnes claims that 'role-immersion games teach students that they can alter the 'course' of humane events. This truth – so hard to learn from history books and lectures – provides an antidote to the apathy that so often deadens our classroom – and poisons our democracy' (2014, 259). This speaks back to one of Rancière's early works: *Disagreement*, where he introduces a definition of politics based upon change and enactment. In this work Rancière claims that 'politics exists because those who have no right to be counted as speaking beings make themselves of some account, setting up a community by the fact of placing in common a wrong that is nothing more than this very confrontation, the contradiction of two worlds in a single world' (1995, 27). In this way, politics is always an active verification of equality and the systems that prevent this are termed the 'police'. The allocation of ways of doing, the order of the visible and the sayable, and the differentiation of discourse and noise that is policed by the police are termed by Rancière the *partage du sensible*:³ the distribution of the perceptible. For him, politics only exists where there is redistribution – where the people who previously were either not counted or miscounted, are now acknowledged. In this way, that which does not redistribute, polices.

Chance and contingency are structural in *Reacting*. For example, passing a particular bit of legislature in the Assembly might lead you closer to completing a victory objective on your role sheet and you need a majority vote. Perhaps members of your faction do not show up to Assembly today. Perhaps they arrive late and thereby do not receive as many votes. Maybe when it comes to the vote, a citizen of Athens at the last minute decides not to honour their promise to you. The direction of the game can change quickly and you must adapt to achieve your victory objectives. In Ming China, perhaps the frustration felt by the First Grand Secretary leads to the persuading of the Emperor to have you whipped at the Meridian Gate. Perhaps your military expedition to restore the Athenian empire meets disaster due to the roll of the dice; perhaps it means great success. Carnes suggests that historians

> often reduce individuals to mere flotsam and jetsam upon heaving seas of casual absolutes. Particular individuals may swim against the currents or be borne up by them, but their own exertions matter little. Students often regard the future fatalistically. If history is driven by titanic forces, why bother to vote, work on political campaign, or help out in a soup kitchen? But this fatalism is wrong. (2014, 258)

And this fatalism is challenged when one performs a historical role within a play world.

'History could have gone many different ways' and 'outcomes can never be guaranteed' are resounding comments on student feedback from my *Reacting* classes. 'It gave us the freedom to discuss and debate,' one student wrote. Because the students have to find their way through a particular time period in the role of someone else, they are able to make discoveries they would not have otherwise. One student reflected that had they been cast in a role 'more similar to myself, I would not have learned what I learned from the experience'.

When discussing the *Poetics* of Aristotle on a day in Greek tragedy class dedicated to investigating dramatic structure, one student was struck by his distinction between history and poetry: 'One tells us what happened and the other the sort of thing that would happen' (1451b). 'That's what happens when we play the game,' they commented. In the role-immersion game we only learn what 'was' after we learn what might have been and what may be. As students research the ideas, develop and hone the articulation of an argument, and create a character, they recognize that they can similarly approach the politics of our time and develop their own character in this world. Having performed in role during liminal historical moments, students rehearse a redistribution of the perceptible.

GAMEFUL DESIGN: WHERE THERE'S A WILL

Evidence has shown that 'reacting students become fully engaged because the elements of bad play – the pressure of social obligation, the joyous liberation of taking on a new identity, the thrill of subverting customary hierarchies and conventions – are so powerful' (Carnes 2015, 393). This is supported by an independent study on *Reacting* published in the *Journal of Educational Psychology*, which found that the pedagogy increases motivation and engagement with course materials (Stroessner, Beckman and Whittaker 2009, 617). It is precisely the elements of play – a difficult challenge, an essential vote, that contribute to the fun and drive students feel in *Reacting*. Recall Rancière's claim that drive is predicated by the demands of external circumstances. Not only does the frame of the game create an environment that necessitates hard work, but it is also reinforced by the social situations. One may be inclined to neither look unprepared while delivering a speech to one's peers nor let the other students in one's faction down by avoiding effort. In this way, the game engages student by the very method which would otherwise distract them from their coursework: play.

Rancière too is concerned with what distracts the pupil in *The Ignorant Schoolmaster*. He argues that 'the mind's original sin is not haste, but distraction' (1991, 55). Furthermore, 'the distracted person *doesn't see why* he should pay attention. Distraction is laziness first, the desire to retire from effort. But laziness itself isn't the torpor of the flesh; it is the act of the mind underestimating its own power' (79, emphasis in original). Rancière writes that 'meaning is the work of the will. This is the secret of universal teaching. It is also the secret of those we call geniuses: the relentless work to bend the body to necessary habits, to compel the intelligence to new ideas, to new ways of expressing them' (56). If the innovative articulation of new ideas is the work of the will, then it is a task of the educator to curate a situation which encourages student drive.

One idea Rancière suggests for curating the will to learn is the demand of the circumstance (51). As such, the challenge becomes cultivating an environment where students are motivated to put in the effort. One student, expostulating in Carnes's book on being Thrasybulus in 403 BCE Athens, said, 'The game was fake; we all knew that. But the goal – influencing your peers, making your voice heard, saying something worth hearing – that was very real' (78). As students are immersed in the game, they become motivated to win the game by accomplishing their victory objectives. Winning is predicated upon doing the necessary prep work, engaging with ideas critically and creatively, and persuading/debating/collaborating with your peers.

In an effort to implement pedagogical transparency, when embarking on the Confucianism game with my students, I had them read Carnes's introduction to *Minds on Fire* to see what *Reacting* was all about and why we were using role-immersion as a pedagogic model. The introduction contains an anecdote of one *Reacting* professor's students voting to hold class at 7:00 a.m. (an hour early) in order to get more game time in. 'I doubt that will happen,' said a student of mine while discussing the chapter.

Well they were right; it did not. Students did, I was told, have midnight Facebook chats debating who could be persuaded to side with the Emperor and whom the First Grand Secretary would try to limit the speaking time of. They held covert meetings underneath stairwells and behind buildings at the start, break and conclusion of class. I even observed one student bow to Katie (who played the Emperor) in the halls, and then realize that they were not in game mode. After the second class, students were sitting up straight without crossed legs, for fear of being reprimanded by the First Grand Secretary. I saw index cards with quotes of Confucius ready to be employed in the rebuttal of anticipated arguments and well-thumbed books to achieve the same ends. I was informed that the library had no remaining copies of the *Analects* by a student who then pleaded to borrow mine so they could trounce their competitors. After the game finished, that same student said to me, 'See, I told you we wouldn't come in at 7:00.' And I was alright with that. While they did not vote to hold class early, it was clear that the game had increased student drive to a level I had not seen before, both as educator and pupil.

In student surveys, when asked, 'What is the number one difference between Reacting classes and other seminars?', nearly all students mentioned the increased engagement: 'It is more engaging and you want to know more and participate more.' Not only do the students seem driven by the game, but they seem driven by the drive of other students: 'Everyone is a lot more engaged with the material as the game took over, and people wanted to do well.' They seemed very pleased that everyone was active and involved. This social aspect of the game also affects the will: be it competitive spirit, social pressure or a combination of them both. And while the gameful design of live action role-immersion games may curate an environment for activating student drive, for Rancière, motivation comes from the scenario of being treated as an intellectual equal: 'a relation of will to will and intelligence to intelligence' (2010, 2).

PERFORMING EQUALITY OR THE EMANCIPATING EDUCATOR

I am; therefore, I think. This is Rancière's invitation to invert Descartes's *cogito ergo sum* (Rancière 1991, 36). We do not need proof of the human's capacity of mind because thought is inherent to being. Again, Rancière's ideas in *The Ignorant Schoolmaster* sit among his wider radical egalitarian project. As such, the notion of equality is paramount to the function of universal education, which means beginning with the foundation that all beings are thinking beings and of the same capacity for learning. Furthermore, for the emancipating educator 'our problem isn't proving that all intelligence is equal. It's seeing what can be done under this assumption' (46). Even if one is not convinced that all people are of the same capacity to learn, one can see that there is potential in addressing people under this premise.

Rancière narrates what happened under presumption of equal capacity with the readers of *Télémaque*: 'Someone has addressed words to them that they want to recognize and respond to, not as students or as learned men, but as people; in the way you respond to someone speaking to you and not to someone examining you: under the sign of equality' (1991, 11). From the onset they were engaged outside of the hierarchy implicit within the explicative order. As such, they returned as people, not pupils.[4]

Carnes addresses the hierarchy within university classrooms in *Minds on Fire*. He writes that in a *Reacting* game 'students usually transform the class into their own subversive play world, and when they do, the walls of authority seem to dissolve' (Carnes 2014, 65). Once in game mode, students are in control of the classroom and the instructor is relegated to the periphery, not allowed to speak – only pass notes. In my performance of universal teaching, these notes tend to say things like 'Do you agree with that?' or 'Let the Assembly know your thoughts on this'. At the onset of the game students give the notes much heed, but as we progress they take them as suggestions addressed to an equal and quite happily might choose to do something different instead.

The dissolution of the hierarchies in relation to college role-immersion games are examined by Cermak-Sassenrath and Walker in their contribution to *Simulations, Games, and Role Play in Higher Education*. They suggest that flat hierarchies 'invite students to manage and evaluate their own learning. They are encouraged to take up critical or experimental positions and articulate their own approach to practice. This, in turn, often leads them to understand that their work does not end with the completion of assignments, but rather opens new research questions' (2012, 143). For them, learning in role challenges the artificial/extrinsic curriculum requirements (148). In this way, learning by performing in role works to dismantle Rancière's explicative order and address what he claims is a mode of learning 'no one wants to cope with' (Rancière 1991, 16).

Rancière says that equality is the only way in which universal education can work. 'One can teach what one doesn't know if the student is emancipated, that is to say, if he is obliged to use his own intelligence' (1991, 15). In order for me to embark on an intellectual adventure with my students into the forest of ideas where we will discover what might have been, I need to work towards eliminating, subverting or making visible the hierarchies at work. For students, the most glaring issue of hierarchy at work in the university classroom is the mark. While I am obliged to give the students a mark on the course, in my version all of the work done on and around the game is strictly formative. This differs from how most teachers employ the game, where the prepared speeches function as small, summative assessments. The instructor's manual also recommends using bonus points as a carrot for success in the game and I do not.

My students take ownership of the class. As I am relegated to the sidelines, the scenario demands it. In the first day of the Athens game, it is common for the primary assembly president to glance over to me, sitting in the far corner of the room, and ask if they can begin. I shrug and look at my notebook. They take a moment. They begin. This too contributes to the subversive aspects of the pedagogy. A game is being played inside the classroom and it is being directed by the students. When students learn among themselves, as in *Reacting*, there is a no hierarchical structure or explicative order; there is reasoning between equals.

Doubtful of a dissolution of hierarchies, Pelletier endorses Nina Power's argument: that Rancière/Jacotot's model does not remove hierarchy, but rather that by assigning a side-by-side translation as a means of learning French, the power of the 'master' simply shifts from the teacher to the book/author (Pelletier 2012a, 103). But Rancière addresses this very concern: 'The intelligence of the book [becomes] the thing in common, the egalitarian intellectual link between master and student' (Rancière 1991, 13). In *Reacting*, the game becomes this link. As mentioned in the section on chance, even though the games have designers, 'the experience of playing the game gives potential to deconstruct the author's interpretation of the texts and interrogate the alternatives' (Carnes 2014, 255).

Furthermore, Carnes's notion of role-immersion games in universities fit within a trajectory of pedagogic inquiry that suggests the work of constructivism is not yet complete, as Pelletier alludes. Alison King's seminal notion of moving from 'sage on the stage' to 'guide on the side' is taken further by Anthony Weston who advocates for an 'impresario with a scenario'. Weston advances dramaturgically and dialectally structured role-immersion games because of their interactive, contextual and skills-based experiences, with the tutor serving a directorial function in the producing of the enterprise (2015, 99–100). Independent researchers Stroessner, Beckman and Whittaker conducted several examinations of students who participated in *Reacting* classes against control students in the same course who did not play the games, and published their findings in the *Journal of Educational Psychology* (2009). Their research suggests that in comparison to the control classroom *Reacting* increased motivation and engagement. According to tests administered to *Reacting* and control students before and after the course, this had the effect of producing several benefits typically associated with academic success, including elevated self-esteem, empathy, more external locus of control, enhanced rhetorical skills and a greater endorsement of the belief that human characteristics are malleable (617). This supports Carnes's claim that 'we experience deep learning by acquiring additional selves; these internal conversations generate deep critical thinking' (2014, 12). That students have increasingly demonstrated an understanding of their own characteristics as malleable falls in line precisely with the main tenets of *The Ignorant Schoolmaster*: learning that one is indeed capable. As Rancière summarizes, 'The problem is not to create scholars. It is to raise up those who believe themselves inferior in intelligence' (1991, 101).

Awareness of a malleable self has been proven to lead to deep learning.

> Malleable selves regard failure as evidence of poor effort or mistaken strategy rather than innate incapacity. [...] This outlook encourages [students] to explore new fields and helps them summon up the effort to do better. Even if they fail, malleable selves may appreciate that they have improved and learned. (Carnes 2014, 164)

In Carnes's words, the student will never 'speak truth to power [...] unless they believe that they can prevail' (2014, 50). Having the embodied knowledge from the game that they effected change in both the fictional, historic threshold moment and order and hierarchies of the classroom, undergraduates may find an awareness of and confidence in their capacity outside of the classroom to redistribute the perceptible.

WHOEVER TEACHES WITHOUT EMANCIPATING STULTIFIES

> The Master asked, 'If one cannot run a country by making use of the deferential attitudes induced by ritual, what point is there in ritual?' (Confucius 4.13).

Like the quotes of Confucius that the students in the Ming China game used to persuade the Wanli Emperor, they too enacted. Because they performed deference to an emperor – lowered voices, uncrossed legs, a kowtow, subtle suggestions – they experienced with their bodies a bit of the social control that the Ming dynasty used to maintain order in a land so vast, one person could hardly visit all of it in their lifetime. At the end of one of the sessions, a Confucian purist came up to me, after being particularly remonstrated by the First Grand Secretary for advising the Emperor too strongly. 'How can you make change in a society where you don't have a voice?' they asked. I don't think I could have taught that lesson, not in the deep way they clearly understood it, without the game – without that student having had to perform and play. Feeling the rigid social control used to maintain order in their bodies, the student could better appreciate the notion of decorum qua governance, a performance tradition as precise as moving a certain finger when saying a particular word, and why the protagonist nun is longing for worldly pleasures. The bodily constraints of the game provided the external circumstances for activating the will and discovering additional selves.

As Rancière espouses the integral elements of chance, will and equality in universal education, *Reacting* is structured around the features of contingency, student drive and the subversion of classroom hierarchies. As universal education is criticized for its incapability of reconciling itself with the current regime of higher education, Carnes is fighting back against 2,000 years of educational role-play prejudice, including those who claim Dewey's emphasis on play (and by extension Froebel and Huizinga) did not work. However, elements of universal education are seen in the success of *Reacting to the Past*, and the theories behind both sit within a trajectory of progressive higher education pedagogy.

Universal education has been seen at work elsewhere in contemporary forays into pedagogic advancement. Richard Stamp's article 'Of Slumdogs and Schoolmasters' compares Rancière's ideas in *The Ignorant Schoolmaster* to Sugata Mitra's hole-in-the-wall experiment, where computers were provided through walls on the streets of urban India and kids were able to learn how to use them on their own. For Mitra, more than learning a skill, this cultivates a concept of social change within the pupil (Stamp 2013, 649). They learn that the world of computers can be their world; Rancière's pupil's recognition of their own capacity, 'me too, I am a painter' (Rancière 1991, 65), becomes me too, I am tech-literate. Lorraine Otoide and Steve Alsop in *Canadian Journal of Science, Mathematics, and Technology Education* outline how they tailored an elementary science class curriculum around the ideas of universal education. They too pinpointed the performance of their teaching role as the most essential component of demonstrating equality: 'We had to let go and redistribute how as teachers-researchers we speak and perform science education' (Otoide and Alsop 2015, 246). A shift in the dramaturgy of the classroom and performance of the pedagogue was necessary. Like Stamp, Otoide and Alsop, I position my use of *Reacting* within the discourse of universal education in practice.

And it is not an easy feat. I hope not to have given the impression that all of my classes are gameplay, subversion and 'what-ifs'. I am a product of the explicative order as well. Bingham and Biesta write that 'the scholar is an adult who has gone to school. Because of this attendance, this adult knows how to school others with his or her own thought. This adult knows how to explain' (Bingham and Biesta 2010, 148). The explicative order pressures the tutor into performing within its monolithic structure. It persuades the teacher to find security in the intellectual distance the order creates between tutor and pupil. As the explicative order instils the idea that someone will always be more of a master, experts too can at times feel imposter syndrome.

Why is it important to pursue or remain vigilant about pedagogic models based upon an initial premise of intellectual equality? Above, Confucius notes the power of performing rituals to inculcate. So too does the performance of the classroom teacher who does not build their curriculum upon the premise of equal intellectual capacity inculcate the explicative order. When a student says 'I can't', they mean 'I have been taught that I can't and I believe it'. And this has implications outside of the academy. Rancière suggests that 'the pedagogic inequality learned by the student continues in perpetuating/disguising forms of social inequality' (Rancière 2010, 5). He summarizes the social impact of the explicative order thus:

> Scholarly progression is the art of limiting the transmission of knowledge, of organizing delay, of deferring equality. The pedagogical paradigm of the master explicator, adapted to the level and needs of students, provides a model of the scholarly institution's social function, which itself translates to a general model of society ordered by progress. (8)

Rancière describes a shift away from the explicative order where a distance in intellectual capacity is taught to students, where the groundwork is laid for the myth that the academy distributes knowledge equally rather than favouring those with social privilege, and thereby perpetuating the notion that those who succeed in the academy are those of greater intellectual capacity. To achieve this shift, a shift in the dramaturgy of the classroom and the performance of the pedagogue is necessary. Otherwise, the educator is complicit in policing the distribution of the perceptible. 'Whoever teaches without emancipating stultifies' (Rancière 1991, 16).

In a complex higher education role-immersion game, the educator is not bringing a pupil by degrees to their level of expertise, because no one is a specialist in what may be. The game element gives the tutor space to erase, subvert or make visible classroom hierarchies. Players are excited by elements of chance, driven by the circumstances provided by the gameful design, and progress with the educator into the forest of ideas as equals. And discourse thus.

NOTES

1. Surveying the top ten U.S. Drama and Theatre programmes which offer PhDs according to the QS World University Rankings, nine of ten require oral examinations of this kind as progression requirements. One university website describes it as a ninety-minute 'oral qualifying examination covering general knowledge in the field'.
2. Bowen and Watson suggest that it is far from common practice for university teachers to say to students: let me do more research before I respond to your question (2017, 32).
3. In Rancière's *Disagreement*, Julie Rose translates *partage du sensible* as 'partition of the perceptible', whereas it is more popularly translated elsewhere as 'distribution of the sensible' (Gabriel Rockhill, *Politics of Aesthetics*; Steven Corcoran, *Aesthetics and Its Disconnects* and *Dissensus*). I would suggest that a combination of the two translations best captures its meaning in English, hence my use of 'distribution of the perceptible'.
4. In fact, Bingham and Biesta suggest a semantic shift from 'student' to 'speaker' (144).

REFERENCES

Aristotle. 1998. *Poetics*. Translated by M. E. Hubbard. In *Classical Literary Criticism*, edited by D. A. Russell and M. Winterbottom, 51–90. Oxford: Oxford University Press.
Arum, Richard, and Josipa Roksa. 2010. *Academically Adrift: Limited Learning on College Campuses*. Chicago, IL: University of Chicago Press.
Bain, Ken. 2004. *What the Best College Teachers Do*. Cambridge, MA: Harvard University Press.
Biesta, Gert, and Charles Bingham. 2012. 'Response to Caroline Pelletier's Review of Jacques Rancière: Education, Truth, Emancipation'. *Studies in Philosophical Education* 31, no. 6: 621–623.
Bingham, Charles, and Gert Biesta. 2010. *Jacques Rancière: Education, Truth, Emancipation*. London: Continuum.
Bok, Derek. 2006. *Our Underachieving Colleges: A Candid Look at How Much Students Learn and Why They Should Be Learning More*. Princeton, NJ: Princeton University Press.
Bowen, José Antonio, and C. Edward Watson. 2017. 'Teaching Naked Techniques: Leveraging Research on Learning to Improve the Effectiveness of Teaching'. *Change: The Magazine of Higher Learning* 49, no. 5: 26–35.

Carnes, Mark C. 2015. 'From Plato to Erikson: How the War on 'Bad Play' has Impoverished Higher Education'. *Arts & Humanities in Higher Education* 14, no. 4: 383–397.

Carnes, Mark C. 2014. *Minds on Fire: How Role-Immersion Games Transform College*. Cambridge, MA: Harvard University Press.

Cermak-Sassenrath, Daniel, and Charles Walker. 2012. 'S(t)imulating Interdisciplinarity'. In *Simulations, Games and Role Play in University Education. The Learning in Higher Education (LIHE) Series*, edited by C. Nygaard, N. Courtney, and E. Leigh, 139–149. Faringdon: Libri Publishing.

Cohen, David. 1993. *The Development of Play*. London: Routledge.

Collini, Stefan. 2012. *What Are Universities For?* London: Penguin.

Confucius. 1993. *Analects*. Translated by Raymond Dawson. Oxford: Oxford University Press.

Erikson, Erik H. 1950. *Childhood and Society*, 1995. London: Vintage.

Freire, Paulo. 1970. *Pedagogy of the Oppressed*. Translated by Myra Bergman Ramos, 2017. London: Penguin.

Huizinga, Johan. 1980. *Homo Ludens: Study of the Play Element in Culture*. New York, NY: Routledge.

King, Alison. 1993. 'From Sage on the Stage to Guide on the Side'. *College Teaching* 41, no. 1: 30–35.

Moreno, Roxana, and Richard Mayer. 2007. 'Interactive Multimodal Learning Environments'. *Educational Psychology Review* 19, no. 3: 309–326.

Nygaard, Claus, Nigel Courtney, and Elizabeth Leigh, editors. 2012. *Simulations, Games, and Role Play in University Education*. Oxford: Libri.

Oioide, Lorraine, and Steve Alsop. 2015. 'Moments with Jacques Rancière: Sketches from a Lived Pedagogical Experiment in an Elementary Science Classroom'. *Canadian Journal of Science, Mathematics, and Technology Education* 15, no. 3: 234–247.

Pelletier, Caroline. 2009. 'Emancipation, Equality, and Education: Rancière's Critique of Bourdieu and the Question of Performativity'. *Discourse: Studies in the Cultural Politics of Education* 30, no. 2: 137–150.

Pelletier, Caroline. 2012a. 'No Time or Place for Universal Teaching: The Ignorant Schoolmaster and Contemporary Work on Pedagogy'. In *Jacques Rancière and the Contemporary Scene*, edited by Jean-Phillipe Deranty and Alison Ross, 99–115. London: Continuum.

Pelletier, Caroline. 2012b. 'Review of Charles Bingham and Gert Biesta, Jacques Rancière: Education, Truth, Emancipation'. *Studies in Philosophical Education* 31, no. 6: 613–619.

Power, Nina. 2009. 'Axiomatic Equality: Rancière and the Politics of Contemporary Education'. *Polygraph*, 21.

Rancière, Jacques. 1995. *Disagreement: Politics and Philosophy*. Translated by Julie Rose. Minneapolis, MN: University of Minnesota.

Rancière, Jacques. 1991. *The Ignorant Schoolmaster*. Translated by Kristin Ross. Stanford, CA: Stanford University Press.

Rancière, Jacques. 2010. 'On Ignorant Schoolmasters'. In *Jacques Rancière: Education, Truth, Emancipation*, edited by C. Bingham and Gert J. J. Biesta, 1–24. London: Continuum.

Rancière, Jacques, with Andrea Benvenuto, Laurence Cornu, and Patrice Vermeren. 2005. 'The Actuality of the The Ignorant Schoolmaster'. In *Dissenting Words: Interviews with Jacques Rancière*, edited by Emiliano Battista, 173–190, 2017. London: Bloomsbury.

Reacting.Barnard.Edu. Barnard College, Columbia University.

Rossi, Andrew. 2014. *Ivory Tower*. CNN Films.

Schumpeter, Joseph. 2017. *Theory of Economic Development*. New York, NY: Routledge.

Scott, A. C. 1969. *Traditional Chinese Plays*, Vol. 2. Madison, WI: University of Wisconsin Press.

Stamp, Richard. 2013. 'Of Slumdogs and Schoolmasters: Jacotot, Rancière, and Mitra on Self-Organised Learning'. *Educational Philosophy and Theory* 45, no. 6: 647–662.

Stroessner, Steven J., Laurie Susser Beckman, and Alexis Whittaker. 2009. 'All the World's a Stage? Consequences of a Role-Playing Pedagogy on Psychological Factors and Writing and Rhetorical Skills in College Undergraduates'. *Journal of Educational Psychology* 101, no. 3: 605–620.

Weston, Anthony. 2015. 'From Guide on the Side to Impresario with a Scenario'. *College Teaching* 63, no. 3: 99–104.

Wills, Sandra. 2012. 'The Simulation Triad'. In *Simulations, Games and Role Play in University Education*, edited by C. Nygaard, N. Courtney, and E. Leigh, 23–40. Faringdon, UK: Libri.

Part IV

PERFORMANCE AS POLITICAL DISRUPTION

Chapter 8

Resisting Rancière

Janelle Reinelt

No recent political thinker has influenced performance scholarship as much as Rancière. Many of the key concepts in his work (dissensus, the redistribution of the sensible, equality and the emancipated spectator) are extraordinarily suggestive for performance scholars who seek a post-identitarian, post-dramatic or post-political performance practice. However, I do not think the consequences of embracing his ideas will lead to an effective political engagement through performance, and prefer a differently configured understanding of the relationship between politics and performance. This chapter, while not wholly hostile to Rancière's ideas, attempts to offer a critique of any wholehearted embrace of his theoretical categories for use in our field. In a book dedicated to acknowledging and celebrating the influence of Jacques Rancière on theatre and performance studies, I intend this chapter to act as a kind of counterpoint.

In what follows, I begin with some broad comments on the relationship between politics and theatre and performance studies in order to identify reasons why Rancière's thought has been attractive to scholars in our field. Turning next to three critical issues in political theory, I analyse the meaning of dissensus (and consensus) in the context of political activism, the problem of identity and the 'part of those who have no part' in the context of citizenship, and Rancière's critique of democracy in the context of the contemporary neoliberal conjuncture. Along the way, I will rely on performance scholars to examine how Rancière's ideas have been deployed in our field of theatre and performance.

I

The reasons Rancière has appealed to scholars in our discipline are several, but perhaps the most important have to do with the claim for theatre and performance to a history and tradition of important political activity. Usually beginning with the Greek theatre and its undoubted role in public life, and then focusing on the European Enlightenment – the rise of eighteenth-century bourgeois culture and its public sphere – it has been possible to show how Western theatre 'mattered' politically in specific historical situations. Similarly, the 1960s and 1970s saw activist theatres engaged in political struggles from the United States and Europe to South Africa and India. While the amount of impact or efficacy of such performances has always been debated,[1] they certainly highlight a genealogy of performance imbricated in the sociopolitical ballast of significant struggles.

However, a gradual disillusionment with 'political theatre' has grown up after postmodernism and during neoliberalism, combined with a long-standing critique of institutional and commercial theatre (e.g. Kershaw 1999) in favour of a range of alternative or experimental performance practices. Hans-Thies Lehmann's well-known theorization of postdramatic theatre (1999), asserting a breakdown of political potential for drama, has also proved highly influential. According to Lehmann, 'Political conflicts increasingly elude intuitive perception and cognition and consequently scenic representation' (2006, 175).[2] Moreover, the recent focus on spectatorship combined with theoretical interest in affect studies has contributed to an emphasis on individual experiential possibilities rather than collective address and discursive signification. These strands come together in a tendency to minimize or denigrate the political impact of theatre – we can see this in Joe Kelleher's reluctance to attribute direct political affect to the theatre (2009),[3] or Tony Fisher's scepticism about their connection (2017),[4] or Alan Read's outright rejection of the combination of theatre and the political (2008).[5] Writing in a special issue on 'The Politicality of Performance' in the Serbian journal *TKH*, Ana Vujanović opines that while performance may not be apolitical, under the current regime of neoliberal capitalism, performance has become a 'model of production' rather than political practice, thus rendering 'its politicality [. . .] indirect and dubious' (2011, 120). These views, while individually different from each other, entail both a degree of rejection and regret; they have been collected and summed up well by Tony Fisher in his call for a 'critical politics of the visible', and explicitly linked to *The Emancipated Spectator*, in particular Read's and Rancière's denial of theatre's instrumentality (Fisher 2017, 15ff). Fisher aligns himself with a recognition of

> aesthetic singularities, each attuned to the political task of performance and theatre insofar as it embraces a tragic conception; understanding, that is, that

forms of theatrical performance – but also the performance of the radical politics of the street – necessarily must take place in a space defined by contingency, vulnerability and eventuality. What is essential to such a standpoint is the understanding that no Archimedean point exists beyond the social that would preserve 'radical art' and its gestures from the threat of co-option. (16)

My discomfort with these propositions is that they dampen expectations about the political potentialities of performance and lead to a kind of quietism where one neither expects too much nor ventures too far in the name of a politics of performance. First, an emphasis on aesthetic singularity and denial of theatre's communitarian possibilities isolates individuals in exactly the same way that neoliberalism does – it throws them back on their own resources and encourages self-absorption or even narcissism. Focus on individuals' experience and meaning in performance rather than collective experiences of a posited 'We' may heighten the sense of unique sensory intake, but it thins out the grounds for building common insights and perceptions that are fundamental to sociopolitical subjectification. Second, in diminishing expectations for efficacy because we cannot secure meaning or impact in a directly instrumental sense, these critics help produce a climate in which striving for such effects appears naive and futile. Instead of pointing out the serendipity of performances that have contributed to specific political contexts or celebrating those occasions when performances matter to outcomes, this form of theory can discourage sustained and engaged political artistry. And this is the worst bit: in a discipline like ours, 'dissensus' can be valorized as the only political goal available to performance while any positive politics with content or a programme is dismissed as overreaching. One might think of Howard Barker, whose plays I find stimulating and rich, but whose rejection of 'political theatre' is rooted in a notion that clear, persuasive political content denies power or agency to the audience: put crudely, by telling them what to think. Of course this tends to privilege a particular kind of highbrow experimental theatre and art practice, and dismisses a range of popular performances as well as mainstream ones, not to mention the dedicated political theatres of community, identity and 'applied' theatre. Rancière seems to offer the field of theatre and performance studies a way to abandon politics as usual (governance, organizing, coalition building, representation) while maintaining a political capacity for performance, refigured in line with Rancière's ideas about the differences between politics and the police. Because some scholars in our field still wish to preserve a notional politicality for theatre and performance without being tethered to what Fisher calls the 'efficacy argument' (the burden of having instrumental impact) the Rancièrian landscape is understandably attractive. In the next part of this chapter, we will look more closely at specific aspects of Rancière's thought that will help flesh out his positions and my objections.

II

Among performance scholars, the most highly appreciated concept in Rancière's lexicon is undoubtedly 'dissensus' (e.g. Haedicke 2013; Kear 2013; Lavender 2016). As with most of Rancière's ideas, this one has developed across several of his key writings, an early articulation appearing in 'Who is the Subject of the Rights of Man?' (2004), expanded and revised for *Dissensus: On Politics and Aesthetics* (2010). It is, moreover, an interlocking category with other key ideas such as 'the distribution of the sensible' and 'the police'. Not surprisingly, it also gathers import from its contrast to 'consensus', a highly disparaged object of Rancièrian attack. Along with parsing the term 'dissensus' in order to understand what Rancière is saying through the word and how performance scholars appropriate the term, we should also note the binary structure of contrast (dissensus to consensus), a typical rhetorical technique in Rancière's prose: two terms are posed as opposite and a choice is forced between them, without gradations in between. Often accompanied by a value reversal, Rancière relishes flipping familiar relations on their head.

Before we can approach dissensus, however, we first need to deploy one of his other key contrasts between 'politics' and 'the police'. The police is best understood as the hegemonic, status-quo, sociopolitical organization. With its hierarchies and authorities, it is a regime of governance that can only be opposed and interrupted:

> Politics is generally seen as the set of procedures whereby aggregation and consent of collectivities is achieved, the organization of powers, the distribution of places and roles, and the systems for legitimizing this distribution. I propose to give this system of distribution and legitimization another name. I propose to call it the police. (2009, 28)

Calling it 'the police' is polemical, economical and succinct. It aligns common-sense meanings of policing with the Foucauldian concept of governmentality and makes it impossible to separate out more-or-less benign components of such a system. This neologism is one of the most radical lynchpins of Rancière's thought. To the police, he opposes 'politics', defined as 'an extremely determined activity antagonistic to policing: whatever breaks with the tangible configuration whereby parties and parts or lack of them are defined by a presupposition that, by definition, has no place in that configuration – that of the part that has no part' (2009, 29–30). In this pair of concepts, Rancière disallows any contemplation of working within conventional politics – elections, parties, regulatory bodies, local government, social services or even non-governmental organizations that exist in relation to more codified bodies. Nor does he advocate any alternative organizational effort or method of building a movement or sustaining a position. It is the individual act of dissensus, of breaking relations, that is considered the quintessential political act.

In setting up this definition of dissensus, Rancière draws the figure of the political subject through the example of Olympe de Gouges. A playwright and literary figure, she wrote 'Declaration of the Rights of Woman and the Female Citizen' in 1791, and was guillotined for sedition in 1793. Rancière characterizes her as the political subject, the one who forces a key contradiction to erupt in public:

> Her point was that women, who were apparently born equal, were in fact not equal as citizens. They could neither vote nor stand for election. Olympe de Gouges's argument showed that it was not possible to draw the border separating bare life and political life so clearly. At least one point existed where 'bare life' proved to be 'political': when women were sentenced to death as enemies of the revolution. If they could lose their 'bare life' thanks to a politically motivated public judgment, this meant that even their bare life – their life from the standpoint of its being able to be put to death – was political. [. . .] This is what I call a dissensus. [...] A political subject is a capacity for staging scenes of dissensus. (2010, 68–69)

The fundamental political act is a disruption of the 'normal' order of things by a subject who has not been previously recognized as a subject – an act of insurrection by taking a part by those who have no part.

In contrast to dissensus which is disruptive and, according to Rancière, always political, consensus is a process of depoliticization. Again reversing a familiar meaning, he insists that consensus is not

> the simple attempt to settle political conflicts reasonably and practically through forms of negotiation and agreement. [...] Consensus consists in the attempt to dismiss politics by expelling surplus subjects and replacing them with real partners, social and identity groups and so on. The result is that conflicts are turned into problems to be resolved by learned expertise and the negotiated adjustment of interests. Consensus means closing spaces of dissensus by plugging intervals and patching up any possible gaps between appearance and reality, law and fact. (2010, 70–71)

Rancière here appears to be describing a state of affairs under neoliberalism familiar to its many 'post-political' critics:

> Technocratic mechanisms and consensual procedures [. . .] operate within an unquestioned framework of representative democracy, free market economics and cosmopolitan liberalism. In post-politics, political contradictions are reduced to policy problems to be managed by experts and legitimated through participatory processes in which the scope of possible outcomes is narrowly defined in advance. (Wilson and Swyngedouw 2015, 6)

Rancière's careful argument-building creates a tautology: he defines consensus as manipulative and oppressive, and links the two terms, 'dissensus' and 'consensus'. You cannot have dissensus without a prior consensus, and consensus implies at least an implicit dissensus. But there are other ways of defining consensus – for instance, where the key element is not to enforce agreement and silence dissent but rather to work on pragmatic group interaction, sometimes within institutions and systems, in order to shift them. This kind of collective action is often disruptive to some extent, not aimed at dismantling things and leaving them broken in bits on the floor – but instead using the pieces that are questioned/disturbed to make something else that is 'better' for those in that social context.[6]

Another important aspect of Rancière's position is his mistrust of any 'negotiated adjustment of interests', based on the danger that the weak lose out to the strong who marshal their strengths (often 'learned expertise' and a dominant community of speech) to dismiss or overlook the challenger. In *Dissensus*, Rancière makes this point clearly:

> If there is someone you do not wish to recognize as a political being, you begin by not seeing him as the bearer of signs of politicity, by not understanding what he says, by not hearing what issues from his mouth as discourse. […] A political demonstration is therefore always of the moment and its subjects are always precarious. A political difference is always on the shore of its own disappearance. (2010, 38–39)

The fear of dilution or simple invisibility if one does not stand up and fight is obvious. And it calls for the kind of confrontative politics for which the concept of dissensus is made. It is, however, only one kind of political strategy; by discounting other kinds, he narrows the meaning of politics. As I argue later in this chapter, the ability to be heard, to be intelligible, is determined by the very distribution of the sensible Rancière wishes to contest (see p.182).

The thrust of Rancière's political agenda is always disruptive – he is more concerned with breaking apart than reassembling. This runs throughout his work from his early definition of equality to his most recent statements. In 1992,[7] he writes that 'the essence of equality is not so much to unify as to declassify, to undo the supposed naturalness of orders and replace it with controversial figures of division. Equality is the power of inconsistent, disintegrative and ever replayed division' (1995, 32–33). In 2017, he says in an interview, 'If there are parties and long-term strategies, it is because there are moments of rupture, moments of delegitimation of the powers in place, of the distribution of powers, of the division of powers between those who govern and those who are governed, of the separation between political spaces and those that are not. Revolutionary or subversive moments are what makes politics' (quoted in Gavroche 2017).

A number of commentators have identified Rancière with anarchism (May 2007, 2008; Hallward 2005, 2006; Petrović Lotina 2018), and indeed Rancière has occasionally associated himself with anarchism as well: 'I proposed a definition of democracy that is anarchistic in the strong sense: there is no power authorised or legitimated to exercise power' (quoted in Gavroche 2017). Todd May, who has written extensively theorizing a poststructuralist anarchism, has embraced Rancière's work as an example of anarchism that is not simply anti-state: 'Anarchism [. . .] should be seen as a critique of domination, rather than as a critique of the state'(May 2005, 21). May finds that Rancière's concept of the police extends beyond the state to corporate elites and systems beyond formal government. What is wrong with 'mainstream politics' on this view is that it presupposes inequality – rather than seeing representative government as enabling, May sees it as 'predicated on a refusal to recognize that people can run their own affairs, and so must have them run for them' (2005, 24). Rancière's presumptive equality turns this state of affairs on its head. Democracy becomes the practice of politics by dissensus – confronting and rejecting the contradictions of the hegemonic systems of inequality Rancière calls the police.

However, I do not think that the principle of equality that drives dissensus solves all the problems anarchy poses as a serious political position. The stark binary of power and resistance that is the conceptual driver of both anarchy and dissensus does not recognize the complex and interrelational components of hegemony that an alternative radical theorist such as Chantal Mouffe embraces as the basis for creating lasting change: she argues against total rupture with the existing political regime in favour of a transformational approach to the existing hegemony.[8] Based on Gramsci's notion of the 'integral state', she writes, 'Such a hegemonic strategy engages with the existing political institutions in view of transforming them through democratic procedures and it rejects the false dilemma between reform and revolution' (Mouffe 2018, 45).

In addition to the argument that politics should challenge, but ultimately work to change not destroy or abandon existing political formations and institutions, another argument considers the serious and immediate harm that can result from the rejection of the state and its larger civil and institutional frameworks. I offer an example from my home context: the struggle over healthcare insurance in the United States is a protracted fight. When the Obama administration finally succeeded in passing 'Obamacare'(the Patient Protection and Affordable Care Act, signed in 2010 to take effect in 2014), it extended health insurance to 30,000 million uninsured Americans.

Adequate healthcare coverage had been a political struggle in the United States for seventy-five years. While European social welfare systems were the cornerstone of post-war reconstruction, in the United States, an alliance of conservatives, insurance companies and many medical interests succeeded in making a national health insurance programme impossible to realize, branding European systems 'socialized medicine'. It took Supreme Court rulings in 2016 that most of the provisions of the Affordable Care Act were constitutional to finally confirm it as law. Trump and Republicans campaigned on a vow to 'repeal and replace Obamacare', and after the 2016 election, the majority Republican Congress tried in every way possible to accomplish this task. However, even if the law was weak, inadequate and under-resourced as a Left view would have it, or whether, on the other hand, it created too much federal regulation and interference in the 'market' as the Right would have it, doing away with it altogether would have removed healthcare from millions of people who previously did not have it at all. Furthermore, specific injustices in insurance practices had been addressed in the legislation such as charging anyone with a pre-existing medical condition higher premiums or refusing coverage altogether. In addition, the health coverage especially helped women, Hispanics and African Americans (Cole 2015).

The Congressional battle in 2017 to preserve or destroy these gains was a typical party-based struggle between Democrats and Republicans led by President Trump. American citizens protested, demonstrated, wrote letters to their senators and representatives, and made donations to both party-based organizations and other non-affiliated groups who were fighting the attempt to destroy this legislation. Moderate republicans sided with Democrats (and ultra-conservatives who found the new bill too liberal) to defeat the attempt to replace Obamacare in a decisive vote. In 2018 in the run-up to the November midterm elections, many Republicans were suddenly talking about the need to protect people with pre-existing conditions – even Trump tweeted, 'Republicans will totally protect people with Pre-Existing Conditions, Democrats will not! Vote Republican'(24 October 2018).

From a Rancièrian position, it could be argued that this entire issue falls within the realm of the 'police', since the struggle was conducted largely within the existing legislative and legal structures by means of overwhelmingly partisan political activity. To follow party politics (that is, to know where congress people and senators stood on these issues, to watch and try to influence their votes, even to engage on the streets since demonstrations were planned and executed in tandem with the flashpoints in debate and votes on Capitol Hill) – is this not a course of action confirming rather than challenging or refusing the 'distribution of the sensible'? I think Rancière would not see this as being a valuable space of struggle for political activism as he conceives it – it is entirely too institutional in nature. However, a great deal is at stake in this struggle, and significant and widespread damage would accrue if the system breaks down. One estimate is that the Affordable Care Act is saving 24,000 lives a year (Cole 2015). That is not negligible; it is a major social good through governance.

Rancière argues that politics always exists in a specific situation, and the context determines the possibilities for political action. I agree with this situated logic, which is why I offered a familiar and local 'for instance' to argue that dissensus does not offer a pathway to address a complex institutionally embedded issue like healthcare.[9] The more general critique would then be that there are a multiplicity of ways to address this situation, but that engagement with institutions must be at least part of a possible scene of play. Chantal Mouffe, who can sometimes seem aligned with Rancière, in some matters, parts company by clearly recognizing the limitations of refusing to engage:

> Movements cannot be left just to the streets. I am very critical of the idea of politics as fomenting a moment of total rupture with the existing status quo. This is not how revolutions work. At some point, mobilizations will lose steam. You cannot change things only on the horizontal level of social movements. […] Left-wing populism should see a relationship between the horizontal in the streets and vertical in the institutions. (Quoted in Shahid 2016)

This idea that one must struggle within the 'police' as well as agitate from outside seems more pressing than ever in light of the political divisions that have emerged in Western democracies within the last few years. A heightened sense of antagonism in the wake of right-wing ascendency has put paid to the notion that there is no real difference between left and right, a complaint once voiced by Mouffe (2005, 64–72) as well as by the post-political crowd. The 2018 electoral struggles in, for example, Italy, Sweden and Austria have made it clear that a well-defined antagonism exists around issues of immigration and national interest (unfortunately, at the moment, the upsurgence of the Right seems to be winning). A new 'agon' is certainly possible and the conditions that have previously been described as post-political have been rapidly changing into what might yet become a neo-political moment for which we will need a wide range of political options. Peter Hallward, one of the most thoughtful of Rancière's critics, has put this succinctly: 'Rancière's emphasis on division and interruption makes it difficult to account for qualities that are just as fundamental to any sustainable political sequence: organization, simplification, mobilization, decision, polarization, to name a few' (2006, 126).

This political debate about whether to operate within or against existing institutions plays out with implications for theatre and performance. The either/or terms of Rancière's theories leave traditional 'political theatre' open to the charge it is only conspiring with the police and will be co-opted by the distribution of the sensible it contests. This approach reintroduces an old debate about aesthetics and politics that invokes Theodor Adorno's view of art as autonomous, that is, containing its own internal rules and values, and not subject to any political or social purpose or function: 'Insofar as a social function may be predicated of works of art, it is the function of having no function' (1997, 227). It seems to me that Lehmann, for example, channels this Adorno when he rejects political drama. Claire Bishop, leaning heavily on Adorno and Rancière, also rejects art that has taken the 'social turn' for being instrumental and banal. On the other hand, Adorno himself held a more complex understanding of art than is often attributed to him. Andy Hamilton expresses it thus:

> To talk of something as an artwork is to separate it from other things, and yet those other things do remain connected with it. This is a paradox, that is, an apparent contradiction that is not a genuine one – just as the liberation of the artist through commodification of the artwork is paradoxical, but since capitalism liberates as well as constricts, not a genuine contradiction. Adorno's account is one of the most brilliant attempts to explain this connection and disconnection, an account that overcomes the dichotomy between aestheticism and social functionalism. (2008, 263)

Shannon Jackson has argued persuasively against this dichotomy in *Social Works: Performing Art, Supporting Publics* (2011). In this important volume, she examines art practice through a performance studies lens to argue against critics such as Claire Bishop. Jackson identifies four antimonies that structure the contemporary crossroads of performance aesthetics and social engagement: social celebration versus social antagonism, legibility versus illegibility, radical functionality versus radical unfunctionality and artistic heteronomy versus artistic autonomy. Jackson argues against conceptualizing these as binaries from the perspective of an intermedial understanding of art events, drawing on her performance studies training to blur the boundaries of inside and outside that structure the antinomies. By examining how both the formal aesthetics and the social engagement of a work converge, she rejects the conceptual oppositions that value one set over another. This in turn also allows her to undo an anti-institutional bias as well:

This book questions models of political engagement that measure artistic radicality by its degree of anti-institutionality. While the activist orientation of some social practice displays the importance of an anti-institutional stance in political art, I am equally interested in art forms that help us to imagine sustainable social institutions. [...] When a political art discourse too often celebrates social disruption at the expense of social coordination, we lose a more complex sense of how art practices contribute to inter-dependent social imagining. (14)

Jackson's method throughout the book is to take contrasting art works that seem to embody the antinomies she has identified and deconstruct the oppositions between them – for example, the work of Santiago Sierra and Shannon Flattery, or the 'stage management' of Allan Sekula, Andrea Fraser and William Pope. L. (who can be seen either as institutional critics or as social artists). Specific to theatre, she analyses The Builder's Association and Rimini Protokoll as theatrical groups who work within professional theatre networks and yet challenge many formal conventions of the medium. They address in subject matter some global political topics while foregrounding the medium itself in the role of affective labour under globalization.[10] The point of her critique throughout is to show that supportive interaction is a key modality of performance and that it is capable of politics beyond co-option or defiance. Consensus and dissensus can be better employed to describe aspects of the social processes these artists engage with rather than seeing them as mutually exclusive options for either ethics or politics.

III

Rancière's most valued political concept and ultimate commitment is found in his articulation of the principle of equality. Variously stated as 'the part of one who has no part', or sometimes 'those who fall outside the count' (2009, 2004), Rancière argues that every distribution of the sensible excludes by nature of its hierarchical arithmetic. To counter this, only the presumption of radical equality can reveal the 'demos'. Roughly similar to 'the people', the demos, as explained very well by performance scholar Maurya Wickstrom,

> are not the poor and it is not a class identification. These are not individuals, or individual collectivities, identity groups, or citizens. They are those who fall outside the count. The count, as in Badiou, is what structures power by organizing and managing certain kinds of belonging. Rancière calls the count 'the police'. This demos – those who stage dissensus and in the process become true political subjects – questions the count itself, who is included in it. (2012, 22–23)

To see how the various interlocking parts of this precept of equality build up to Rancière's theory of politics, it is useful to go to his early pedagogical writing about Joseph Jacotot (1770–1840) in *The Ignorant Schoolmaster*. Here Rancière speaks through the historical figure to posit that all human beings have equal intelligence and that from this supposition, a political act challenging any social order can take place when one asserts one's equality and establishes the logic by which equality may be demonstrated (or not). The act of the challenge is a demand for verification of the equality claim. Here is how Rancière describes this process:

> The process of emancipation is the verification of the equality of any speaking being with any other speaking being. It is always enacted in the name of a category [that denies] either the principle or the consequences of that equality: workers, women, people of colour, or others. But the enactment of equality is not, for all that, the enactment of the self, of the attributes or properties of the community in question. The name of an injured community that invokes its rights is always the name of the anonym, the name of anyone. (1992, 59–60)

Thus the syllogism follows the well-known form: All 'men' are equal. But this 'man' (Olympe de Gouges, for instance) is not equal; therefore, not all men are equal. In the insistence on this logic, and in the refusal to specify any particular 'man', Rancière reverts to a kind of universalism that is the basis for his rejection of identity politics. But this is also, I would argue, where his theory stumbles.

While on one hand certainly the 'anyone' who has no part can try to speak to challenge the veracity of the claim to equality, it is always within a given order, society, distribution of the sensible that one intervenes to speak, if the speech is to be intelligible. Rancière himself notes the problem in *Dissensus*, as I noted above (p.176) in this book, but does not address how one gets heard beyond disruption, in other words, how to enter the discourse. Furthermore, the specific challenger will be marked by certain attributes or characteristics on the basis of which he/she is being excluded. These must be named to make an argument about the unjust exclusion. Citizenship theory has been decisively split between those who advocate a 'liberal' universal definition of inclusion (think John Rawls) and those who insist that 'anyone'/'everyone' is always already marked by attributes which may in fact be differentiated, leading to differences in the practices of exclusion and calling for different modes of remedy (think Iris Marion Young).[11] While there is a way in which one can act on the part of all those who have no part, most politics involves identifying specific beings or categories of beings who have no part. This makes for different struggles, for sure. But the very specificity of the claims are where the reproach to power lies: in our time, for instance, Black Lives Matter and the Me Too Movement invoke very concrete attributes of those who have no part. While overlap and solidarity among these challengers is both possible and politically desirable, it would not be efficacious if race or gender were removed as the markers of these political actors. This seems obvious to me, but in light of a strong anti-identitarian critique not only in political theory but also in some performance theory, this point needs to be made again and again. Rancière seeks to override this critique by denying he is talking about specific selves, but I find it unconvincing:

> The process of equality is a process of difference. But difference does not mean the assumption of a different identity or the plain confrontation of two identities. The place for working out the difference is not the 'self' or the culture of a group. It is the *topos* of an argument. And the place for such an argument is an interval. The place of a political subject is an interval or a gap: being *together* to the extent that we are *in between* – between names, identities, cultures, and so on. (italics in original, 1992, 62)

To shift 'the place' for this argument to an 'interval' or a 'gap' removes the materiality of the 'self' or 'culture' that is the raison d'être of the argument in the first place. I see this as an avoidance of embodiment and performative concreteness in favour of a rational and logical formalism that does not describe emancipatory political processes adequately. It might, of course, be possible to focus on its spatiality as a metaphor for something like an empty signifier that can 'quilt' together a first-person plural address – this would be following up on basic ideas from both Mouffe and Laclou (1985, chapters 3 and 4) and Zizek (1989, 87ff). However, there are significant differences among these theorists, and Rancière seems to be much more connected to the abstractions of language and logic than to the phenomenological aspects of lived subjectivization.

For theatre and performance, the most obvious outcome of following Rancière's theories of subjectivization would be to reject representation of particular groups (identities) because the categories are themselves part of the distribution of the sensible with which Rancière would wish us to break. When he writes about these matters, he insists on a difference between identification and subjectification (the former is a category designation controlled and described by the police). To form a collective subject capable of speaking in the name of equality seems to require a unique, previously unrecognized name to emerge and disrupt the normalized distribution of identities:

> A political subject is not a group that 'becomes aware' of itself, find its voice, imposes its weight on society. It is an operator that connects and disconnects different areas, regions, identities, functions, and capacities existing in the

configuration of a given experience – that is, in the nexus of distributions of the police order and whatever equality is already inscribed there, however fragile and fleeting such inscriptions may be. (Rancière 2009, 40)

This 'operator' seems inhuman, disembodied, more like a lever – and in any case, this term constructs a Rancièrian logic that is not susceptible to modifications: another tautology. Todd May, attempting to explain and defend Rancière, uses the gay rights movement as his example. He admits it could not be called the Burma rights movement but insists that 'the gay rights movement is not about gayness, but equality'. (On the contrary, it seems to me to be clearly about both since the reason equality has been withheld has been prejudice against gays.) However May goes on:

In that sense, then the name of a subjectification is not the name of a group that becomes aware of itself, but of a group that is created through a variety of people's connections to one another and disconnections from previous stereotypes in order to proceed in sayings and doings under the banner of equality. (2010, 49)

This reading of Rancière's meaning is somewhat helpful, I admit, but it still pushes us towards an unembodied and unmarked subject, an empty signifier of sorts which would not require 'gay' as a crucial descriptor, since that would be the name of a group that has become aware of itself (which indeed it has). The symptom of an appeal to a universalism arises here – when Rancière cites, approvingly, the French students in 1968 who said 'We are all German Jews' (Rancière 2009, 59), he does not parse the occasions on which this might be considered presumptuous or offensive, nor does he try out the valences of similarly constructed statements with different categories: when 'Black Lives Matter' is countered with 'All Lives Matter', there is a universalism that denies the inequality asserted by the first term rather than an 'operator that connects'. 'Black Lives Matter' insists that they *should* matter in circumstances where police shootings demonstrate they do not; while 'All Lives Matter' is an attempt by whites to pretend blacks are included within the universal 'all' – the slogan is a reproach and a charge of separatism. However, one can imagine Rancière insisting that 'All Lives Matter' is the very principle of equality and the proper proclamation of politics (although he would certainly not support the racial politics). This is where I get restive with Rancière.

In theatre and performance studies, there are many committed artists and scholars who are worrying about this problematic in different ways. For some, identity politics have divided possible constituencies and diluted progressive politics. For others, the appeal to universalism seems to be an appropriate response to an overly particularized world. Alan Read goes so far as to say that 'every politics that grounds itself in reference to some substantial particularity (whether that be ethnic, religious, sexual or concerned with lifestyle) is by definition reactionary' (85). This charge is over the top, but has achieved notice in our field.

While Matthew Causey and Fintan Walsh quote Read, they establish a far more careful exposition in support of their critique of identity politics in the realm of theatre and performance. While they acknowledge the valuable history of identity politics in our field, their book puts forward a number of examples of scholars who are trying to find new ways of thinking about political subjectivity (beyond identity), and re-politicize the relations between theatre, performance and identity (Causey and Walsh 2011, 1). This is a genuinely worthy investigation, and some of the essays, in particular Petra Kuppers's essay on disability dance writing and Fintan Walsh's essay on Antony Hegarty, definitely contribute to expanding political considerations of performance.

In Kuppers's case, she carefully parses the difference between the legitimate and necessary attention to the creativity of disability arts while refusing to delimit and essentialize disabled identity. In Walsh's case, he has selected a performer who is exploring the insufficiency of fixed sexual identities. A transgender-identifying performer whose work is often imbued with a queer sensibility, Hegarty is engaged in the creation of music which presages ethical and political entailments of a world of connection beyond human and non-human, let alone gender or sexuality. Reading his appeal through environmental ethics, referencing the dissolving identities theorized by Guattari in particular, Walsh is wanting performance politics to reach beyond human subjectivity and identity. He sums up Hegarty's value for this project: 'He rehearses a model of being in the world that is premised on a heightened awareness of the constitutive materiality of all things, animated and distributed through multi-sensory intensity and affect, including his own performances'(225).

I selected these two examples from the Causey and Walsh collection because they (colloquially) 'do not throw out the baby with the bathwater'. Both Kuppers and Walsh include the importance of identity markers (disability and transgender vocal registers, respectively), even as they urge a transcendence of essentialist or stolid meanings/attributes in order to expand community through ethical and political call and response. These approaches maintain the possibility of keeping on stage the claims of 'those who have no part' while also evoking solidarity beyond the particular attribute in whose name attention is being paid. And that is the key thing: to establish a collective subject or series of subjects that can challenge inequality and build a certain kind of – dare I say it – consensus. Not a consensus that silences all antagonism but an agreement among differing positions and perspectives to collaborate on a coalition to demand equality and to fashion tactics and strategies both inside and outside of institutions to produce change.

IV

The emphasis on dissensus, the binary of police versus politics that rejects working with institutions, and a notion of equality that is flawed as much as it is admirable makes Rancière's ideas about democracy similarly problematic. They lack a theory of building collectivity, a means of sustaining organizations or institutions, and they undermine representational structures of democracy based on hierarchical (to Rancière) presumptions of expertise, office and party. To understand better the way these problems accrue to a Rancièrian position, I turn to the critique of Oliver Marchart who argues that democracy has to be established against competing political projects and maintained – therefore, it needs institutions as only they can sustain over time. Because Rancière refuses to consider democracy a *regime* ('the institutional framework of democracy and a democratic "way of life"' [Marchart 2011, 142]), he has no way to theorize substantial, enduring successful politics (substantial' here means duration as well as structure). As Marchart puts it, if this mode of substantial democracy is acknowledged as a regime, then (with reference to Rancière's own words in *Disagreement*),

> It becomes impossible to describe democratic institutions in terms of 'fleeting' inscriptions (Rancière 1999, 40). Nor can it be plausibly claimed, as Rancière repeatedly does, that (necessarily democratic) politics 'in its specificity is rare', that it 'is always local and occasional' (1999, 139), and 'doesn't always happen – it actually happens very little or rarely'. (1999, 17) (Marchart 2011, 140)

By compiling key descriptions of the individual, occasional and quick characteristics that mark dissensual practice together with the absence of structuring principles (regime), Marchart illustrates the weakness in Rancière's thinking for the project of developing an actual democratic politics, one that involves the long slow slog of organization, maintenance, collective consultation, and repeated actions and gestures at least as much as the individual, infrequent and fast flashes of rupture advocated by Rancière. I also worry that Rancière's emphasis on individual action, on the one hand, and the distrust of expertise as criterion of the ability to govern, on the other hand, plays into current neoliberal individualism and its distribution of the sensible.

And what about theatre and democracy? At the beginning of this chapter I complained about the denigration of the ability of theatre and performance to achieve political efficacy and that the notion of dissensus valued and advocated by many scholars privileges the kind of post-dramatic, non-rhetorical, 'open' dramaturgy of nondecidability and the aesthetics of ambivalence. Also worrisome: if the project of working within as well as against existing structures of governance and institutions is dismissed as insufficiently radical, the fact that many times theatre's infrastructural operations are supported and supportive of the other arts, and that often it serves as a bridging activity between already existing governance structures and institutions and the larger demos of the body politic can also be dismissed as of little (political) value. In closing this chapter, I wish to consider a juxtaposition of Rancière's theories to a current subject of concern in our field to illustrate how a counterpoint to a Rancièrian politics of performance is possible. To quote Jackson one last time, the goal will be 'to join performance's routinized discourse of disruption and de-materialization to one that also emphasizes sustenance, coordination, and re-materialization' (29).

One of the most pressing issues confronting us internationally is the situation of inequality and injustice facing millions of displaced persons now, and the likely prospect of increasingly intensified global migration due to many factors including war, economic inequality; repressive governmental actions based on race, ethnicity, religion, sexuality or other factors; and climate change. The current figure of 65.3 million displaced people is larger than the populations of the UK, Argentina, Canada, Australia or Kenya. 'If this displaced population were a nation, it would be the 21st most populous in the world' (Bhabha 2018, 10). The vocabulary used to describe migrants is itself deeply politicized, and appears on theatrical stages and in performance scholarship as well as public and official discourses under such names as immigrants, refugees, illegals, undocumented persons, aliens, asylum-seekers or economic migrants – to mention only some – depending on where in the world is being referenced, and who is doing the referring.[12]

The specificity of saying 'we are all Immigrants' in California at this moment might work in the way Rancière would like – the Mexican and Central American immigrants who are being targeted for deportation by the Trump administration could benefit from the solidarity of the proclamation, but I would note the irony that most older Californians are already indeed immigrants, but from a wide variety of other places (such as Italy, Ireland, Sweden etc.), and hardly share the current conditions of inequality that the new ones face. In addition, this proclamation would not touch the complexity of the current situation of those who are currently, for example, 'Dreamers' who were born in the United States but whose parents are illegal residents and whose right to remain is now in limbo, or the persons without documents who were trafficked into forced labour or sexual slavery in a number of border areas, and who now must decide whether they are more at risk from the violence of their captivity or from collateral damage during legal action against their abductors (which may identify them and lead to deportation back to unsafe countries of origin).

Arguably, theatre and performance are well suited to contribute to creative expression of the complex dynamics facing particular contexts and peoples living in present conditions of embodied 'irregular motion' as well as those who are positioned more statically as their 'hosts' or as citizens in settlement states. However, as Emma Cox points out, 'The identification of asylum as a category subject to artistic and political representation, regardless of the emancipatory ideals of that representation, does not merely *describe* but is also *generative* of the category' (2015, 2, emphasis in original), and that would be true for other appellations as well. Thus the decision to represent as well as the nature of the representation is clearly an ethical and political matter.

That migration and performance is currently a 'hot topic' in our field can be seen in a number of important recent publications (including Cox 2014, 2015; Jeffers 2012; Balfour et al. 2015), a special journal issue of *RiDE: Research in Drama Education* (2018), and in summer 2018 the International Federation for Theatre Research's annual conference in Belgrade on 'Theatre and Migration; Theatre, Nation, Identity: Between Migration and Stasis'.[13] At the same time, many activists have been engaged in making performances by and/or about migrants, as well as participating in local and national political activities ranging from protests and marches to volunteer work in refugee centres, legal aid centres and municipal, state or national political organizations. This, I would argue, is a critically important terrain for theatre and performance scholars but also one that is severely fraught with difficulties in 'getting it right'. What might we say about this field of activity, taking into account Rancière's ideas and their critique?

To begin with, we should ask, is the subject matter appropriate to performance? Followers of Rancière might be dubious because (a) migrants and other named variants constitute an identity category, not a proper political subjectivation and (b) to represent them on stage could set up a spurious relation between those on stage and the audiences watching because it would be based on delineated roles (citizen, host, fellow migrant, etc.) that come from the 'distribution of the sensible' controlled by the police, and would also risk, as Cox writes, further consolidating the category. (This representation is further complicated if authors and actors are/are not themselves migrants.)

In reply we might respond as follows: The very difference and variety of persons designated as migrants might in fact allow the act of challenging inequality to give rise to political subjectification. How different would this be from Olympe de Gouges becoming a political subject by virtue of demonstrating (by her very death) that she was not a part of the count, appearing on behalf of those who have no part? In other words, the ability to trigger a collective subject must certainly be a possibility although it cannot be a certainty. (It would depend on the concrete details of situation and person(s) involved in any particular performance, and the way a plurality might aggregate into a proper collectivity.) As for the second matter, Rancière, ventriloquizing Jacotot, might consider the performance illustrative of the 'principle of enforced stultification' (1991, 7): Performances about migration, asylum, detention and so on can certainly suffer from overly didactic messages directed at supposed ignorant spectators by presumptuous producers, but can we not imagine another scenario in which embodied representation/ presentation of migrant experiences might be richly varied on the part of the artists and sought out to be thoughtfully contemplated by spectators who are engaged in trying to think through and feel deeply the specificity of the issues and their own situatedness in relation to them? In fact, there are many examples of such performances.[14]

The contingency and open possibility involved in these answers may seem like a weak response to the more categorical objections, but surely this is what Tony Fisher means when he avows that 'forms of theatrical performance – but also the performance of the radical politics of the street – necessarily must take place in a space defined by contingency, vulnerability and eventuality' (Fisher 2016, 16). For Fisher, this is a 'tragic conception' but for me it is more of a promise – that there is still a possibility of forming political affinities among diverse constituencies through performances that illuminate injustice, push back against power and evoke a political 'we'. This optimism may only be Gramscian (pessimism of the intellect, optimism of the will),[15] but it can be warranted in the wake of some exemplary examples of actual performances that achieve these ends. I'll finish by recalling one such performance.

Emma Cox has written perceptively about the solo work *Nine Lives* (2016) by Zimbabwean British playwright Zodwa Nyoni. Ishmael, the gay protagonist, must reveal and perform his gay-ness in order to secure his asylum case, but outside the legal context, chooses to conceal it in order to make a new friend in a social situation where he is a stranger and a cultural outsider. Ostensibly about how gay identity is codified and coerced by the asylum process which demands not only revelation but intimate 'evidence', it is also about how the strategic choice to conceal sexuality in a new unfamiliar civil context (making friends in Leeds) may eventually lead to improvising a new gay identity in response to encounters with British life. Thus the play is about both migration law as a domain of intimate and closely watched performances produced for the state and its agents, and at the same time, about the challenges of migrant resettlement in the micro-political daily life of someone attempting to find a new place and space to be himself.

In addition to the complex configuration of the (political) subject in Ishmael, *Nine Lives* also illustrates how a 'small' bit of efficacy can generate a larger political effect. The production in London (2016) affiliated with a number of local organizations and networks doing overtly political work on behalf of the LGBT community and refugee activists, such as UK Lesbian and Gay Immigration Group, Platforma Arts and Refugees Network, and City of Sanctuary. These kinds of affiliations in connection with the explicitly theatrical work of *Nine Lives* directly address social injustice. Seeing the theatre as a 'worksite of democracy', to gloss Etienne Balibar as I have done at length elsewhere (Reinelt 2015), it is possible to contrast a collaborative model of political process to the disconnected alternatives of Rancière's ruptures. Here, instead, deliberate connecting and supporting between and among groups creates a stronger collective subject and also a multifaceted approach to achieving social justice. Perhaps theatre is not capable of acting by itself to achieve large political objectives but it is efficacious when it uses its own best tools, affective and embodied relations among artists and audiences, in concert with other organs of political discourse and change such as but not limited to the groups incorporated into the *Nine Lives* effort. This effort draws specifically on theatre's strengths while transcending its limitations in several ways. Cox concludes her discussion of *Nine Lives* thus:

> Its event-quality (as, among other things, the intensification of imaginative and emotional capacities) working in conduit with its accumulative and associative function as representation flanked by prior and ongoing engagements[, illustrates theatre's multi-functionality]. As far as leveraging justice is concerned, then, the potential power of refugee-responsive theatre might most usefully be recognized as embedded dynamically in networks of friends and associates. (Cox 2016)

This production, of course, is only one example of a successful theatrical intervention that can be called 'political theatre' without any cringing. But it is not so different from the productions that Kuppers and Walsh value that I have discussed previously. It also makes use of those qualities of organization and mobilization that Hallward notes are missing in Rancière's conception of politics, and that Jackson finds necessary to the interdependent social imagining of the performing arts.

For us theatre scholars, could we not theorize a larger theatrical terrain where many forms of theatre and performance can be valued for their political potential and recognized for the contingent, vulnerable, but also potentially powerful resources they are? – especially when allied with each other and with other individuals, networks and organizations to address the contemporary situation in which we find ourselves.

NOTES

1. Looking back to an excellent essay addressing this efficacy debate, I would cite Tim Miller and David Román's 1995 essay, 'Preaching to the Converted', addressing the disparagement of gay and lesbian theatre and dismissal of politically engaged art more generally. They wrote, in part:

> The idea that an artist is preaching to the converted sets into motion a no-win discursive dynamic that implicates both the artist and the audience. The dismissive 'preaching to the converted' response assumes queer artists to be didactic and queer audiences to be static. Mainstream reviewers who employ the phrase position queer people as needing to be preached to, while queer people who employ the phrase position queer audiences as defiantly against being preached at. Regardless of how the phrase is employed – whether it be to insist that queer artists are propagandists and queer audiences infantile, or to insist that queer artists are didactic and queer audiences bored with it all – lesbian and gay theatre that supposedly preaches to the converted is never understood as a valuable, or even viable, activity. Instead, the uncontested phrase shuts down discussions around the important cultural work that queer artists perform for their queer audiences. (1995, 173)

2. For a more recent look at how Lehmann's original ideas have developed and how performance scholars have grappled with the politics of his theory, see *Postdramatic Theatre and the Political* (Jürs-Munby, Carroll, and Giles eds. 2013).

3. 'There is no guarantee that its [theatre's] theatrical effects will "work" in the way they are supposed to or that its carefully constructed political message will be understood in the ways they are to be understood' (Kelleher 2009, 24).

4. 'For it is not, in my view, particularly helpful to draw together too tightly the tenuous threads that connect the forms of representation involved in theatre and performance with those of representative politics' (Fisher 2017, 8).

5. 'To politicise performance requires us to do away with the idea of political theatre, if not political theatre itself. ... Down with political theatre!' (Read 2008, 27).

6. I am grateful to Lynette Hunter and Peter Lichtenfels for suggesting these insights about consensus, coming out of their early reading of this text.

7. 1992 refers to the original French publication.

8. For a clear and definitive contrast between the positions of Rancière and Mouffe, see Petrović Lotina (2018). He writes, in part, 'While Rancière's distinction between the principle of democracy and the principle of the state forecloses the possibility of politics to engage with the police order, the reciprocal relationship between democracy and the state, suggested by Mouffe, allows for an engagement with existing politics' (145).

9. It is not only the United States of course: a similarly concrete situation concerning healthcare in Britain (the NHS) or the anti-immigrant situation in Germany with a weak Merkel-led government and a far-right party in parliament for the first time, or the 2018 general election in Italy where neo-fascists made large gains would offer equally appropriate European examples – any situation would in which opposition must work with as well as against governing institutions or established

leadership. Arguably another layer of argument can be made on a global level concerning the politics of combatting extreme weather events due to global warming, or the protracted refugee crisis across the globe: both legislative/juridical efforts and mass mobilization and protest are urgently needed, and a way to connect those 'horizontal' and 'vertical' efforts is similarly critical.

10. Jackson identifies both companies as prime examples of postdramatic theatre, but goes on to show how their work is political in that it demonstrates the very imbrication of the 'old' material theatre with the 'new' immaterial affect and technology of new media. Her case studies are performances by both companies dealing with call centres, affect and material labour: *Alladeen* (The Builders Association) and *Call Cutta in a Box* (Rimini Protocol).

11. John Rawls is perhaps the best known Western philosopher of political liberalism. He argues that justice can only be determined by deliberating under a 'veil of ignorance' that ignores markers of difference (1971). Iris Marion Young, on the contrary, argues that justice can only be determined when differences are acknowledged and taken into account (2011). For a full discussion of citizenship theories, highlighting feminist viewpoints, see Dutt, Reinelt and Sahai, eds. (2017), Introduction, 1–23.

12. Cox and Wake's introduction to their special issue of RiDE (2018) contains the best summary I have seen of up-to-date data about the numbers and growth of displaced persons over the last decade. I have varied terminology in this chapter, painfully aware of its sometimes imprecision; my default term has been 'migrant', but I do recognize the problematics of that terminology.

13. It is worth noticing that Cox, Balfour et al., and Wake – leading voices in this arena – have been working deeply within the Australian context, where immigration policy of successive governments has been especially divisive and harmful to migrants. Cox discusses a wide range of theatre productions from highly subsidized international productions to locally produced solo work (often well beyond Australia) while Balfour et al are concerned with a specific applied theatre project to use drama techniques in support of resettlement with young people, funded by the Australian Research Council and local refugee assistance programmes. Cox and Wake (2018), in their jointly edited special issue of RiDE, make note ironically of how after a large amount of work by theatre makers and scholars on Australia's punitive detention and deterrence policies, the focus of this work has now shifted away from Australia although 'the brutal reality is that Australia has redoubled its hard-line measures'.

14. See, for example, the Australian plays collected in Cox (2013) or for the African context, see Fleishman (2015).

15. Antonio Gramsci used this phrase, attributed to the novelist Romain Rolland, as a slogan and key concept as early as 1921 (Hoare and Smith (eds). 1989, 175).

REFERENCES

Balfour, Michael, Penny Bundy, Bruce Burton, Julie Dunn, Nina Woodrow. 2015. *Applied Theatre: Resettlement Drama, Refugees and Resilience.* London and New York, NY: Bloomsbury.

Bhabha, Jacqueline. 2018. *Can We Solve the Migration Crisis?* Cambridge: Polity Press.

Causey, Matthew, and Fintan Walsh, Eds. 2013. *Performance, Identity, and the Neo-Political Subject*. London and New York, NY: Routledge.

Cole, Juan. 2015. 'Top 6 Achievements of Obamacare: (Hint, Millions More Insured)'. *Informed Comment*, 26 June 2015. https://www.juancole.com/2015/06/achievements-obamacare-millions.html [Accessed 20 February 2018].

Cox, Emma. 2014. *Theatre & Migration*. Basingstoke: Palgrave Macmillan.

Cox, Emma. 2015. *Performing Noncitizenship: Asylum Seekers in Australian Theatre, Film and Activism*. London and New York, NY: Anthem Press.

Cox, Emma. 2016. 'Concealment, Revelation and Masquerade in Europe's Asylum Apparatus: Intimate Life at the Border'. *Lateral: Journal of the Cultural Studies Association* 5(2) (special issue, 'Leveraging Justice'). http://csalateral.org/wp/archive/issue/5-2/ [Accessed 26 May 2018].

Cox, Emma, and Caroline Wake, Eds. 2018. 'Envisioning Asylum/Engendering Crisis: Or, Performance and Forced Migration Ten Years On'. Special issue of *RiDE: Research in Drama Education* 23(2): 137–147. https://0-www-tandfonline-com.pugwash.lib.warwick.ac.uk/doi/full/10.1080/13569783.2018.1442714?src=recsys [Accessed 28 May 2018].

Dutt, Bishnupriya, Janelle Reinelt, and Shrinkhla Sahai, Eds. 2017. *Gendered Citizenship: Manifestations and Performance*. London: Palgrave Macmillan.

Fisher, Tony. 2017. 'Introduction: Performance and the Tragic Politics of the Agōn'. In *Performing Antagonism: Theatre, Performance & Radical Democracy*, edited by Tony Fisher and Eve Katsouraki, 1–24. London: Palgrave Macmillan.

Gavroche, Julian. 2017. 'Jacques Rancière: The Anarchy of Democracy'. *Autonomies*, 10 May 2017. http://autonomies.org/2017/05/jacques-ranciere-the-anarchy-of-democracy/ [Accessed 20 February 2018].

Hallward, Peter. 2005. 'Jacques Rancière and the Subversion of Mastery'. *Paragraph* 28(1): 26–45.

Hallward, Peter. 2006. 'Staging Equality: Rancière's Theatrocracy'. *New Left Review* 37(January–February): 109–129.

Jackson, Shannon. 2011. *Social Works: Performing Art, Supporting Publics*. New York, NY and London: Routledge.

Jeffers, Alison. 2012. *Refugees, Theatre and Crisis: Performing Global Identities*. Basingstoke: Palgrave Macmillan.

Kelleher, Joe. 2009. *Theatre & Politics*. Basingstoke: Palgrave Macmillan.

Kershaw, Baz. 1999. *The Radical in Performance: Between Brecht and Baudrillard*. London and New York, NY: Routledge.

Kuppers, Petra. 2013. 'The Bone's Pirouette: Disability Dance Writing and the Crip Relic'. In *Performance, Identity, and the Neo-Political Subject*, edited by L. Causey and C. Walsh, 154–165. London and New York, NY: Routledge.

Lehmann, Hans-Thies. 2006. *Postdramatic Theatre*. Translated by Karen Jürs-Munby. London and New York, NY: Routledge.

Marchart, Oliver. 2011. 'The Second Return of the Political: Democracy and the Syllogism of Equality'. In *Reading Rancière*, edited by Paul Bowman and Richard Stamp, 129–147. London and New York, NY: Continuum.

May, Todd. 2007. 'Jacques Rancière and the Ethics of Equality.' *SubStance* 36(2): 20–36.
May, Todd. 2008. *The Political Thought of Jacques Rancière: Creating Equality*. Edinburgh: Edinburgh University Press.
May, Todd. 2010. *Contemporary Political Movements and the Thought of Jacques Rancière: Equality in Action*. Edinburgh: Edinburgh University Press.
Merriam Webster Dictionary. 2018. *Archê*. https://www.merriam-webster.com/dictionary/arche [Accessed 15 April 2018].
Oxford Living Dictionaries. 2018. *Anarchism*. https://en.oxforddictionaries.com/definition/anarchism [Accessed 20 February 2018].
Rai, Shirin M., and Janelle Reinelt, Ed. 2015. *The Grammar of Politics and Performance*. London and New York, NY: Routledge.
Reinelt, Janelle. 2015. 'Performance at the Crossroads of Citizenship'. In *The Grammar of Politics and Performance*, edited by S. Rai and J. Reinelt, 34–50. London and New York, NY: Routledge.
Rancière, Jacques. 1991. *The Ignorant Schoolmaster: Five Lessons in Intellectual Emancipation*. Translated by Kristin Ross. Stanford, CA: Stanford University Press.
Rancière, Jacques. 1992. 'Politics, Identification, and Subjectivisation'. *October* 16: 58–64.
Rancière, Jacques. 1995. *On the Shores of Politics*. Translated by Liz Heron. London: Verso.
Rancière, Jacques. 2004. 'Who is the Subject of the Rights of Man'. *South Atlantic Quarterly* 103(2/3): 297–310.
Rancière, Jacques. 2009. *Disagreement*. Translated by Julie Rose. Minneapolis, MN: University of Minnesota Press.
Rancière, Jacques. 2010. *Dissensus: On Politics and Aesthetics*. Translated by Steven Corcoran. London and New York, NY: Continuum.
Read, Alan. 2008. *Theatre, Intimacy & Engagement: The Last Human Venue*. Basingstoke: Palgrave Macmillan.
Ridout, Nicholas. 2006. *Stage Fright, Animals and Other Theatrical Problems*. Cambridge: Cambridge University Press.
Shahid, W. 2016. 'America in Populist Times: An Interview With Chantal Mouffe'. *The Nation*, 15 December. https://www.thenation.com/article/america-in-populist-times-an-interview-with-chantal-mouffe/ [Accessed 26 May 2018].
Vujanović, Ana. 2011. '*Vita Performactiva*, on the Stage of Neoliberal Democratic Society'. *TkH* 19: 116–123.
Walsh, Fintan. 2013. 'The Matter of Queer Politics and Ethics: Antony Hegarty and The Crying Light'. In *Performance, Identity, and the Neo-Political Subject*, edited by L. Causey and C. Walsh, 215–229. London and New York, NY: Routledge.
Wickstrom, Maurya. 2012. *Performance in the Blockades of Neoliberalism: Thinking the Political Anew*. Basingstoke: Palgrave Macmillan.
Wilson, Japhy, and Erik Swyngedouw, Eds. 2015. *The Post-Political and Its Discontents: Spaces of Depoliticisation, Spectres of Radical Politics*. Edinburgh: Edinburgh University Press.

Chapter 9

Dissensual Reproductions in You Should See the Other Guy's *Land of the Three Towers*

Caoimhe Mader McGuinness

In September and October 2014, a group of single mothers alongside their children, friends and allies occupied a half-emptied council estate in Stratford, in the East London borough of Newham.[1] This action was part of a local campaign operating under the name Focus E15 mothers. This campaign, led by the group of single mothers, had started organizing when these women collectively decide to challenge Stratford council's decision to rehouse them outside of the borough, and in certain cases, outside of London itself. Spurred by local support, the women decided to occupy two flats in the Carpenters estate for just over two weeks.[2]

The estate had slowly been emptied of most of its residents in preparation for a fabled regeneration that would see the publicly owned housing complex demolished or renovated in a joint venture with private enterprises. Angered by the fact that Stratford council was refusing to house local residents locally as it was letting the estate's flats decay in waiting for the highest bidder, the women took matters into their own hands by squatting the flats in the Carpenters under the slogan: 'These homes need people, these people need homes.' A highly mediatized occupation followed, as the occupied flats became a temporary social centre where childcare and cooking was collectivized, people could attend evening events such as film screenings and open-mic nights and where skill-shares and workshops transformed the space into a hub for London-wide housing groups. On 7 October, after a legal battle with the council, the women were able to leave on their own terms, obtaining certain concessions to their demands, including the temporary housing of several families on the estate.

The campaign remains active on many fronts in 2018, continuing to support other London housing struggles and gathering more members and supporters themselves – not least through the weekly outreach stall which the mothers have been running since the inception of the campaign in 2013. Another way the campaign and the occupation have remained visible is through performances – most prominently in work about the 2014 occupation. One of these performances, You Should See the Other Guy's *Land of the Three Towers*, emerged directly out of the protest itself; the work was created by active members of the campaign Emer Mary Morris and Nina Scott, and was performed mostly by Focus E15 activists. *Land of the Three Towers*' use of song, audience participation and site specificity created a piece of work which moved beyond a piece of agit-prop or community theatre, offering a certain amount of self-reflexivity about its own constitution, which in turn raised important questions about the representation of struggle and working-class expression. The show premiered in the community hall of the Carpenters estate in 2016 and has continued to tour, primarily to other estates fighting council-led regeneration efforts. As I will argue, certain staging choices in the performance demonstrated not only how some aspects of the campaign itself manifested Rancièrian dissensus but was also predicated on rendering visible socially reproductive labour, so as to valorize this type of labour. This in turn raises interesting questions on particular affinities between protest, social reproduction and artistic labour in a way that both corresponds with – and perhaps expands – Rancière's own articulations of dissensual practices.

Jacques Rancière defines dissensus in the following terms:

> It is a demonstration (*manifestation*) of a gap in the sensible itself. Political demonstrations make visible that which had no reason to be seen; it places one world in another – for instance the world where the factory is a public space in that where it is considered private, the world where workers speak, and speak about the community, in that where their voices are mere cries expressing pain. (2010, 38, emphasis in original)

Dissensus is then the public articulation of speech by categories of people deemed incapable of public speech, people rendered invisible due to being relegated to the realm of the private. As he elaborates: 'Tracing a line between a political sphere of citizenship and a social sphere ruled by private arrangements also means deciding who is able and who unable to address public affairs' (2010, 58). It is this relationship to who and what is deemed to belong to the realm of the private, and thus incapable, which renders the protest strategies of the Focus E15 campaign especially dissensual. Not only did the group of mothers highlight the inherent public nature of the 'home' in relationship to housing policy, but, especially during the occupation, the public nature of the activities that happen within it. In this regard, this specific occupation not only highlighted the dispossession and displacement of impoverished Londoners, especially single mothers, but also made visible the amount of reproductive labour – cleaning, childcare and other so-called domestic activities – that maintains the putatively private idea of the home. *Land of the Three Towers* also highlighted this through specific staging devices which foregrounded the public nature of reproductive labour as well as gesturing to how the occupation itself had enabled the performance not only in content but also form.

Furthermore, the ways in which both the campaign and its representation in *Land of the Three Towers* centred on questions of social reproduction – motherhood and childrearing but also cleaning, cooking and domestic labour – might also further expand understandings of Rancièrian dissensus through grounding dissensus in interventions offered by materialist feminism. I deploy social reproduction in the Marxist feminist sense, understood as the bearing and rearing of children, as well as housework, caring, and to a certain extent affective and sexual labour necessary to the reproduction of workers under capitalism. As Tithi Battacharya has recently argued, 'Social reproduction theorists perceive the relation between labour dispensed to produce commodities and labour dispensed to produce people as part of the systemic totality of capitalism' (2017, 2). Thus the term designates areas of typically feminized labour which isn't valued to the same extent as productive work is, remaining either unpaid or, increasingly, low-waged and racialized (Federici 2012, 65–75). I will consider theorizations of the relationship between work, social reproduction and primitive accumulation articulated by Silvia Federici alongside considerations surrounding artistic labour offered by Dave Beech due to their interplay in the work and their potential to expand the dissensual frame of the performance.

Furthermore, Rancière's historical work, most notably *Proletarian Nights*, which traces instances of French worker's literary and political self-expression throughout the nineteenth century – and which seems to pre-empt his conception of dissensus – also seems partly grounded in a similar quest to trace and theorize the ways in which working-class experience and culture open interstices within the capitalist mode of production, classification and domination; importantly, Rancière's earlier writings also analyse the relationship between militancy, expression and forms of devalued productive labour in a way that offers a useful parallel to socially reproductive activities. In order to set up this argument, I will first focus on the dissensual nature of the occupation itself, as well as the central role of social reproduction took during the campaign. I will then offer a description of *Land of the Three Towers* and how it figured both social reproduction as well as the disparate community enabled by the occupation. Finally, I will consider how social reproduction can be put into dialogue with both contemporary housing struggles and Rancière's historical research, through focusing on the question of labour and subsequently the question of cultural expression.

THESE HOMES NEED PEOPLE

The Focus E15 mothers had grabbed media headlines in October 2014 as soon this group of activists occupied empty council flats in the East London borough of Newham. The coverage ranged from local newspapers and sympathetic left-leaning newspapers such as the *Independent* to national television and platforms such as the *Financial Times* who used it to question London's 'Olympic Legacy'. *Guardian* journalist Aditya Chakrabortty was a particularly prolific and enthusiastic chronicler of the women's occupation and campaign as a whole. In an article titled 'For Real Politics, Don't Look to Parliament but to an Empty London Council Estate' (2014) published a few days after the flats had been occupied, he writes:

> Perhaps, like me, you look at the party conferences and despair at the minute positioning that passes as politics. In which case, turn your gaze to a flat on an abandoned council estate in east London. Thanks to a group of self-taught, radicalised women, real political action is happening there.

Chakrabortty's understanding of the political as something which is to be found away from the traditional centres of power, as well as his focus on of how the Focus E15 mothers are both radical and self-taught here resonates with aspects of Rancière's thinking. Part of Rancière's project has been to identify how Platonic understandings underpin conceptions of politics and democracy in Western thought, whether from right- or left-wing perspectives. While he uncovers Platonic tendencies in the work of philosophers ranging from Edward Burke to Giorgio Agamben to Hannah Arendt to Karl Marx, one of his strongest critiques of this tendency is to found in his reflections on contemporary French sociology and philosophy. According to Rancière, contemporary French thought, in railing against 'the apolitical life of the indifferent consumer of commodities' comes to identify democracy 'purely and simply with "modern society", which in the same blow is transformed into a homogenous anthropological configuration' (2014, 29). What Rancière identifies in this critical tendency is an anxiety about claims to equality by disparate elements and people in society, a society which comes to stand in for what democracy is supposed to be and figured as a collection of thoughtless individualists and consumers in need of expert guidance and democratic leadership. Thus, to sublate democracy into the social thus reveals an anxiety around the full equality of all people, as the mindless consumer comes to be identified with the mass of people incapable of making correct choices. According to Rancière, this harks back to Plato's pronouncements against democracy in the *Republic* as a 'regime that overturns all the relations that structure human society' (2014, 36). These Platonic conceptions implicitly or explicitly seek to organize society according to 'a natural order' dividing the world between those who need to be governed and those who possess the right titles to govern, due to a combination of kinship and wealth, evoking an oligarchic form of rule (2014, 46). This way of dividing the world between those who are seen as fit to rule and those who can only be ruled is what he calls the logic of the police, a logic 'predicated on a given distribution of qualifications, places and competencies' (2014, 53). Rancière argues that contemporary Western governments based on universal suffrage and representative democracy are thus a combination between oligarchy and democracy, 'redirected by democratic combats and perpetually reconquered by oligarchy' (2014, 54). This mixed aspect of contemporary Western liberal democracies means that paradoxically, these forms of rule 'cannot function without referring in the last instance to that power of incompetents who form the basis and negate the power of the competent, to this equality which is necessary to the very functioning of the inegalitarian machine' (2014, 54–55).

What he identifies here is a peculiar double bind in which those not deemed to be of the right status to govern still remain necessary to the egalitarian basis Western liberal democracies claim to be founded on. This contradiction leads Rancière to identify democratic practice being initiated precisely beyond state institutions and juridico-political forms of governance, manifesting exactly when these institutions get challenged, for example, through protest and demonstrations. Such actions, according to him, fundamentally transform a space which has been defined by the police as one simply to 'move along' in, into a space for the appearance of a subject: the people, the workers, the citizens (2010, 37). This consists, he further argues, 'in re-figuring space, that is in what is to be done, to be seen and to be named in it' (2010, 37). Thus, for Rancière, *'the essential work of politics is the configuration of its own space'*, a space which can only be created through dissensual practice as those considered incapable to speak lay out the validity of their political claims (2010, 37, emphasis in original).

Inhabiting a part of the half-emptied estate, the Focus E15 mothers claimed their right as social tenants and members of Stratford's community while directing the media and the public's attention towards their exclusion from both, making themselves appear as legitimate subjects. The impromptu and open space enabled by the weekly stall provides an additional example of this. Paul Watt describes the stall as a space where random connections 'occur between those suffering from housing distress and visiting journalists, playwrights, filmmakers, students and academics' and as a 'socio-material assemblage of a small table with leaflets, voices and music from the PA system, multiple colourful banners, coupled with a lively, ever-shifting melange of adults and children' (2016, 313). Despite the welcoming atmosphere of the stall, local police have demanded it be shut down several times; yet refusing 'to move along', they appropriated the space they were denied, turning a space of circulation and consumption into a spot where claims could be staked and further battles plotted.

Yet, it is not only the appropriation of denied space which rendered the Focus E15 occupation essentially political, and *dissensual*, but also how the occupation and its representations in the media made public the supposedly private activities of quotidian domestic labour. The occupation started under the guise of a 'family fun day', as the mothers chose to make children central to what could potentially be a risky action, setting the conditions for the space to remain organized around collective childcare most of the time. The filmed coverage of the occupation itself also shows various women involved in the campaign carrying children as they show journalists around the crowded but pristine flat on the Carpenters estate. As Watt argues, 'The women made strenuous efforts to keep the flats clean' in order to neither 'alienate the local population' but also highlight the 'the disingenuousness of Newham Council's claim that the estate was not "viable"' (2016, 311). This strategy in turn appeared to unsettle the possibility of framing the occupation as unwelcoming or overly aggressive in the media, as the images of the occupation that circulated inevitably painted a relatively familiar picture of a domestic interior – albeit a very public one.

Fundamentally, for Rancière, dissensus, the 'presence of two worlds in one', hinges upon 'struggling against the distribution of the public and the private that shores up the twofold domination of the oligarchy in the State and in society' (2014, 55). He argues that

> traditionally, in order to deny the political quality of a category – workers, women and so on – all that was required was to assert that they belonged to a 'domestic' space that was separated from public life. [...] And the political aspect of these categories always consists in re-qualifying these spaces, in getting them to be seen as the places of a community. (2010, 38)

The occupation, as well as the campaign as a whole, was organized around requalifying the supposedly private on three fronts. In the first instance, the mothers pushed back against the individualization of their housing claims, finding a community of struggle as they refused to obediently accept the inadequate housing solutions offered to them by the council. Secondly, their occupation is part of a wider activist movement preoccupied with showing that the wider housing crisis befalling Londoners is not the result of individual failings but of austerity measures and decisions made by local councils. Finally, and perhaps most importantly, the centrality of social reproduction to the occupation and how it was valorized, acutely revealed how the obscured sphere of domestic activities is fundamental to public life – an aspect of the occupation also crucial to *Land of the Three Towers*' staging.

IN THE *LAND OF THE THREE TOWERS*

Since the occupation, the mothers and their allies have continued to work in coalition with other London based housing groups and in Newham itself, opening a small organizing space in Stratford for local activist groups and continuing to hold their weekly stalls. The Focus E15 mothers have continued to remain visible in London's political and cultural landscape through the use of performance, both as part of their protest tactics and in separate productions narrating their struggle.[3] Since the occupation, three different performances narrating aspects of the campaign have been shown in Edinburgh and London: *E 15* by Lung Theatre (2016), *E 15* by FYSA Theatre (2015) and You Should See the Other Guy's *Land of the Three Towers*, which I saw in January 2016. All of these performances developed in collaboration with the campaigners, the first two used interviews with the mothers to create verbatim theatre pieces. *Land of the Three Towers* stands out as it was devised by and with members of the campaign itself and, except for a small stint at London's Camden's People Theatre in October 2016, was performed in sites of local housing struggles, including the carpenter's estate itself. *You Should See the Other Guy*'s artistic directors Emer Mary Morris and Nina Scott are both core members of the campaign, as are the other performers. As Elena Marchevska argues, the choices made by *You Should See the Other Guy* made this work an 'extension of the protest' due to its direct relationship to the campaigning group and the use of banners and space tied to the protest itself (2016, 115). This was enhanced when I saw the show in January 2016 at the Carpenters and Docklands centre community hall, in very close proximity to the site of the occupation itself, drawing a large audience from the local residents as well as people who had actively participated in the campaign. The night I saw the show was its first performance. After getting lost in the confusing and ever-changing landscape of Stratford, I arrived at the community hall after making my way through the quiet streets around the Carpenters estate, which felt dwarfed by the surrounding towering cranes. The space was draped with placards that have become a recognizable feature of the campaign, most prominently a large red and white banner which read 'Repopulate the Carpenters Estate'. The show's style was tongue in cheek, poking fun not only at the mayor of Stratford's hypocrisies but also the process of the occupation itself and the sustained media attention. The action follows not only the campaigners, but also showcases stories from the few inhabitants who remain on the estate. One of these narratives opened the show, just after the onstage guitar player briefly summarized what the Focus E15 campaign achieved. After this speech, one of the performers emerged from the audience wearing a pink dressing gown and introduced herself as Mary Finch, who has lived on the estate for forty-three years. As she slowly got up she tells spectators in a shaky voice how she was 'over the moon' when she first saw her new council home, advising us to not to trust the current run-down appearance of the area. Thus, as well as narrating the process of the occupation itself, the anecdotes from the neighbours account for how life was lived on the estate before it was emptied of most of its residents. While this element of the show was partly grounded in nostalgic visions of an idealized past, the detail given about how the streets I had just run through to reach the community hall might have looked and felt like created a tangible relation between the images conjured by the inhabitants and the space I found myself in right now. The picture she painted was one of neighbourly cooperation and liveliness, in contrast to the still, abandoned, streets I had just travelled through.

This gesture towards the past is also manifested in the show's name, 'Land of the Three Towers'. As one of the performers informed us, this used to be the name given to Stratford by its residents, as the three tower blocks of the carpenter's Estate used to dominate Stratford's horizon. This aspect of the show, using local residents' words verbatim, in turns contrasted with the more stylized staging of the occupation, with its inclusion of song and elements of physical theatre. For example, in a scene depicting how days unfolded during the occupation, spectators were told that much of the media, as well as supporters of the campaign, seemed to largely be composed of 'citizen journalists'. Placards and direct address were used to narrate the action as well as skilful choral singing and witty songs. One of these songs took as its starting point the specific speech pattern of one of the activists and performers. She narrated her experiences with the council's housing services, continually punctuating her story with 'like, you know'. This 'like, you know' is picked up by all the performers as a vocal leitmotiv over which different women discuss rental situations in Newham, most memorably with the line 'If you can't afford to live in Newham, then you can't afford to live in Newham.' Here, the performers transformed the supposedly unsophisticated speech pattern which punctuated one of the activists' expression with 'yeah, you know' into a skilful and humorous song. This device subverted stereotypes framing working-class women as inarticulate, transforming an apparent unrefined way of speaking and apparent naivety regarding rental prices into the leitmotiv for a song forcefully articulating the need for more housing provision in Newham.

As journalist Dawn Foster (2016) notes, 'Working-class women [...] are too often viewed as the recipients of feminist action rather than as actors in their own right, reliant on middle-class activists to articulate their demands because they are considered too unsophisticated to do so for themselves.' Yet, as narrated in the performance, the process leading up to the occupation and the occupation itself were conversely a potent and successful exercise in persuading the local Stratford community, neighbours on the estate and broader society of the validity of their mothers' claims and actions. This persuasion was constituted by dissent but also crucially through foregrounding that which would appear to make the E15 Mothers less valuable, highlighting 'mundane' domestic labour to demonstrate their resilience and ultimately their power. In terms of theatrical representation, the 'yeah you know' song can in this instance be understood as another example of dissensus, following from Rancière. Drawing from an experience of dejection at the housing office, one in which the young woman was reminded of her 'place' – a place which could no longer be Newham – she turns this experience into a refusal. This refusal is enacted not only through political action but also subsequently through her own creative expression.

Another notable device used in the performance is the recreation of the occupation's open-mic nights. The performers turn to spectators, inviting participation from the stage. Whether previously agreed or not, this device effectively evokes the slapdash, if spontaneous and supportive atmosphere of the original open-mic nights; a shy girl reads a poem from her smartphone, an angry campaigner rants at the lack of housing provision in London, an acoustic guitar player shares the song he wrote about E15 as people join in the chorus: 'A woman led revolution, taking on the boys at the top.' Most memorably, a single mother gets up and shakily sings of the drudgery of housework and the difficulty of raising a teenage daughter, a moment which becomes a bittersweet ode to familial love as her daughter joins in to declare her appreciation for her mother's efforts. The tentative singing stands in sharp contrast to the coordinated and polished feel of most of the rehearsed songs in the performance, the shyness and gentleness of the woman's voice offering a more intimate quality than the rousing musical numbers by the main performers. Yet this particular moment of expressed motherly and daughterly love, as well as the whole open-mic scene as a whole feels central to what the work aims to achieve. Although the spontaneity may perhaps have been lost, the fact that Mary Morris and Scott chose to invite this performance to be part of the show as a whole gives some indication they wanted to foreground both mother-child relationships and housework, keeping in line with the feel of the occupation. Overall, insofar as the 'official' performers and makers of the show are active members of the campaign, this recreation of the open-mic nights, seemingly with the same participants that had attended them during the occupation, reveals the pre-existing space given to performance during the occupation as well as acting as a homage of sorts to these past nights. This establishes not only a direct dialogic link between the campaign and the performance but also to the exchanges between people and forms of life which had existed during the occupation, conjured again on this particular evening – forms of life predicated on ongoing attention given to the relationship between social reproduction and militancy.

DISSENSUAL REPRODUCTIONS

Before returning to *Land of the Three Towers*, more attention needs to be given to how social reproduction has been theorized in relationship to property and labour relations, as well as how it might sit alongside Rancière's earlier historical work. Indeed, Federici's consideration of the relationship between social reproduction and the enclosure of the commons is relevant to the Focus E15 mothers own struggle. Moreover, her articulation of socially reproductive labour as labour might productively build on Rancière's arguments on devalued productive labour in his study of nineteenth-century artisans and its links to militant expression.

A key aspect of Federici's understanding of social reproduction is how necessary this form of labour is to capital. Moving away from feminist demands that push for more inclusion of women into productive work, she and her comrades declared instead that housework should be a remunerated activity. As Kathi Weeks argues, 'as a perspective, the demand [of wages for housework] was an attempt to demystify and deromanticise domestic labour, while simultaneously insisting on its necessity and value' (2011, 129). This approach thus functions on several levels: underlining the fundamental necessity of reproductive labour for both the functioning of capital and life itself, Federici points to how this is obscured by a naturalization of feminine behaviour while simultaneously insisting on the undesirability of productive work itself.

The question of women's bodies is also vital to Federici as it relates to primitive accumulation – the transition from feudalism to capitalism and importantly its attendant enclosure of the medieval commons, the land available to serfs for subsistence farming – among other activities. Federici's project departs from Karl Marx's study of primitive accumulation which focuses on the institution of new class relationships through the emergence of wage labour and the expansion of private property. Her contention is that Marx lacks attentiveness to how this process relied on new forms of control of women's bodies for the reproduction of labour power. She uncovers how sorcery became a placeholder for forms of social life not yet instrumentalized by the capitalist development, forms of life that needed to be violently eliminated and which were primarily the domain of women. Thus the enclosures of the commons – spaces mostly maintained by women – have a direct link to witch hunts, additionally destroying the ways women and workers could reproduce themselves more or less autonomously from capital. This is where her historical analysis relates back to the contemporary organization of social reproduction. The progressive dismantlement of benefits, free government–provided childcare and social housing have left working-class women increasingly unsupported outside of family networks. While Federici has never claimed that the social democratic welfare state was a form of commons or the abolition of patriarchal power relationships, it did alleviate aspects of women's lives in ways which are now being entirely overturned, as the original fate of the Focus E15 mothers shows.

As previously noted, the occupation was in keeping with Rancière's understanding of dissensus insofar as the mothers refused to let their housing issues be relegated to a set of private circumstances, choosing instead to make these issues a public question. Yet, the attention drawn to social reproduction by the Focus E15 campaign, starting with the fact those leading it strongly foregrounded their identity as working-class single mothers, performed an additional requalifying of what is perceived as belonging to the private sphere. During the occupation itself the home was figured in large parts through the domestic labour that goes into maintaining it, as the campaigners insisted on showing how these emptied homes could be transformed through the attention given to them. Thus, the occupation made visible the large amounts of putatively private domestic labour to make a statement about its necessity as a public resource. This is exactly what gave the action its strength and potential, as exemplified in an article by sociologists Kate Hardy, Tom Gillepsie and Paul Watt. Their article is based on both their own involvement with the campaign and interviews with other activists, including You Should See the Other Guy's co-director, Emer Mary Morris. Drawing from Morris's claims, they write:

> This collectivisation of social reproduction was also fundamental to the affective atmosphere of the occupation. Emer describes the tone of the occupation as 'celebratory' and argues that the Focus E15 campaign is characterised by 'a lot of love and joy and looking after each other', with children playing a central role in setting this tone. (2018, 824)

What transpires in this account is not only that foregrounding domestic labour was the result of the need to rehabilitate the formerly abandoned flats in the face of sustained and potentially hostile media attention. Rather, social reproduction and its collectivization functioned as a *fundamental characteristic* of the campaign, and through this shifted understandings of how participating in devalued collective care can create a particularly effective form of militancy. The openness suggested by the celebratory and child friendly environment, ended up drawing many disparate people to the Carpenters estate. This strategy, counter-intuitively enabled by the core activists' strong identification as mothers, enabled according Hardie, Gillepsie and Watt to shift 'register to become a broadened out demand to provide social housing for all who need it, making the mothers champions of social justice far beyond their own specific interests' (2018, 822). In relationship to Rancière's arguments, this helpfully complements the question of dissensual actions with a material focus on socially reproductive labour and can in turn be read through his historical work explored in *Proletarian Nights* and subsequent comments made in his short essay *The Myth of the Artisan*. Indeed, in both these texts Rancière also focuses on historically devalued forms of labour and their links to the militant expressiveness of some workers involved in these forms of labour.

As Rancière discusses the early nineteenth-century writings by the locksmith Gilland and the typographer Corbon, described as the 'loudest at singing the glory of work' through articulating a 'worker's ideal' he nevertheless detects a contradiction, stating, 'The representation of the worker that they bring out in the press and in politics is the fallout from an impossible fallout to escape the "culture" of their everyday working lives' (1983, 14). His observation here is meant as an intervention into social histories which contend that there was a direct link between militancy and the levels of skill of particular workers during the nineteenth century – an argument based on the understanding that the most respected and organized a worker's guild might have been, the most likely its members would have been to resist the proletarianization brought about by rapid industrialization. Rancière refutes this, through exploring the writing of a recurring figure in both aforementioned texts, the carpenter Gauny, who describes 'the experience of a life "imprisoned" by the "trap" of the proletariat' (1984, 6). Thus, at the heart of Gauny and other nineteenth-century worker's writing, is the tension between 'all those who are forced, by their place in workshop guild, neighbourhood, organization, or journal, to daily compare their dreams of the absolute with the countless shabby things in the order of the work and family' (2012, 124). In turn, Rancière argues that the verses, letters and articles written by these workers as an 'escape', a means to travel between worlds in a way he describes as 'a symbolic rupture which is constituted by the entry into writing, that is, into the domain of the literate' (2012, 13). Rancière thus argues that the desire to write proudly about a worker's culture in order to defend it stemmed in many cases from specific workers' dissatisfaction with their trade, often originating from the guilds perceived as lesser skilled and with the most repetitive work patterns, or even individuals' indifference to manual labour in general.

This 'symbolic rupture' seems to prefigure Rancière's work on dissensus, especially his critique of Platonic understandings of both social organization and aesthetics. What is already at stake in Rancière's earlier historical writings is to seek out what he later identifies as dissensual practices which 'remove[s] the artisan from "his" place, the domestic space of work, and give[s] him "time" to occupy the space of public discussions and take on the identity of a deliberative citizen' (2006, 43). Yet it is not only the foreshadowing of dissensus which is useful in this case, but also its relationship to both social reproduction and to *Land of the Three Towers*, as I will elaborate.

Weeks's aforementioned comments on the wages for housework campaign, in which she argues that these demands both refused to romanticize domestic labour while insisting on its value, offer a useful productive starting point to discuss this relationship. Her argument can be seen to echo what Rancière is identifying in earlier workers' movements: to discuss emancipation through centring certain types of labour, as the Focus E15 mothers did during the occupation, might not stem from a quest to glorify work, paid or unpaid. Rather, to return to Rancière's own formulation, it might be a means to 'escape' that work's everyday culture and imagine it anew. Following from this, the celebratory quality of the Focus E15 occupation as it is qualified by a collectivization of care in Morris's account might be understood in as similar vein. This affirmed collectivization of care is less a desire to claim that socially reproductive activities are to be taken pride in, in and for themselves. Rather, foregrounding their collectivization might momentarily offer a glimpse of some better, other organization of society that draws from the qualities of reproductive labour.

The specific nature of social reproduction as being both a form of work and a challenge to productive work also echoes remarks made by Rancière on the actuality of communism. The philosopher critiques approaches that consider there to be 'an "objective" communism already at work in the forms of capitalist production or able to be anticipated in the logic of capitalism' (2010, 82). Rather, recognizing the pervasiveness of the capitalist mode of production, he argues for being *'intempestive* or *a-topian* communists [...] occupying a site that is both outside and inside [...] framing with our thoughts, acts and struggles – a certain world of material and immaterial communism' (2010, 83, emphasis in original). Intempestive here means to belong and not to belong to a time, just as a-topian means to belong and not to belong to a place. The question posed by Rancière, is the recognition of 'an equality of intelligences', a recognition of anyone's capacity to act and think in the world. According to him 'the only communist legacy that is worth examining is the multiplicity of forms of experimentation of the capacity of anybody, yesterday and today' (2010, 171). Thus, the intempestive communism that Rancière discusses here is one not strictly tied to forms of political action and experimentation per se, but also to how people's recognition of their ability to act is fundamentally linked to their ability to think and articulate themselves as equals.

The Focus E15 campaign might be thought of as example of such an experiment, demonstrating an equality of intelligence and capacity on a variety of levels. Firstly, this was manifested in how the occupation became a hub for a huge range of people to draw from each other in order to organize for better housing provision, and affirming their expertise on housing issues against the practices of the local government. Secondly, the way the campaign interacted with the media, and aspects of the performance, reversed a specific impotence assigned to working-class women. Most productively however, it is the highlighting of social reproduction by the Focus E15 campaign which shows that beyond 'experimentation', it is the constancy of the subordinated aspect of this labour, uniquely constituted as both inside and outside of the realm of commodity production, which might render it most potent for an *intempestive* communism, to use Rancière's formulation. Through figuring social reproductive activities as a means of resistance, the campaign showed that the recognition of the capacity of everybody and anybody must be grounded in an understanding of feminized and domestic labour *as labour* but more crucially that it can be especially generative for emancipation. Beyond the occupation and the campaign itself, this reimagining of work also happened through performance, in a manner which also created a 'symbolic rupture' in the sense that Rancière understands it, constituted here by an entry into theatrical representation.

INTEMPESTIVE ENCHANTMENTS

A key question at the heart of Rancière's *Proletarian Nights* is posed thus:

> Perhaps there is a real point in letting the scene unfold as weavers and shoemakers, joiners or smiths, ask themselves about their identity and their right to speak. [...] Such is their venture as they seek to reappropriate for themselves the night of those who can stay awake, the language of those who do not have to beg, and the image of those who do not need to be flattered. (2012, 22)

It seems to me that the open-mic nights, both during the occupation and in their theatrical re-enactment, created a space in which the participants were invited to ask themselves about their right to speak. Indeed, the re-enactment of these nights invited a recognition of how performance and theatrical representation might also have functioned as a form of activist practice during the occupation. This explicitly comes up in the interviews conducted by Hardy, Gillepsie and Watt. In their article they quote another campaign member, Andrew, who states:

> We can resist a hundred evictions ... but we're not creating a culture alongside it where people can feel included ... we're just sweeping up all the mess that the government's causing. [It is important to have a space for] culture ... music, theatre ... all the things that we're not supposed to be doing because they don't produce surplus value [*sic*]. We need to reclaim that, we need to produce surplus that's for enjoyment. (2018, 825)

Similarly to the role given to social reproduction within the occupation it appears that making space for cultural expression was also a specific characteristic of the campaign. Importantly, in *Land of the Three Towers*, the forms of self-expression these open-mic nights enabled during the occupation were not presented as subordinate in the performance, but rather central to what the occupation achieved politically. Inviting the amateur performers into *Land of the Three Towers* revealed how the original impromptu acts of the open-mic nights might have provided some of the material of the show. Thus, in interrupting the virtuosity of the main performance, these raw and seemingly unrehearsed acts pointed towards how forms of unpaid and amateur labour, whether activist, performative or domestic, had enabled the creation of the show itself. Conversely, the fact that You Should See the Other Guy have also toured to show in other estates as a means to support other housing campaigns, also underlines how the performance seeks to enable and support further resistances. Drawing from the specific militant and creative space of the Carpenters Estate occupation, the performance then might serve to hopefully help engender or maintain different activist locales.

Apart from a brief stint at the Camden's People Theatre, You Should See the Other Guy has also shown the work in estates across London to tenants facing their own threats of refurbishment which would see residents 'decanted'. The performances are accompanied by workshops with housing activists teaching resistance strategies to people facing evictions. Thus, *Land of the Three Towers* is suspended between community theatre and protest performance, fitting within, yet also escaping strict definitions of both traditions. Insofar as the performance is billed alongside explicit organizing workshops, the show itself is also a sleek piece of theatre which also function as such. While You Should See the Other Guy have also performed some scenes of the show as part of protests with E15, it also offers an escape from the hardship of organizing simultaneously drawing from the labour which constitutes this organizing. Rancière contends that what might constitute the political in art is how it 'weaves a new sensory fabric by tearing precepts and affects that constitute the fabric of ordinary experience' rather than any direct attempt to intervene in 'life' (2018). Thus, rather than offering a 'toolkit' for organizing within the show itself, the politics of *Land of the Three Towers* might be locatable how it makes social reproduction visible, tearing it from ordinary experience to weave a new sensory fabric through the aesthetics of theatre. The 'usefulness' of the show to other campaigns can then also be simply understood through the types of representation it enables, and whom it offers the space to ask themselves 'about their identity and their right to speak'.

It is the question of what a performance made by and mostly performed to other activists and which draws on social reproduction as a major theme might do which I now wish to explore more closely. In the 2012 introduction to *Proletarian Nights*, Rancière argues that the poems, articles, letters and other modes of workers' artistic and philosophical expressions he uncovers were not marginal but fundamental to workers' struggles, writing,

> For the workers of the 1830s, the question was not to demand the impossible, but to realise it themselves, to take back the time that was refused them by educating their perceptions and their thought in order to free themselves in the very exercise of everyday work, or by winning from nightly rest the time to discuss, write, compose verses or develop philosophies. (2012, ix)

For Rancière here, the time claimed by workers to engage in expressions and debates typically denied to them becomes in itself a manifestation of resistance. This reconsideration of what is understood to constitute a challenge to the existing order is useful when considering the space given to artistic expression during the Focus E15 campaign and in *Land of the Three Towers* recreation of the open-mic nights. Disrupting the display of vocal and performance skill, this moment conjured aspects of togetherness modelled on what had occurred during those nights, inviting those who had originally participated as a way to remember the utopian promise of the now dispersed community of the occupation. Additionally, making space for this re-enactment might also fit with Rancière's assertions surrounding the importance of taking workers' self-expression seriously as a mode of emancipation.

The disruption engineered by the recreation of the open-mic night is also fundamental here, as it interrupted the glossier ensemble work performed by the main cast. While the 'interruption' offered by the open-mic night was seamless, the seemingly unrehearsed and sometimes timid quality of the performances was in sharp contrast to the main ensemble's work which made use of harmonious choral singing and tightly choreographed movement sequences. I would thus like to frame this interruption as a break in 'theatrical magic', as this moment drew attention to the skill and the work of the main performers, while also perhaps stressing its qualities as a piece of theatre. This deployment of the term will allow me to offer a comparison between artistic and socially reproductive labour; the concept of magic is useful in this context in relationship to how one might understand magic as predicated on masking its actual material operations through dissimulation. I thus draw on the term to refer to both social reproduction and artistic practice as both have the capacity to similarly conceal their relationship to aspects of the material conditions of capitalism, as I will discuss below. In Federici's analysis, the conjuring of magic as a threat posed by women served to obscure the shift in relationships of production in the era of primitive accumulation. She writes, 'Magic was also an obstacle to the rationalisation of the work process, and a threat to the establishment of individual responsibility. Above all, magic seems a refusal of work, of insubordination, and an instrument of grassroots resistance to power' (2017, 174). Federici argues that the persecution of sorcery is not only linked to processes of capitalist rationalization, but also as a means to suppress other ways of being together and different futures enabled by the commons, for which sorcery becomes a handy bogeyman. Thus her project demonstrates that the fear of magic is not a fear of magic at all, but essentially a means to both subordinate reproductive labour and quash the utopian possibilities implicit in this form labour. This ambiguity Federici identifies in social reproduction – the paradoxical possibilities it offers as a subordinate form of labour that does not have a straightforward relationship to other modes of capitalist production – mirrors how Dave Beech has recently discussed the contradictions of artistic labour. He recognizes that art is today a bourgeois concept implicated in capitalism, yet also argues that 'artistic labour has been allocated a specific location within the social division of labour, as abstract as abstract labour but not reducible to socially necessary average labour time' (2016, 18). The ambiguity of artistic labour is that it escapes the rationalization of time in relationship to commodity production, something Beech has recently suggested might be comparable to the ambiguity of social reproduction as a form of labour (2017). Both socially reproductive labour and artistic labour evade aspects of the capitalist rationalization process due to the difficulty of quantifying what they produce in relationship to surplus value. Perhaps both then can occupy this site, this outside/inside space which Rancière evokes, an *intempestive* site which might already hold within it a glimpse of communism.

Beech's comments also map back onto Rancière's excavating of cultural and intellectual productions of nineteenth-century workers. Insofar as interventions regarding the recognition of artistic work *as work* have been hugely important, his project, just as Beech's, is an attempt to think through why forms of cultural production might also feel, and be, emancipatory. To take back the language of those who do not have to beg is also, for Rancière 'to subvert the order of time prescribed by domination, to interrupt its continuities and transform the pauses it imposes into regained freedom [...] asserting, against the rationality imposed by the managers, their governments and experts, a capacity for thought and action that is common to all' (2012, xi–xii). Key to Rancière's project is to account for why appropriating forms of thought and expression are not seen to be proper to one's position in society. Even as workers need to find interstices within the temporal organization of commodity production which dominates the organization of their lives, these moments stolen to think and write interrupt both this temporality and their social position. Beech's suggestion that there might be a correlation between the interruption of capitalist temporality offered by forms of artistic production and the activities comprising social reproduction, and the question of valorization of the capacity of everyone and anyone offered by Rancière, materialized in *Land of the Three Towers*. The specific space given to social reproduction through artistic production, the combination showing them both to be integral to activist organizing against the state and capital, evoked how these two forms of labour might contain within them glimpses of emancipation. Thus it not only makes 'visible that which had no reason to be seen' but also indicates that to understand the domestic as a site of labour is to recognize it as a site of collective transformation beyond the walls of the home.

Federici remarks that the 'world had to be "disenchanted" in order to be dominated', yet the disenchantment of the world is paradoxically also its own enchantment (2017, 174). Thus, it is necessary, as Federici and Beech do, to demystify those forms of labour in capitalist society which might present themselves as most detached from commodity production. Conversely in relationship to the performance, to reenchant aspects of artistic and socially reproductive labour through combining both together underlines their emancipatory potential, offering strategies not only to ensure the valuation of these forms of labour, but also hints at how this valuation might point to freer ways of world-making – or, to return to Rancière's understanding of intempestive communism, the 'ability to invent worlds that are not yet imaginable' (2010, 177).

NOTES

1. I would like to first and foremost Lynne McCarthy for taking me to see *Land of the Three Towers*, aware as she is of the most exciting political and applied work happening in London as well as Nic Fryer and Colette Conroy for inviting me to participate in this collection. Additionally, my thanks goes to Louise Owen, Bryce Lease and most prominently Broderick Chow for inviting me to present a version of this chapter at London Theatre Seminar and offering probing questions about the role of magic. Thanks also to the members of TAPRA's Performing Bodies group for comments on the early stages of development of this work, as well as Shane Boyle for suggesting I read *Proletarian Nights*. Thank you of course to Catherine Silverstone and Nicholas Ridout for their initial comments on what was then my PhD conclusion. Finally, I want to express my eternal gratitude to Faisal Hamadah and Martin Young, alongside the rest of my brilliant PhD cohort for unrelenting yet critical support and engagement with the entire process of writing this chapter.

2. There are many newspaper articles and blogs discussing the campaign, including Focus E15 campaign own blog which traces the history of their activism. *Focus E15 Campaign Blog*, https://focuse15.org/ (accessed 19 November 2017).

3. See, for example, the piece of street theatre in which the activists performed snippets of the play in the Stratford Shopping Centre as a means to highlight housing issues in Newham. Focus E15 blog (2016). 'Actors Occupy Shopping Centre To Speak Out Against Social Cleansing', *Focus E15 Blog*, https://focuse15.org/2016/10/17/actors-occupy-shopping-centre-to-speak-out-against-social-cleansing/ (accessed 9 November 2018).

REFERENCES

Battacharya, Tithi. 2017. 'Introduction'. In *Social Reproduction Theory: Remapping Class, Recentring Oppression*, edited by Tithi Battacharya, 1–20. London: Pluto Press.
Beech, Dave. 2016. 'Art, Labour and Revolution'. *Art & the Public Sphere*, 5 (1): 7–21.
Beech, Dave. 2017. Untitled Conference Paper given at *Anti-Social Reproduction Conference*, Common House, 4 November 2017.
Chakraborrty, Aditya. 2014. 'For Real Politics, Don't Look to Parliament But to Empty London Council Estate'. *Guardian*. https://www.theguardian.com/commentisfree/2014/sep/23/real-politics-empty-london-housing-estate. Accessed 9 May 2019.
Federici, Silvia. 2004. *Caliban and the Witch*. Oakland, CA: Autonomedia.
Federici, Silvia. 2012. *Revolution at Point Zero*. Oakland, CA: Autonomedia.
Foster, Dawn. 2016. 'Mums Against Austerity in the UK'. *Dissent Magazine*. https://www.dissentmagazine.org/article/focus-e15-mums-against-austerity-uk. Accessed 19 November 2017.
Gillepsie, Tom, Kate Hardy, and Paul Watt. 2018. 'Austerity Urbanism and Olympic Counter-Legacies: Gendering, Defending and Expanding the Urban Commons in East London'. *Environment and Planning D: Society and Space*, 36 (5): 812–830.
Marchevska, Elena. 2016. 'Performing Inequality: Feminist Performative Acts as Protest Gestures'. *Journal of Arts & Communities*, 8 (1&2): 107–119.
Rancière, Jacques. 1983. 'The Myth of the Artisan Critical Reflections on a Category of Social History'. *International Labour and Working-Class History*, 24: 1–16.
Rancière, Jacques. 2006. *Hatred of Democracy*. Translated by Steve Corcoran. London: Verso.
Rancière, Jacques. 2006. *The Politics of Aesthetics: The Distribution of the Sensible*. Translated by Gabriel Rockhill. London/New York, NY: Continuum.
Rancière, Jacques. 2008. 'Aesthetic Separation, Aesthetic Community: Scenes from the Aesthetic Regime of Art'. *Art & Research*. http://www.artandresearch.org.uk/v2n1/ranciere.html. Accessed 9 November 2018.
Rancière, Jacques. 2010. 'Communists without Communism'. In *The Idea of Communism*, edited by Costas Douzinas and Slavoj Zizek, 167–177. London: Verso.
Rancière, Jacques. 2010. *Dissensus: On Politics and Aesthetics*. Translated and edited by Steven Corcoran. London: Continuum.
Rancière, Jacques. 2012. *Proletarian Nights: The Workers' Dream in Nineteenth Century France*. Translated by Zakir Paul. London/New York, NY: Verso.
Watt, Paul. 2016. 'A Nomadic War Machine in the Metropolis'. *City*, 20 (2): 297–320.
Weeks, Kathi. 2011. *The Problem with Work: Feminism, Marxism, Antiwork Politics and Postwork Imaginaries*. Durham, NC: Duke University Press.

Chapter 10

The Paradoxes of Performing Activism
Art, Oil and Liberate Tate
Stephen Scott-Bottoms

Dear Tate,

> *Happy Birthday. We wish we could celebrate with you. But we can't. As we write, your corporate sponsor BP is creating the largest oil painting in the world, inspired by profit margins and a culture that puts money in front of life, its shadowy stain shimmers across the Gulf of Mexico. ... Every day Tate scrubs clean BP's public image with the detergent of cool progressive culture. But there is nothing innovative or cutting edge about a company that knowingly feeds our addiction to fossil fuels despite a climate crisis.*
>
> —Liberate Tate, 'Communique #1' (May 2010)

In April 2010, BP's ultra-deep-water drilling rig, Deepwater Horizon, suffered a catastrophic failure in the Gulf of Mexico. Eleven crew members died in the resulting fire, as oil began to gush into the ocean, creating the largest-ever oil slick in U.S. territorial waters. The following month, to mark the tenth anniversary of the opening of London's Tate Modern gallery, an activist collective called Liberate Tate announced itself to the world with its first Communique, and with an unsanctioned performance action titled *Dead in the Water*. Protesters released a collection of black helium balloons inside Tate Modern's enormous Turbine Hall, which floated up to lodge against the high ceiling, where they were extremely difficult for staff to retrieve. Hanging from the balloons were the carcasses of rotting fish, whose aroma permeated the hall. In making a stink, quite literally, about BP's impact on the Gulf of Mexico's ecosystem, Liberate Tate launched what was to become a sustained campaign with a single, highly targeted objective: to persuade Tate Galleries to end its longstanding sponsorship arrangement with British Petroleum. A further fifteen performances were staged in support of this mission over the next six years, always within the precincts of either Tate Modern or its sister gallery, Tate Britain.

This chapter attempts to read Liberate Tate's campaign through the lens of Jacques Rancière's essay 'The Paradoxes of Political Art' (which, coincidentally, first appeared in English translation in 2010). Presented in three parts, the discussion marks out what I see as three key stages in the evolution of Liberate Tate's work as a collective: first 'disruption' (*of* the institution), secondly 'curation' (*for* the institution – albeit uninvited), and finally 'complicity' (*with* the institution – kind of). These stages map conveniently onto three approaches to political art discussed by Rancière in his essay: respectively, 'representational mediation', 'aesthetic distance', and 'ethical immediacy'. Although, for reasons we will come to, his own preference is clearly for the second of these modes, I hope to show that they are not neatly separable, and that each one may be strategically deployed in changing contexts. In examining Liberate Tate's campaign via Rancière's thinking, the ensuing discussion seeks to shed a constructive light on both, and to argue for the collective's performed activism to be read in distinctly Rancièrean terms – as an exemplary blending of the 'politics of aesthetics' and the 'aesthetics of politics'.

Before continuing with this mission, though, I must acknowledge a caveat. 'The Paradoxes of Political Art' has become a key reference point for anyone seeking to engage with Rancière's perspective on contemporary art, yet it is not – at first glance – the most obvious critical 'fit' for examining performance activism. Arguing for the ontological autonomy of the artwork, and thus its separation from cause-and-effect chains of political action, Rancière is openly dismissive towards 'forms of art that claim to have overcome the separation ... between artistic performance and social activism' (2010, 146). He also disparages 'the sculpture-performance model' of political art favoured by Liberate Tate (149), while valorizing film and video art. I would venture to suggest, however, that Rancière's personal artistic prejudices should not be confused with – or allowed to detract from – his aesthetic theorizing. Furthermore, a clear distinction needs to be made between the individual performance action, which may indeed be aesthetically autonomous, and the wider, activist campaign to which it relates. The former need not seek to achieve the objectives of the latter. It is this apparent paradox around which the following analysis coheres.

DISRUPTION ('REPRESENTATIONAL MEDIATION')

To understand Rancière's apparent dis-ease with art activism, it is necessary to examine his long-standing disagreement with Guy Debord and the Situationist International (SI). Although dissolved in 1972, the SI's legacy is still very much apparent: 'Today', Rancière observes, 'calls for the need to struggle against the society of the spectacle, to develop practices of *détournement*, continue to come from all quarters' (2010, 144). The Situationist tactic of *détournement*, which involves hijacking the symbols of power, in order to re-mediate what they represent (hence 'representational mediation'), is indeed a commonplace in contemporary activism, and was a recognizable element of Liberate Tate's approach from the outset. With *Dead in the Water*, for example, the polarities between (dirty) oil company and (clean) art gallery were strategically reversed by labelling the Gulf spillage as 'the world's largest oil painting', while suspending dead fish from the lofty ceiling of the Tate. Over the next six years, the gallery's distinctive logo and typeface were regularly plagiarized in the creation of literature 'interpreting' Liberate Tate's performances, and opposing BP sponsorship.

'Capital produces a culture in its own image,' writes McKenzie Wark, but through *détournement* 'its own image turns against it' (2011, 39). Rancière's objections to Debord are neatly contained in the illogic of this nutshell. An image, after all, is just an image: it cannot 'turn against' capitalism, only people can. Debord and the SI – whose 'Definitions' (1958) describe *détournement* as a 'method of propaganda' – seem to have imagined that people might be prompted into action *by* such images. Jerked out of the somnolent passivity brought on by 'the society of the spectacle', 'the spectator is supposedly induced into a specific reading of the world around us ... and ultimately [to] intervening into the situation staged' (Rancière 2010, 136). As Rancière points out, however, such assumptions are rooted in a *'pedagogical* model of the efficacy of art' which was 'debunked ... as early as the 1760s' (ibid, emphasis in original). Too often, he continues, artists and writers still postulate a 'relationship between cause and effect, intention and consequence', even though there has never been any evidence to support such a model. His most pithily sarcastic formulation of this idea recalls the stinking fish of *Dead in the Water*: 'Art compels us to revolt when it shows us revolting things' (135).

Rancière's objection to such pedagogic illogic is consistent with both *The Emancipated Spectator* (2009) and his earlier book *The Ignorant Schoolmaster* (1991). These texts present learning not as a one-way transferral of information from enlightened teacher (or artist) to obedient pupil (or spectator), but as a collaborative process of mutual enrichment. A novel or painting may be presented for the learner's consideration, but if the teacher seeks to dictate a 'correct' or 'appropriate' interpretation of the work, he is guilty of 'stultifying' the learner – by failing to acknowledge her own intelligence and the autonomy of her responses. A reader or spectator is never simply a passive receptacle for communicable contents, Rancière maintains, but is always already active: 'She observes, selects, compares, interprets. … She composes her own poem with the elements of the poem before her' (Rancière 2009, 13). Emancipation thus consists, at root, of letting people be, to respond on their own terms, rather than trying to cajole them into responding as you want them to.

It might be easy to conclude, from such arguments, that 'activists' are simply stultifying teachers, noisily trying to impose their own reading of the world on unsuspecting others who didn't ask their opinion. Certainly that seems to be the inference drawn by Alana Jelinek, who cites Rancière's critique of pedagogical art in support of her arguments in *This Is Not Art: Activism and Other 'Not-Art'* (Jelinek 2013, 152). The book's title doubly underscores a rhetorical separation of art-making and activism into separate universes. These are ontologically distinct activities, she contends, with mutually exclusive objectives. To evidence her case, Jelinek references her experience of working with Platform London on an exhibition for Bristol's Arnolfini gallery in 2009. Platform is a long-standing activist collective whose research into the oil industry has strongly informed Liberate Tate's campaign against BP. Yet Jelinek's experiences with them prompted considerable discomfort: 'I realised how "artworld" were my assumptions, methodologies and knowledge base. However political I thought I was, I had to learn from scratch the assumptions and methodologies of activism' (2013, 2).

Jelinek's emphasis on training and methods inadvertently undermines her own argument, in that it highlights institutional procedures more than ontological differences. As curator Nato Thompson contends in his book *Seeing Power* (2015), the art world's routine preference for more abstract or politically 'ambiguous' art cannot be separated from the fact that galleries and museums rely on the goodwill of wealthy donors and sponsors. Since these gift-horses are assumed to be averse to political controversy, it is no coincidence that overtly political art is so often characterized as 'didactic' – a term which, Thompson suggests, operates as 'a second cousin to "banal"', and which is 'thrown around at all things embarrassing, naïve and painfully obvious. This places the didactic outside the realm of art' (Thompson 2015, 36). This ruling dispensation needs actively to be challenged, Thompson suggests, and yet is too often consented to by radical artists who simply embrace their marginalized, outsider status as a badge of honour. In developing this argument, Thompson cites Rancière's concept of 'the distribution of the sensible' – 'the sensory self-evidence of the "natural" order [which] destines specific individuals and groups to occupy positions of rule or of being ruled' (Rancière 2010, 139). If the ruled consent to being ruled, excluded or disempowered, it is because they have accepted 'common-sense' attitudes about their place in the world, which may merely be consensual fictions (note here the linguistic links: *consent, consensus, common sense*). Politics, for Rancière, is precisely that which disrupts such established 'norms' by introducing alternative forms of sense-making.

He thus articulates the central, animating question of 'The Paradoxes of Political Art' as follows: 'Which models of the efficacy of art govern our strategies, hopes and judgements regarding the political import of artistic practice?' (2010, 135). Art can and does have political import, he maintains. Yet 'pedagogic' uses of art, in seeking to *teach* us something (else), locate art's purpose outside of itself. Such cause-and-effect thinking leaves intact the 'common-sense' separation between the art gallery and the political realities beyond its walls, which art simply comments on. But for Rancière, crucially, 'there is no "real world" that functions as the outside of art. Instead, there is a multiplicity of folds in the sensory fabric of the common', which 'passes itself off as the real' (2010, 148). Perceptions of reality are learned, and thus, to the extent that art offers different ways of seeing, alternative modes of sense-making, 'aesthetic experience has a political effect. ... What it produces is not rhetorical persuasion about what must be done. It is a multiplication of connections and disconnections that reframe the relation between bodies [and] the world they live in' (Rancière 2009, 72). By rejecting the idea that there is some causal chain of effect from 'art world' to 'real world', Rancière returns politics to art itself: 'Politics, before all else, is an intervention in the visible and the sayable' (2010, 37).

By way of illustration, Rancière offers the example of Martha Rosler's Vietnam War-era collages, which juxtapose 'photographs of the war ... with advertisements for petty-bourgeois furniture and household goods – the epitome of American happiness'. A 'pedagogical' reading of Rosler's work would argue that it functions 'to reveal the realities of imperialist war that lie underneath the standardized images of individual happiness' (Rancière 2010, 142–3): the shock of such juxtapositions is said to prompt intellectual awareness of the situation, and thus to galvanize the anti-war effort. And yet, Rancière insists, there is 'no calculable transmission between artistic shock, intellectual awareness and political mobilization' (Rancière 2010, 143). Instead, he returns to the visual shock value of the work itself to argue that the 'real forms of effectiveness' of critical art lie here, in aesthetic experience. Nobody is necessarily 'taught' anything specific by Rosler's collages, but our 'common-sense' separation of places and peoples, war and peace, is nonetheless disturbed: 'What comes to pass is a rupture in the specific configuration that allows us to stay in "our" assigned places in a given state of things' (2010, 143).

It seems clear enough, extrapolating the logic of this argument, that art and activism are not as readily separable as Jelinek suggests. For activism too, just as much as art, relies on paradoxical notions of efficacy. There is no straightforward, causal link between an activist protest and its 'real-world' effects, because there is no reason to assume that a spectator or passer-by hailed by activists (traditionally, through a placard slogan or verbal rhetoric) will necessarily be persuaded of the cause in question – let alone act on it. Indeed, what frequently neutralizes activism, politically, is the very conventionality and familiarity of the protest methods employed, which render those protesting as an expected, anticipated, *consensual* element within an existing distribution of the sensible (in short: '*we* agree that *you* will protest and that *I* will ignore you'). As Nato Thompson puts it, 'Simple protest chants [can] ring like the tedious drone of a weary, hollowed-out mass repeating itself. And to some extent, that's exactly what it is' (2015, 51). Efficacious activism thus needs better *aesthetic* strategies: 'Art and politics each [involve] a dissensual reconfiguration of the common experience of the sensible,' Rancière notes (2010, 140). Which is, I think, to imply that – far from being 'not-art' – activism is itself a mode of artistic intervention. 'Within *any given framework*,' he continues (emphasis mine), 'artists are those whose strategies aim to change the frames, speeds and scales according to which we perceive the visible' (141).

These points are illustrated powerfully by the second Liberate Tate action, *License to Spill*, which took place on the occasion of a summer party at Tate Britain in June 2010. This event marked the twentieth anniversary of Tate's sponsorship relationship with BP, and the guest list included prominent names from the worlds of art, government, finance, pop music and so forth – all there to celebrate the ongoing union of gallery and corporation. More than just a party, this was also a form of political sense-making. As Platform's research on the oil industry has established (Marriott 2011), fossil fuel companies knowingly curry favour with 'special publics' – with leaders and taste-makers – in order to maintain their 'social license to operate' (a term coined by marketing company Fishburn Hedges, for their work with Shell). A standard means of doing this is to align with the 'cool', the 'smart', the 'progressive' – tropes central to Tate's own brand as an institution – which is why association through sponsorship can amount to a kind of reputation laundering, or 'artwash' (Evans 2015). In this era of climate change and ecological breakdown, argue activists, there is a pressing need to challenge such 'common-sense' marketing tactics. Not so long ago, after all, tobacco companies seemed like perfectly 'natural' sponsors for cultural events of all sorts. Might oil companies, too, be perceptually 're-branded' as a global health hazard?

With oil still carpeting ocean and shoreline in the Gulf of Mexico, Liberate Tate devised a highly visual disruption of the summer party. A phalanx of black-veiled figures converged on Tate Britain's entrance ramp (the route into the party) to dump out gallons of a black, viscous substance from oil drums bearing the BP logo. This 'oil slick' (the material was actually molasses – treacle) oozed across the steps and entrance paths leading to the gallery, forcing them to be closed off as a safety risk. Meanwhile, inside the party, two female members of the Liberate Tate collective (who had entered legitimately with tickets) released another floor slick from containers concealed under their bouffant skirts, creating chaos for the party-goers. They then made an elaborate clown-show of attempting to 'clean up the mess', while succeeding only in spreading the substance further around the floor (see Evans 2015, 1–4).

Like Rosler's collages, *License to Spill* was essentially an exercise in juxtaposition, in which the viscous creep of the black molasses (as artist's 'material') was starkly contrasted with the pale, marbled floors of the gallery (as 'canvas'). BP's disarmingly eco-friendly sunflower logo, emblazoned on the 'oil drums', was *détourned* as a clarifying referent for anyone with a short memory about Deepwater Horizon. The visual rhetoric of the piece seems clear, but I would argue that it was the raw, sensory impact of the spill image – more than any implied interpretation – that invited its wide dissemination in press and media outlets. Correctly anticipating that photographs of the exterior spill would be widely reproduced, Liberate Tate ensured that these pictures 'spoke' for themselves: the veiled, black-clad activists outside the gallery were seen but not heard, refraining from words. In *The Future of the Image*, Rancière argues that the emotive impact of figures in still photographs derives from their 'obstinate silence', which can seem 'more truthful than any discourse proffered by a mouth' (2007, 13).

While visually forceful, *License to Spill* was not designed to persuade anyone, 'pedagogically', of the activists' cause. Although Rancière tends to assume that *détournement* or representational mediation of this sort aligns directly with pedagogic intent, Liberate Tate seem to have been well aware that making a mess of Tate properties was as likely to irritate casual spectators as it was to intrigue them. Indeed, the primary audience for this piece was the guests attending Tate's summer party, who were personally inconvenienced by the action. A larger, secondary audience saw images in the press, but the activists had no control over how these would be framed editorially. It was thus the simple fact of their presence, not what anyone made of it, that was key here. At this early stage of their campaign, Liberate Tate seem to have been less interested in teacherly persuasion than in defiant disruption – throwing an oily spanner into the smooth workings of the institution as an open expression of dissent. The previously unchallenged consensus, which allowed bosom relations between an art gallery and an oil company to be passed off as 'normal', was thus replaced by a highly visible state of *dissensus* – 'not a designation of conflict as such', Rancière specifies, but 'a conflict between a sensory presentation and a way of making sense of it', 'the presence of two worlds in one' (Rancière 2010, 139, 37).

In several subsequent pieces, such as *Sunflower* (Tate Modern, September 2010) and *Human Cost* (Tate Britain, April 2011), Liberate Tate played further variations on the textural and visual contrasts between gallery floors, messy molasses, corporate logo and silent figures in black. The group could not predict any specific outcomes for these actions – any more than they could control the trajectory of the 'oil' they spilled – but they could and did register vivid disagreement with the very institution they used as backdrop. In doing so, they interpolated onlookers as active respondents, whether pro or con. Take the example of a Channel 4 News report on the *Human Cost* action, which featured 'vox pop' responses from two gallery visitors, both of whom defended Tate's acceptance of BP money.[1] This pair had not been persuaded of a cause, but they had been asked to pick a side in a dispute that – without Liberate Tate – might not have been seen to exist. 'Political argumentation is at one and the same time the *demonstration* of a possible world in which the argument could count as an argument,' Rancière observes: the addressee 'is required to see the object and to hear the argument that he "normally" has no reason either to see or to hear' (2010, 39, emphasis mine).

CURATION ('AESTHETIC DISTANCE')

Liberate Tate could not continue spilling molasses indefinitely. As Deepwater Horizon faded into the memory of the media cycle, alternative strategies were needed to keep the pressure on Tate. Significantly, the group chose to further assert their identity as artists, as if to 'legitimise' their unlicensed presence within the galleries. This involved stepping back somewhat from overt visual rhetoric and embracing a more nuanced, ambivalent relationship with the Tate and its collections. Indeed, *Human Cost* can be read, with hindsight, as a kind of transitional piece in this evolution. Staged to mark the one-year anniversary of the Gulf explosion, the performance involved a nude figure lying in a foetal position on the floor of Tate Britain's Duveen Gallery, while two other, black-veiled figures poured sticky black liquid all over him. The eighty-seven-minute duration of the action referred to the eighty-seven days it had taken BP to cap the Deepwater Horizon oil leak, but the use of a (white) human body as (blackened) art object created a more ambiguous image than the earlier spill pieces. Was this figure a stand-in for the oil-slicked wildlife on the Florida coast? A metaphor for the 'human cost' of ruined communities? Whatever its representational significance, the figure offered a boldly visual response to the Duveen gallery itself, which in April 2011 was host to an exhibition of mostly female nude statuary. (Indeed, this context explains why the performer's male body was mis-described in several press accounts as female). Photographs of the action were again widely circulated, with the slicked figure carefully framed by the temple-like pillars and arches of the space itself. The activists became increasingly intrigued by the possibilities of capitalizing, aesthetically, on their chosen settings: 'It is the sacredness and neutrality of the gallery that we are able concurrently to utilize and disrupt' (Liberate Tate 2012, 138).

Later the same year, in collaboration with Platform and Art Not Oil, Liberate Tate signalled a more direct interest in the Tate collections by commissioning new, guerrilla audio guides for both London galleries. Launched online in the spring of 2012 under the title *Tate à Tate*, these guides were designed to be parasitic on the existing collections: listeners were invited to download them and walk with their own headphones into the galleries, as a subversive counter to the official audio guide. This intensification of Liberate Tate's dissensual, 'two worlds within one' approach saw the group positioning themselves as alternative *curators*, refusing the distribution of parts that permits only professionally assigned 'experts' the function of commenting on collections.

The relevance of such strategies to the group's campaign was twofold. On the one hand, there was a concern to counter BP's own 'curatorial' presence in the gallery spaces through schemes such as the 'BP Walk Through British Art' at Tate Britain – which entailed the corporation's sunflower logo being placed on walls as a repeating way-finder around the gallery (Evans 2015, 38). On the other hand, Liberate Tate also sought to demonstrate to the Tate's staff and governors that – far from being just an external irritant – they too were art-world insiders, passionately interested in the galleries' collections, and well-versed in art-historical concerns. As Mel Evans (a core member of the collective) explained to me in interview, their paradoxical ethos could be summed up as 'inside / outside / always on the same side':

> Anyone involved in the arts community in London is somehow connected to the Tate. Whether that's as a visitor or a member or a practising artist, you have a connection – you're a stakeholder. Now, as a stakeholder, you could just treat BP's sponsorship as something to feel guilty about, but we've tried to approach it on the level of something we might have some influence over. We're always working between those dimensions of feeling powerless but trying to somehow *gain* power. (Evans 2016)

'Power is not static in institutions,' points out Nato Thompson: 'As someone who worked in a museum, I know that even the slightest provocation demanding accountability would send ripples across the museum boards' (2015, 81). This is particularly the case in galleries which – like Tate

– 'advertise their commitment to the public good', and Thompson argues that this is a reality which political artists should take more advantage of. His point chimes with Rancière's insistence that the inside/outside distinction is itself illusory, that the art world is in and of the real world because art informs perception: 'The efficacy of art resides ... first and foremost in partitions of space and time that it produces to define ways of being together or separate, being in front or in the middle of, being inside or outside, etc.' (2010, 136). The *Tate à Tate* tours set out to explore just such a reconfiguration of 'inside' and 'outside', by using the contents of the Tate collections as a springboard for reflections on BP, the oil industry and the listener's own responsibility for environmental despoliation.

The two audio guides are, however, substantially different in approach. Phil England and Jim Welton's 'Digging the Dirt', for Tate Modern, is essentially a podcast documentary exploring BP's century-long history of ethically dubious involvements in global politics – as the corporation has taken sides in wars and revolutions according to its commercial interests. Fascinating and troubling as this account is, it bears only a tenuous relationship to the artworks that the listener is directed to look at during the guide's various 'chapters' – artworks which are described simply as 'metaphors' for the historical incidents recounted. The effect in situ, at least for this listener, was rather like having Rancière's stultifying schoolmaster lecture me (very much in the 'pedagogic mode') about the deeper meaning of artworks I would rather have experienced on my own terms. Far more successful was Ansuman Biswas's piece for Tate Britain, 'The Panaudicon', which mixes an altogether more complex range of voices, sound effects and poetic textual registers, while foregrounding the listener's own bodily orientation within the gallery.

Biswas's work begins with an establishing sequence in which the listener is encouraged to partition herself, alone, in one of the gallery's basement toilet cubicles. Here, she is provided with contextualizing information about this riverbank site's history – first as a swamp, and then as England's first modern prison, the feared Millbank penitentiary. (The toilet/swamp and cubicle/cell connotations are there if you want them.) Voices then propose that the current gallery edifice, built in the early twentieth century, is secretly a 'panaudicon' – a revision of the penitentiary's Foucauldian 'panopticon'. The playful conceit is that, by using this audio guide to lock down one's spatial co-ordinates, and to look in certain directions *through* the focusing lens of selected paintings, one is able to vastly extend one's hearing range across both geographic space and historical time. Thus, for example, guided to the romantic-period exhibits in the Clore Gallery, the listener is directed to look through J. M. W. Turner's *Childe Harold's Pilgrimage* (1832), in the direction of the Atlantic Ocean, where in Turner's day whales were being ruthlessly hunted for the oil contained in their bodies. The mysterious, lone-tree landscape of the painting becomes infused with mournful whale-song and the sounds of sailors' cries. Turning through 90 degrees on the same gallery bench, we are then invited to look in a sharply different direction, 'through' Joseph Wright's pastoral portrait of the reclining *Sir Brooke Boothby* (1781). This wealthy aristocrat gazes smugly out at the viewer as we tune in to the clanking, grinding sounds of the earliest drilling for fossil oil in the Caspian Sea. The correspondences between these paintings and the sounds heard 'beyond' them are never discussed, but the effect of looking and listening together was, for me, both haunting and disturbing. The aesthetic experience consists, crucially, in the listener's mind, somewhere in the disjunction between what is seen and what is heard. In the process, the paintings cease to mean what the BP Walk Through British Art interpretive boards say the mean, and become something altogether more troubling.

These effects resonate strikingly with Rancière's discussion, in 'The Paradoxes of Political Art', of what he calls 'the aesthetic regime of art'. This way of seeing has its roots in the late eighteenth century, when the thinking of Rousseau, Kant, Schiller and others helped inspire a new romanticism in the arts. Under their aesthetic regime, the artwork becomes more than simply a representation of something in the exterior world; it is now *some thing* – an object of contemplation, a source of 'aesthetic experience'. The object's autonomy demands no specific response on the part of the viewer: indeed, for Rancière, '"aesthetic" designates the suspension of every determinate relation correlating the production of art forms and a specific social function' (Rancière 2010, 138). But this also means that spectatorial experience is treated as autonomous. Kant, for example, distinguished between *beauty*, as a property of an object's physical form, and the *sublime*, which may only be apprehended subjectively. A sense of the sublime may be evoked by art (such as Turner's), but involves the intuition of awe or dread, something beyond perceptible forms. The potential for such powerfully personal responses is key to the aesthetic regime of art, Rancière contends, but it can also be stifled by the gallery context itself, and by the curatorial urge for art-historical pedagogy: 'our museums of fine arts don't display pure specimens of fine art. They display historicized art … a time-space of art as so many moments of the incarnation of thought' (2002, 141). In this process of institutional explanation, the viewer's response can be robbed of autonomy: 'the properties of aesthetic experience are transferred to the work of art itself, cancelling their projection into a new life' (ibid.).

Still, if the museum conventionally assumes 'specific distributions of space and time … that create specific forms of "commonsense"' (2010, 141), it is also possible to challenge such distributions through creative intervention: 'The works of the past can be considered as forms for new contents or raw materials for new formations. They can be re-viewed, re-framed, re-read, re-made' (2002, 143). Liberate Tate's 'Panaudicon' tour does just that, by introducing a self-evidently fictional premise, and inviting the listener to play along. For me, the experience felt at times as if the entire building was spinning around me, even as an uncanny sense of connection emerged between the museum's contents and the history of oil exploitation. The consensual, art-historical 'reality' staged by Tate Britain was thus turned on its head: 'Political and artistic fictions introduce dissensus by hollowing out that "real" and multiplying it in a polemical way' (Rancière 2010, 149).

Note that last phrase: for all his suspicion of 'pedagogic' art, Rancière is certainly not against polemic – against the challenge to existing dispensations that can be offered by politically-oriented provocation. And 'The Panaudicon' is not short on overt polemic: it features a running thread about the need for consciences to be awoken, in the face of environmental crisis, and indeed William Holman Hunt's moralistic Victorian painting 'The Awakening Conscience' (1853) provides the focal point for the guide's final, rapturous riff. Crucially, though, the unnamed voice articulating this struggle of conscience does so in the first person, and wrestles fitfully with its own language – questioning and challenging itself, rather than haranguing the listener. This voice contemplates the difficulty and necessity of change, without quite knowing what form that change should take. 'Art is living so long as it expresses a thought unclear to itself in a matter that resists it,' Rancière suggests (2002, 141). Something is in the process of coming into being.

Whatever *Tate à Tate* achieves as art, it seems to have troubled Tate's conscience enough to prompt its destruction. My initial experience of Biswas's 'Panaudicon', in the spring of 2012, was so affecting (dare I say, 'sublime'?) that I returned in the autumn of 2013, in the hope of re-experiencing it – only to find that every painting the guide refers to had been removed in the interim. Their places had been taken by other pictures from the collection, rendering the audio unnavigable. Some change is to be expected even in permanent collections, of course, but the extent of the tour's erasure was nonetheless striking. It appeared that Tate had acted, systematically, to neutralize the dissensual gambit of this guerrilla guide.

If *Tate à Tate* played provocatively with the institution's existing collection, Liberate Tate's next intervention offered a still more direct challenge to curatorial convention. On 7 July 2012, over one hundred volunteer art-installers converged on Tate Modern from three directions, bringing with them, on improvised trolleys, three severed sections of a single, 16.5 metre-long wind turbine arm. Gently pushing their way past the duty security staff using both weight of numbers and the weight of their freight, the activists convened at the bottom of the gallery's entrance ramp to reassemble the components as a single, large, white sculpture lying across width of the space – like a beached white whale or gargantuan ivory tusk. This was *The Gift*, an artwork 'donated' to Tate Modern; a renewable-energy turbine for the former power station's Turbine Hall. Liberate Tate had even filled out the requisite paperwork for depositing proposed artworks in the national collections. After the activists eventually dispersed, Tate was left with the question of what to do next with this unsolicited offering.

Perhaps the first thing to note about *The Gift*, in relation to every Liberate Tate action that preceded it, is that it makes no overt reference to oil sponsorship, either visually or verbally. The casual observer, on the day, might have remained unaware that this action was 'about' oil, unless they sought out an explanation (like all good curators, Liberate Tate made contextualizing literature available). In donating a found, white object to a museum, the group played knowingly on art-historical reference points such as Marcel Duchamp's *Fountain* – a replica of which features in Tate Modern's permanent collection. This white porcelain urinal, signed with the pseudonym 'R. Mutt', was donated by Duchamp to New York's Society of Independent Artists for their 1917 show, but then famously rejected by the society – despite their claim to be mounting an open-entry exhibition. Duchamp's impish proposal was that the urinal be considered for its aesthetic properties – its ceramic sheen and smooth curves. Just as he had anticipated, however, the society proved uncomfortably conscious of the connotations carried by this object from its function in the outside world. With *The Gift*, Liberate Tate posed a similar question to Tate Modern: will you appreciate the inherent aesthetic qualities of this 'found object', or will its worldly connotations (clean energy, not dirty oil) prove too unsettling?

Such paradoxical tensions between the 'autonomy' of an aesthetic object and the 'heteronomy' of its external relations lie at the heart of Rancière's own writings about old white objects. He reconsiders both the *Juno Ludovisi* and the *Torso* of the Belvedere – fragments of classical statuary that became the focus of philosophical reflections by, respectively, Schiller (on the Juno's torso-less head) and Winckelmann (on the headless torso). Such objects epitomize the aesthetic regime of art, Rancière argues, because they have been divorced from whatever representational function they once served, and can be appreciated now only for the aesthetic appeal of carved stone. 'The paradoxical efficacy of art,' he writes, is apparent in these statues' 'indifference and radical subtraction or withdrawal' (2010, 138); they appear to *mean* less than they *are*. Why is this efficacious? Because, perhaps, it begs questions of us. As Rancière argues in *The Future of the Image*, aesthetic contemplation is possible precisely because the art object itself *exceeds* whatever intentions were invested in it by the person who made it: 'The artistic phenomenon is identified as the identity, in a physical form, of thought and non-thought, of the activity of a will that wishes to realize its idea and of a non-intentionality, a radical passivity of material being-there' (2007, 119).

By the same token, the aesthetic regime of art facilitates the possibility of found objects, such as urinals and turbine arms, being re-framed aesthetically: 'By becoming obsolete, unavailable for everyday consumption, any commodity or familiar article becomes available for art, as a body ciphering a history and an object of "disinterested pleasure"' (Rancière 2002, 144). History and pleasure collide because the object's very autonomy (its subtractive redundancy in relation to external contexts) also paradoxically invokes its heteronomy (by continuing to index the world that made it). For Rancière, this ambiguous in-betweenness of the aesthetic has a strange kind of political efficacy because it 'abolishes the mimetic closure separating the rationale of fictions from that of facts, the sphere of representation from other spheres of existence' (2007, 123). The consensual distribution of the sensible into art and not-art, fiction and fact, gallery interior and worldly exterior, is thus further troubled: 'the "heterogeneous sensible" is everywhere. The prose of everyday life becomes a huge, fantastic poem' (2002, 144).

In the case of *The Gift*, the aesthetic richness of the decommissioned turbine arm's 'radical passivity' is apparent not least in the various documents of the action. For example, two online videos of the day's events tell very different stories. In one piece, for 'Vice News', a documentary narrative follows preparations for, and delivery of, the object to the Tate. Interviews with the activists provide clear statements about the 'gift' of renewable energy and the environmentalist objectives of Liberate Tate. One of the group, Tim Ratcliffe, explains that *The Gift* has been conceived as a self-conscious alternative to 'holding a placard up', because he feels creatively unfulfilled by such traditional activist methods. Yet his observation also begs the question of what exactly is 'written' on the metaphorical placard of *The Gift*, given its blankness as an object and the obstinate silence with which it was delivered. In a second video, made for Liberate Tate by Link-Up Films, the event is framed to emphasize aesthetics over objectives. Accompanied by a stirring musical score (apparently performed live on Millennium Bridge during the approach of one section of the turbine arm), the film follows the forced delivery and assembly of the object in situ. No verbal explanations are offered until, finally, an informal, vox-pop style commentary offers a riff about the action as a retort to the Damien Hirst exhibition then installed at Tate Modern. Echoing familiar critiques of Hirst's frankly mercenary orientation, the speaker suggests that the values of art have become confused with those of commerce and that Tate now seems more concerned with what exhibitions cost than with their aesthetic qualities. We are thus invited to see the arrival of the wind turbine as a low-cost rebuttal; as being – quite literally – art for art's sake. Tellingly, no mention is made of BP or oil sponsorship in this second film, in which Liberate Tate's role as the gallery's unofficial conscience seems to have taken on fresh resonances. Rancière's description of Chantal Akerman's film *De l'autre côté* could thus equally apply to *The Gift*: its 'political impact consists precisely in the way it turns an economic and geopolitical issue into an aesthetic matter, the way in which it produces a confrontation between two sides, and a series of conflicting narratives around the raw materialities of the [object]' (2010, 150).

COMPLICITY ('ETHICAL IMMEDIACY')

The Gift underlined Liberate Tate's double game of playing both outside and inside the institution. By formally requesting that Tate accept their artwork within its collections, the group invited recognition by the institution's own legitimizing discourses – recognition which might be seen to confirm the legitimacy of their cause. If, conversely, *The Gift* was rejected, then Tate could be rhetorically characterized – like the Society of Independent Artists in 1917 – as being on the wrong side of (art) history. Ingenious as it was, though, the gifting gambit also posed risks for Liberate Tate themselves: if the Tate chose to accept this gift into their collections, would the dissensual gesture become swallowed by consensual agreement? In the event, Tate's curators astutely played a double game of their own, by rejecting the turbine arm itself (as too difficult to store) but accepting documentation of the performance action – an action confronting Tate – into the Tate collection. Artists critical of institutions, Rancière writes, often run the risk that 'the mechanism ends up spinning around itself, playing on the very undecidability of its effect' (2010, 144). Liberate Tate, however, proved undeterred by the gallery's ambivalent embrace. *The Gift*'s half-acceptance underlined Tate's now-evident strategy of permitting and absorbing the activists' interventions as quietly as possible, rather than courting adverse publicity by forcibly ejecting protesters. This being the case, just how much was it possible for Liberate Tate to 'get away with'?

In September 2014, with *Hidden Figures*, the group adopted the previously unexplored tactic of advertising an unsanctioned performance in advance. The Turbine Hall, they announced, would play host to an interactive family game. In response to the then-current Tate Modern exhibition of works by Russian revolutionary artist Kazimir Malevich – including his celebrated *Black Square* (1915) – Liberate Tate would unfurl a huge, hundred-metre-square piece of black cloth. Underneath it, visitors young and old could play – just as they might under one of those colourful parachutes used at children's parties. Perhaps because the black square directly complemented the Malevich exhibition, Tate made only a partial attempt at preventing the advertised action occurring, by instituting additional bag checks on the day in question. The cloth, however, was successfully smuggled into the museum in the bottom of a baby stroller, and duly unfurled for the afternoon. 'Hundreds of visitors were playing in it,' Mel Evans recalls, 'mainly because their kids loved it, and really got the game' (2016).

Beneath the swirling, billowing ocean of cloth, visitors were invited to use their bodies to strike numerical poses on the floor – numbers invisible to those watching from above. As was made clear to anyone who enquired, these 'hidden figures' alluded playfully to the numbers hidden beneath black redactions in Tate's financial statements. Platform and Liberate Tate had been attempting for several years to use freedom of information requests to force Tate to reveal the size of its annual donation from BP, which they suspected was far smaller and less vital to the gallery's finances than either partner liked to admit. *Hidden Figures* was staged just days before a scheduled court hearing called by the UK's Information Commissioner, which resulted in Tate being forced to reveal – in January 2015 – that its annual subsidy from BP between 1990 and 2006 amounted to less than 0.3 per cent of its annual operating income (Liberate Tate 2015, 84). Ordinary Tate members collectively donated far more in the same period, and in 2013 close to half of those present at Tate's AGM supported a motion to end the relationship with BP. *Hidden Figures* invoked this wider constituency by involving the gallery's visitors in its game of gentle questioning (why so secret?). It was a striking shift from the earlier tactic of causing inconvenience through disruption.

The following year, the principles of occupying space and inviting participation were taken still further with *Time Piece*. Between the hours of high tide on Saturday and Sunday, 13 and 14 June 2015, a total of seventy-five veiled Liberate Tate activists occupied their favoured spot at the bottom of the Turbine Hall entrance ramp, and used charcoal pencils of varying thickness to write hundreds of selected textual extracts (dealing with art, oil, politics and ecology) onto the floor of the ramp itself. Starting from the bottom and working their way up the slope towards the exit doors, they created a slowly rising tide of carbon. When, at closing time on Saturday (10.00 pm), the group produced sleeping bags and even a chemical toilet from their baggage, and made clear their intention to keep working overnight, no move was made to eject them. The making of their textual artwork thus continued until the designated time for its high-tide conclusion, just before 1.00 pm on Sunday. Meanwhile, throughout day and night, extended participation with the action was invited through the use of social media hashtags. Visitors to the gallery posted online images of the performers and their written texts, while contributors in other time-zones around the world shared these images and volunteered suggestions for further textual inscriptions. Over two million social media 'imprints' were registered over the twenty-four hours, and in London, the performance trended on Twitter.

Given their varying uses of spectatorial participation, *Hidden Figures* and *Time Piece* can both be read as examples of 'relational aesthetics' – the genre christened in 1998 by Nicolas Bourriaud's book of that title, whose many manifestations since have been widely seen as signalling an artistic return to social engagement. In 'The Paradoxes of Political Art', however, Rancière dismisses such practices as further manifestations of 'the pedagogic mode' – as show-and-tell interventions in social situations which seek to model convivial relations and even 'new community bonds' between participants (2010, 147). He queries, in particular, the tactic of 'occupying an exhibition space as a way of proving the real effects of subverting the social order' (2010, 148). Such 'hyper-commitment to "reality"' constitutes, he suggests, a pedagogic tautology: 'The more art ... professes to be engaging in a form of social intervention, the more it anticipates and mimics its own effect. Art thus risks becoming a parody of its alleged efficacy' (2010, 148).[2]

This strikes me as the weakest part of Rancière's argument. If any artist really thinks they are achieving social goals through the presentation of an artwork, they must have peculiarly limited social goals. Certainly in Liberate Tate's case, the sheer scale of the environmental crises to which their work alludes forbids the kind of self-satisfaction which Rancière anticipates. Even the achievement of their stated goal of severing Tate's relationship with BP could only represent a drop in the ocean, in terms of addressing the wider issues. Bringing people together through participatory art, connecting them in (perhaps) a common cause, could only gesture towards the hope – all too little, all too late? – of mitigating the damage wrought by our collective carbon addiction. Liberate Tate's strange complicity with the institution that grew to tolerate their parasitic presence can itself be read as an index of the complicity we all share in the earth's perilous future: 'Inside, outside, always on the same side'.

Rancière's main objection to relational aesthetics seems to be that the framing of public conversations and participatory activities *as* art risks dispensing with aesthetics altogether, by eliminating the fundamental 'cut' between autonomous artwork and autonomous spectator. In 'The Paradoxes of Political Art', he makes clear his own preference for camera-based works (film, video, photography) which necessarily separate the viewer from the object of visual apprehension. Conversely, his use of the term 'ethical immediacy', in reference to relational works, invokes *im-mediate* in the literal sense of 'without separation'. And yet as Gareth White has convincingly argued, one can be completely immersed within a performance event and not lose one's critical objectivity – just as one can dive into water without turning into a fish (White 2012). If, as Rancière himself consistently argues, aesthetic experience is a matter of personal perception, then an autonomous spectator can contemplate the aesthetic in any time or place, no matter how quotidian or enveloping the object of contemplation may be.

Moreover, the sheer scale of the objects that Liberate Tate's work became oriented towards – the great white tusk of the turbine arm, the enormous black cloth of *Hidden Figures*, the rising tide of *Time Piece*'s charcoal textuality – tests the very concept of 'aesthetic distance'. If you're far enough away to see the whole thing at once, you're not close enough to absorb the details (the written words, the folds of the fabric): these are only fully apparent when you're enveloped by the work. I am tempted, here, to appropriate Timothy Morton's term 'hyper-objects', which refers to enveloping realities such as climate change, nuclear waste, oceanic pollution. These are problems engendered by humans but 'massively distributed in time and space relative to humans', and thus of such dimensions that they are literally unrepresentable, even incomprehensible, at the human scale (Morton 2013, 1). They immerse us, with ethical immediacy.

Rancière has elsewhere noted that the urge to visualize the inconceivably huge has been a stimulus for human creativity since (at least) the time of the ancient Egyptians, who sought to express their sense of divinity by building the pyramids, and ended up with sublime failure, a 'surplus of presence'. We cannot represent the unrepresentable today any more than we could then, 'but this maladjustment tends towards more representation, not less: more possibilities for constructing equivalences, for making what is absent present' (2007, 137). The massive black square of *Hidden Figures* is a case in point: beyond its reference to textual redactions, and the continuing connotations of oil slick, it invokes Malevich himself, whose monochrome canvases constituted a revolutionary attempt, in the era of Russian Revolution, 'to replace the production of paintings with attempts to frame new forms of life' (Rancière 2010, 147). Stepping beyond existing strategies of representation, Malevich sought to evoke the unknowable – just as Liberate Tate reference vast global problems through paradoxically circumscribed means. The participatory game aspect of *Hidden Figures* underlines this knot of impossibilities by adopting 'a specific mode of address that delivers the thing represented over to affects of pleasure, play or distance which are incompatible with the gravity of the experience it contains' (Rancière 2007, 110). Conversely, the durational, almost funereal silence of *Time Piece* suggests a vast, oceanic mourning for the rising seas.

'Aesthetic art promises a political accomplishment that it cannot satisfy, and thrives on that ambiguity,' suggests Rancière: 'That is why those who want ... to fulfil its political promise are condemned to a certain melancholy' (2002, 151). As their black garb and veils have signalled from the outset, 'melancholia' is a self-conscious component of Liberate Tate's aesthetic: 'our work grieves the loss of life, habitats, forests, water sources, cultures and communities' brought about by BP specifically, and by capitalist economies more generally (Liberate Tate 2012, 136). A sense of collective responsibility for this great extinction is nowhere more clearly illustrated than in *Birthmark*, made for Tate Britain in December 2015, which turned out to be the final Liberate Tate action before the galleries announced their split with BP the following spring. It was also the only live action made by the group at which I was personally present.

Timed to coincide with the latest exasperating round of inter-governmental climate change talks in Paris, *Birthmark* entailed the group smuggling the contents of a functioning tattoo parlour into Tate Britain's '1840' gallery. In this temple-like space, Liberate Tate set up a 'sacrilegious' juxtaposition of high art and body art – patrician versus plebeian, oil on canvas versus ink on skin. In a roped-off 'altar' area at one end of the gallery, tattoos were administered to participants (like communion) by activists trained in basic tattooing skills. Those of us waiting our turn for the needle sat in the 'nave' of the gallery, adding weight of numbers to the occupation. Each tattoo consisted of just three, small digits, corresponding to the estimated parts per million of carbon dioxide in the earth's atmosphere, during the year of the individual's birth. In my own case, born in 1968, the number was >323, although for younger participants the numbers rose precipitously towards the present.

Birthmark thus invoked the hyper-object of climate change, but the mark itself is small and personal rather than big and intrusive. The piece's conceptual reach extends well beyond the 1840 gallery as the individual participants – now broadly distributed in time and space – continue to carry this branding through daily life. Speaking for myself, I can confirm that conversations about my tattoo occur quite often, in response to questions from friends and strangers alike. In those moments, I usually replay some of what I discussed with Mel Evans, when she inked me. As each of us received our tattoos, we were invited to participate in a contemplative dialogue about what had led us to this moment. It felt to me something like a ceremony of confession, since the increase in atmospheric carbon levels during our own lifetimes is something that each of us is complicit in.

This ritualistic experience in the 1840 Gallery was markedly enhanced by the complicity of Tate itself. Although the action had been planned with characteristic secrecy, Liberate Tate again found that, once they occupied the space, the organisation's security response was simply to permit the action and wait it out. In this case, they closed two of the gallery's three doors, and placed a security guard at the remaining side-entrance to prevent anyone besides Liberate Tate activists from coming in or out. The gallery thus became an exclusive, cloistered space, into which – all day long – curious onlookers peered at the tattooists, or craned their necks round the door to catch a glimpse of this room's most famous painting, John Everett Millais's *Ophelia* (1852).

Meanwhile, identifiable to staff by our uniform black clothing, the occupiers were able to come and go as we pleased – almost as if we had become 'authorised' by the gallery. This blurred relationship between the official and the insurgent was further underlined by the presence, in the open doorway, of stacked copies of an interpretive booklet about *Birthmark*, which as usual hijacked Tate's fonts and design style.

If the relationship between activists and gallery seemed almost uncomfortably close on this occasion, it is worth underlining the very *normalcy* of the situation. Over a period of years, Liberate Tate had succeeded in establishing a new 'common-sense' dispensation within the galleries, whereby they could basically do anything they pleased in Tate's precincts – even scar bodies for life – without any kind of prior permission. As Nato Thompson notes, 'when it is unclear who holds power in a room, the room becomes a space where anything is up for grabs' (2015, 137). The very next weekend (4–6 December 2015), Platform drove a metaphorical truck into this newly cleared room by hosting a three-day festival of talks and events – the 'Deadline Festival' – in spaces all over Tate Modern. This included contributions from playwright Caryl Churchill, geographer Doreen Massey, Green Party leader Natalie Bennett, and a host of others. The Deadline Festival signalled that there was just one year left in Tate's existing deal with BP, and that a deadline for decision was looming on the future of that relationship. Although entirely unsanctioned by the institution, the festival was advertised in advance and went ahead uninterrupted, as a very public, participatory celebration of the need for Tate to change its policies. This was a situation that, from Tate's point of view, had plainly become unsustainable: when you have 'two worlds within one' this publicly, and this persistently, something has to give. In March 2016, Tate Galleries and BP announced that their longstanding sponsorship arrangement would come to an end when the current deal expired at the end of the year. 'What "dissensus" means', Rancière concludes, is 'that every situation can be cracked open from the inside' (2009, 48–49).

CONCLUSION

It is important to underline that no claims are being made here for any direct, cause-and-effect relationship between Liberate Tate's unsanctioned performances and the ending of the gallery's sponsorship deal with BP. Tate itself never acknowledged such a link, and there were also no doubt other factors at play in the decision. Certainly there is plenty of evidence (including minutes of board meetings and personal testimonies) that the campaign prompted extensive arguments and soul-searching within the organization. But no single demonstration – no single artwork – by Liberate Tate necessarily changed anything in terms of direct causality. As Rancière notes, it is vital that 'critical art' not make false assertions as to its efficacy, but is instead 'an art that questions its own limits and powers, that refuses to anticipate its own effects' (2010, 149). Moving stubbornly forward without ever knowing if their goal would be achieved, Liberate Tate's impact was not singular but cumulative, as their dissensual aesthetics gradually normalized other kinds of sense-making than the gallery's own. They did not 'teach' the Tate or its visitors in any pedagogic mode, nor any relational one. What they did was simply present – in action after action, with implacable and usually silent obstinacy – another perspective that previously had no cause to be seen. 'Practices of art do not provide forms of awareness or rebellious impulses *for* politics,' asserts Rancière towards the end of 'The Paradoxes of Political Art': 'Nor do they take leave of themselves to become forms of collective political action. They contribute to the constitution of a form of commonsense ... a new landscape of the visible, the sayable and doable' (2010, 149, emphasis in original).

The inverse of this 'politics of aesthetics' is, as Rancière further notes, the 'aesthetics of politics', which 'lies in a re-configuration of the distribution of the common through political processes of subjectivation' (140). Which is to say, I think, that there is an art to shifting the way people think and feel about who holds power and with whose consent. During the six-year period of Liberate Tate's campaign – as their aesthetic approach shifted from disruption through curation to oblique participation – the campaign to end oil sponsorship of the arts moved from the fringes to the mainstream, and spread to target other museums and theatres. During the same period, wider debates about fossil fuel divestment by universities, pension schemes and other institutions also gathered pace. One index of this shift in 'common sense' is the position of the *Guardian*'s art critic, Jonathan Jones, who had responded to Liberate Tate's earliest performances with deadpan dismissal: 'If [Tate] can get money from Satan himself, they should take it' (Jones 2010). By 2017, following the 'liberation' of the Tate, Jones's process of 'political subjectivation' was apparent in his public call for the National Portrait Gallery, too, to end its sponsorship relationship with BP. 'We should be prepared to say some things matter more than art,' he wrote: 'And they do.'

NOTES

1. See https://vimeo.com/26729208.
2. Note: the original text of Corcoran's translation reads: 'The more it goes into the streets and professes to be engaging in a form of social intervention, and the more anticipates and mimics its own effect.' I have here amended the apparently misprinted dependent clause so as to make grammatical sense of the sentence.

REFERENCES

Evans, Mel. 2015. *Artwash: Big Oil and the Arts*. London: Pluto.
Evans, Mel. 2016. *Unpublished Interview with the Author*, 29 August.
Jelinek, Alana. 2013. *This is Not Art: Activism and Other 'Not-Art'*. London: I. B. Tauris.
Jones, Jonathan. 2010. 'Tate is Right to Take BP's Money'. *The Guardian*, 29 June. https://www.theguardian.com/culture/jonathanjonesblog/2010/jun/29/tate-bp-sponsorship.
Jones, Jonathan. 2017. 'Is it Time for the Arts to Start Saying No to Oil Money?' *The Guardian*, 8 September. https://www.theguardian.com/environment/2017/sep/08/is-it-time-for-the-arts-to-start-saying-no-to-oil-money.
Liberate Tate. 2010. *Communique No. 1*. http://www.liberatetate.org.uk/liberating-tate/about/.
Liberate Tate. 2012. 'Disobedience as Performance'. *Performance Research* 17(1), 135–140.
Liberate Tate. 2015. 'Confronting the Institution in Performance: Liberate Tate's Hidden Figures'. *Performance Research* 20(4), 74–84.
Linkup Films. 2012. 'The Gift'. https://vimeo.com/45369224.
Marriott, James. 2011. 'A Social License to Operate'. *New Left Project*. http://www.newleftproject.org/index.php/site/article_comments/a_social_license_to_operate.
Morton, Timothy. 2013. *Hyperobjects: Philosophy and Ecology after the End of the World*. Minneapolis, MN: University of Minnesota Press.
Rancière, Jacques. 2002. 'The Aesthetic Revolution and Its Outcomes'. *New Left Review* 14, 133–151.
Rancière, Jacques. 2007. *The Future of the Image*. Translated by Gregory Elliott. London: Verso.
Rancière, Jacques. 2009. *The Emancipated Spectator*. Translated by Gregory Elliott. London: Verso.
Rancière, Jacques. 2010. *Dissensus: On Politics and Aesthetics*. Translated and edited by Steven Corcoran. London: Continuum.
Situationist International. 1958. *Definitions*. Translated by Ken Knabb. https://www.cddc.vt.edu/sionline/si/definitions.html.
Thompson, Nato. 2015. *Seeing Power: Art and Activism in the 21st Century*. New York, NY: Melville House.
Vice News. 2012. 'The Gift'. https://vimeo.com/83778146.
Wark, McKenzie. 2011. *The Beach Beneath the Street: The Everyday Life and Glorious Times of the Situational International*. London: Verso.
White, Gareth. 2012. 'On Immersive Theatre'. *Theatre Research International* 37(3), 221–235.

Index

absence, 10, 28, 98, 117, 129, 143
activism, 7, 10, 12, 76, 171, 172, 179, 181, 200–201, 208–9, 212, 215–20, 228. *See also* activists; protest/protesters
activists, 29–30, 128, 188, 190, 196, 198, 202, 205, 209, 218, 220–23, 226–34. *See also* activism; Focus E15; Liberate Tate; protest/protesters
aesthesis, 26, 43
the aesthetic, 20, 22–24, 31, 34, 43, 46, 110, 113, 228, 232
aesthetic community, 101, 109, 111, 113
aesthetic experience, 19, 24–25, 27, 85, 110, 113, 219, 225, 231
aesthetic regime(s), 5–6, 8–9, 18–19, 22, 34, 43, 52, 60, 85, 98, 110, 117–18, 225, 227–28
aesthetics, 1, 8–10, 28, 41, 67, 73, 92, 129, 180, 187, 206, 209, 228, 231, 235; Kantian, 110–11, 113; and politics, 5–9, 20–21, 23–25, 28–31, 33, 35, 41, 43, 62, 67, 81, 83, 86, 89–90, 92–94, 98, 104, 125–26, 180, 216, 223, 235; and theatre/performance, 10, 42, 46, 96, 180, 209, 216, 228
aesthetic strategies/practices, 7–9, 12, 220

affect, 51–52, 69, 72, 77, 143, 172, 181, 185, 190, 192, 197, 205
agency, 85, 101, 105, 108, 112, 117–18
Althusser, Louis/Althusserianism, 21–22, 64–66
anarchy/anarchism, 7, 177
Aristotle, 25, 66, 102, 104, 106, 157; Aristotelian model of acting, 109
audience, 1–4, 6, 10–11, 39, 43, 69, 72, 74–76, 83–88, 93–96, 103, 111, 126, 128–38, 140–41, 143, 173, 188, 190, 201, 221; address, 41, 47–49, 51; participation, 69, 74–77, 196. *See also* spectators/the spectator; spectatorship

Banham, Simon, 87
Barthes, Roland, 52
Beech, Dave, 197, 211, 212
Biswas, Ansuman, *The Panaudicon*, 224–26
blackface minstrelsy, 133–35
Black Lives Matter, 182, 184
bodies/the body, 10, 41, 46–52, 139, 143, 158, 163, 204, 219, 230, 234; and counter-bodies, 10, 41; pensive, 51–53; on stage/of performers, 3, 39–40, 43–44, 49–50, 52–53. *See also* corporeality; embodiment

bots/bot armies, 31–32
BP (British Petroleum), 12, 215, 217–18, 220–25, 228, 230–31, 233–35
Butler, Judith, 89

capitalism/capitalist, 9, 17, 30, 32–35, 40, 128, 130, 172, 180, 197, 204, 207, 210–12, 217, 233. *See also* neoliberalism, neoliberal capitalism
Carnes, Mark C., 151–53, 155–57, 160, 163
Carpenters Estate, 195–96, 200–202, 205, 209
characterization, 67, 69–72
citizens, 48, 91, 102–3, 108, 138, 157, 175, 178, 181, 188, 199, 202, 206
citizenship, 73, 171, 182, 196
Coborn, Charles, 126, 139–42
Collins' Music Hall, 11, 126, 129–30. *See also* music hall; Sprake, Herbert
common sense, 174, 219–20, 225, 235; the common sensorium, 24, 30–31; *sensus communis*, 113
communality, 40, 44
communism, 33, 65, 207–8, 211, 212
community, 10–11, 25, 40, 43–45, 85, 90, 101–15, 119, 156, 182, 185, 197, 199–200, 202, 210, 231; aesthetic, 101, 109, 111; and art/theatre, 10, 102–3, 106, 108–9, 118, 173; 'ethical', 104–5, 112–14; individual's role/place in, 102–3, 109; political, 105–7; representations of, 3, 84, 91, 196; of thought/intelligence/speech, 84, 96, 115, 176
community theatre, 91, 196, 209
Confucius/Confucianism, 154–55, 159, 162–64
consensus, 5, 11, 13, 23, 82, 84, 93–94, 104, 109, 119, 127, 175–76, 185, 219, 221; and dissensus, 11, 171, 174–76, 181
consent, 174, 218–19, 235
constructivism, 149–51, 161

contemporary art, 19–24, 30, 34, 104, 216
corporeality, 10, 41, 47, 53; corporeal intelligence, 41, 51, 52. *See also* bodies; embodiment
Cox, Emma, 188–90

Debord, Guy, 217
Deepwater Horizon, 215, 221–22
de Gouges, Olympe, 175, 182, 188
Deller, Jeremy, 87
democracy, 45, 84–85, 88, 90, 92, 94, 98, 104, 152, 154, 156, 171, 177, 186, 198; and participation/debate, 96, 108; politics/political regime of, 86, 186, 198; post-democracy/the post-democratic, 82–83, 92–94, 98; practice/procedures of, 177, 199, 205; and representation, 82, 89–91, 94, 98; representative, 82, 89–90, 176, 199; and theatre, 86, 186, 190; Western/liberal, 179, 199. *See also* dissensus; theatrocracy
Demolition Incorporada, *Dança Doente*, 39–41, 43–44, 48, 49, 52, 53n1
detournement, 217, 221
didacticism, 11–12, 189, 218
dissensus, 11–12, 104–6, 108, 110, 112, 127, 174–77, 186–87, 196–97, 200, 205, 206–27, 221, 234; and consensus, 11, 13, 171, 174–76, 181; and theatre/performance/artistic practice, 106, 114, 127, 136, 139, 143, 203, 226
distribution of the perceptible. *See* distribution of the sensible
distribution of the sensible, 2–5, 19, 24, 34, 40–43, 45–47, 52, 81, 85, 92, 98, 102–7, 110, 114, 118, 157, 164, 165n3, 174, 176, 179–83, 186, 188, 218, 220, 228
dramatization, 10, 60–61, 63, 69, 76–77, 84
dramaturgy, 9, 41, 47–51, 53, 63, 69, 84, 88, 91, 95–97, 127, 163–64, 187

Duchamp, Marcel, 227

education, 23, 61–62, 73, 77, 105, 110, 116–17, 126, 137, 138, 141, 144n3, 147–50, 152, 154, 156, 163; higher/ university, 11, 147, 150–51, 155–56, 160, 163–64; models/systems/ processes of, 62, 66–67, 72–73, 75, 77, 148; universal, 11, 147–51, 155–56, 160–61, 163–64. *See also* Jacotot, Joseph; Rancière, *The Ignorant Schoolmaster*
educational roleplay/games/simulation, 143
educational theatre, 77, 125
emancipation, 23, 28–29, 32, 62, 64–65, 72, 77, 96, 112, 115, 148, 150, 182, 188, 207–8, 210–12, 208; emancipated spectatorship, 46, 49, 85, 131, 171; emancipating educator(s), 151, 160–62, 164; emancipatory politics, 20, 27, 183; intellectual, 62, 64, 68, 155
embodiment, 10, 46, 50–51, 84–85, 88–89, 92–93, 97, 183, 188–90; embodied experience/ perceptions, 47, 52; embodied knowledge, 41, 162. *See also* bodies; corporeality
Emperor Wanli. *See* Ming dynasty
equality, 11, 31, 45, 59, 62, 66, 68–69, 73, 77, 84, 86, 116, 127, 142–43, 148, 151, 156, 160–64, 171, 176–77, 181–84, 186, 198–99; of intelligence/ intellect, 21, 62, 70, 73, 75, 116, 147, 150–51, 164, 207; presumed, 62–63, 86, 199; radical, 19, 66, 68, 115, 181. *See also* theatrocracy
ethics/the ethical, 42, 104, 109–10, 181, 185, 188, 216; and community, 104, 107, 109, 112, 114, 185; 'the ethical turn' 104; immediacy, 216, 229–34; regime of art, 6
Evans, Mel, 223, 230, 233
Evelin, Marcelo, 39–40, 49, 54n10

Fan, Ssu, *Longing for Worldly Pleasures*, 155
Federici, Silvia, 219, 226, 233–34
feeling, 19, 110, 117, 135, 163. *See also* affect
Fénelon, François, *Les Aventures de Télémaque*, 62, 68, 72, 148, 156, 160. *See also* Jacotot, Joseph; Rancière, *The Ignorant Schoolmaster*
Fisher, Tony, 89, 172–73, 189
Focus E15, 195–96, 198–201, 204–5, 207–8
Fox News, 4
Freitas, Marlene Monteiro, 51; *Bacchae-Prelude to a Purge*, 41, 44, 48–49, 52–53
Freire, Paulo, 150–51

Gameful design, 152–53, 155, 158–59, 165
game theory, 152
genius, 158
global migration. *See* migration
Gregory, Richard, 87

Hallward, Peter, 1, 7, 12, 59, 65, 102, 106–7, 115, 125, 142, 177, 179, 190
Hamilton: An American Musical, 1–2, 6–7
Hegarty, Antony, 185
heterology, 44
heteronomy, 18, 190, 227–28
Hirst, Damien, 228
historiography, 11, 126, 131, 143, 156
history/histories, 1, 6, 29, 65, 69–70, 96, 125–28, 131, 137, 151, 154, 156–57, 197, 204, 206, 224, 226, 228–29; art, 17, 19, 43, 223–27, 229; (post) colonial, 41, 45; in roleplay/games, 154–58; social/labour, 83, 126–28; theatre, 9, 11, 47, 119, 126, 127–32, 140, 143, 172, 185
Ho Rui An, *Solar: A Meltdown*, 41, 44–45, 50–53

humour, 45, 61, 69–71, 132, 134, 137, 139, 202

inequality, 19, 35, 62, 66, 73–74, 76, 85, 125–26, 148, 164, 177, 184, 185, 187–88
irony, 61, 69–71, 187

Jackson, Shannon, 180–81, 187, 190
Jacotot, Joseph, 21, 61–64, 66–77, 147–48, 155–56, 161, 182, 189. *See also* Rancière, *The Ignorant Schoolmaster*

Kant, Immanuel, 110–11, 225
Kantian aesthetics. *See* aesthetics
King, Alison, 149, 161
Kuppers, Petra, 185, 190

labour, 9, 11, 25, 28, 65, 92–93, 97, 126–28, 134–36, 138–39, 141, 143, 187, 196–97, 204, 206–9, 211–12; affective, 181, 197; artistic/theatrical, 12, 23, 97, 126–27, 133, 135, 138–39, 143, 196–97, 210–11; domestic, 197, 200, 203–8, 212; labouring class/labourers, 5, 128, 143; relations, 91, 204; socially reproductive, 12, 97, 196–97, 204, 206, 210–12. *See also* Rancière: *The Nights of Labour/Proletarian Nights*
Liberate Tate, 7, 12, 215–35; *Birthmark*, 233–34; *Dead in the Water*, 215–17; *The Gift*, 226–29; *Hidden Figures*, 229–32; *Human Cost*, 222–23; *License to Spill*, 220–22; *Sunflower*, 222; *Tate à Tate*, 223–26; *Time Piece*, 230–32
logos, 25–26, 31, 66

Mackenzie, Iain and Robert Porter, 10, 60–61, 63–64, 67, 69–71, 76
Macmillan, Duncan, *People, Places and Things*, 10, 101, 108–9, 114, 119–20
Malevich, Kazimir, 229, 232
Mallarmé, 101, 113

May 1968 uprisings, 20–21, 33–34, 65, 127, 184
May, Todd, 177, 184
Michelet, Jules, 84, 86
migration, 187–89
mimesis/the mimetic, 18, 43, 46, 52, 102, 128, 142, 228
Ming dynasty, 154–55, 157, 162–63
Morris, Emer Mary, 196, 201, 203, 205
Mouffe, Chantal, 177, 179, 183, 191n8
music hall, 11, 126–30, 134–41

neoliberalism, 10, 29, 40–41, 43, 171–73, 175; neoliberal capitalism, 21, 30, 172; neoliberal individualism, 118, 186
Nyoni, Zodwa, *Nine Lives*, 189–90

Obamacare (the Affordable Care Act), 178
the Occupy movement, 89, 107

participation, 2, 4, 11, 44, 67, 69, 74–76, 84, 96, 102, 130, 159, 176, 196, 203, 230–35
pedagogy, 11, 62, 74–75, 77, 114–15, 117, 147–51, 153, 158–59, 161, 163–64, 182, 217, 231; models/theories of, 62–63, 68–70, 72–73, 77, 149–50, 156, 159, 164, 217; pedagogic theatre/art, 218–19, 221, 225–26; 'the pedagogue'/the pedagogic mode, 147–48, 164, 224, 231, 235. *See also* education
Pence, Mike, 1–7
pensiveness, 10, 41, 51–53; pensive bodies, 9, 51–53; the pensive image, 10, 51
'the people', 10, 31, 65, 81–86, 88–90, 92–95, 97–98, 142, 181, 199. *See also* Rancière, *Staging the People*
people's theatre, 84–86
phonê. *See logos*
Platform London (Platform), 218, 223, 230, 234

Plato, 12, 28, 62, 65–66, 102–6, 128, 154, 198, 206; *The Laws*, 84; *The Republic*, 28, 84, 102, 104, 152, 198
play, 5, 11, 19, 41, 44, 48–49, 67, 96, 134–35, 143, 147, 151–58, 160–64, 226, 229–30, 232. See also role-play
playfulness, 51, 134
poiesis, 19
police, 2, 6, 11, 26–30, 33–34, 45, 50, 106, 156–57, 173–74, 177–81, 183–84, 186, 188, 199
the political, 5, 22–23, 66, 76, 83, 89, 92, 172, 198, 209
political agency. See agency
political art, 5–6, 22, 23, 50, 54n12, 112, 173, 181, 216, 218, 224. See also Rancière, 'The Paradoxes of Political Art'
political philosophy, 7, 10, 59–60, 107, 128
political subjectivation, 5, 44–45, 49, 89, 91–92, 188, 235
political theatre, 6, 131, 172, 173, 180, 190
politics, 2, 6–7, 9, 11–12, 23–28, 31, 34–35, 42–43, 45, 50, 65, 73–74, 82–83, 90, 92–94, 98, 104–5, 112–13, 115, 125, 127, 138–40, 156–58, 173, 175–79, 181–86, 189–90, 198–99, 206, 209, 219, 224, 230; and aesthetics, 5–9, 20–21, 23–25, 28–31, 33, 35, 41, 43, 62, 67, 81, 83, 86, 89–90, 92–94, 98, 104, 125–26, 180, 216, 223, 235; and/of art, 5–7, 9, 12, 20–25, 27, 34, 73, 219–20, 235; and/ of perception, 3, 25, 40–42, 47, 53; and police, 2, 6, 11, 29, 106, 196, 208; and/of theatre/performance, 3, 8, 9, 11–12, 20, 28, 41–42, 60, 81, 89, 102, 104, 125, 126, 171–73, 181, 185, 187, 189, 209. See also political art; political theatre
populism, 42, 82–83, 179
Porter, Robert. See Mackenzie, Iain

post-dramatic, 41–42, 46–47, 86, 92, 94, 98, 171–72, 187
post-identitarianism/anti-identitarianism, 171, 183
post-political, 171, 175, 179
protest/protesters, 12, 29, 32, 43, 65, 188, 192n9, 196, 199, 201, 209, 215, 220, 229. See also activism; activists
the Pylades, 126, 136–39, 142

quarantine: *Quartet (Summer, Autumn, Winter, Spring)*, 87, 94–98; *See-Saw*, 86–87; *What Is the City but the People?*, 87–89

Rancière, Jacques, published works of: 'The Actuality of *The Ignorant Schoolmaster*', 148; *Aesthetics and its Discontents*, 110, 112–13; 'Aesthetics and Politics', 104; 'Aesthetic Separation, Aesthetic Community', 101–11, 113; *Aisthesis: Scenes from the Aesthetic Regime of Art*, 8, 18, 43, 45–46, 53, 54n14; *Althusser's Lesson*, 20, 64, 65; *Disagreement: Politics and Philosophy*, 115, 156, 165n3, 186; *Dissensus: On Politics and Aesthetics*, 174, 176, 182; *The Emancipated Spectator* (collection), 101, 112, 172, 217; 'The Emancipated Spectator' (essay), 4, 6, 45–46, 51, 112, 115–17; 'The Ethical Turn of Aesthetics and Politics', 104; *The Future of the Image*, 221, 227; 'Good Times, or Pleasure at the Barriers', 105; *The Ignorant Schoolmaster: Five Lessons in Intellectual Emancipation*, 10, 11, 59–61, 63–64, 66–67, 76–77, 105, 112, 114–17, 120, 147–51, 155, 158, 160, 162–63, 182, 217; 'The Misadventures of Critical Thought', 112; 'The Myth of the Artisan', 206; *The Nights of Labour/Proletarian*

Nights: The Worker's Dream in Nineteenth Century France, 5, 11–12, 66, 70, 127, 128, 144n2, 197, 206, 208, 210; 'On Ignorant Schoolmasters', 148; 'The Pensive Image', 51; *The Philosopher and His Poor*, 11, 66, 128; *The Politics of Aesthetics: The Distribution of the Sensible*, 5, 40, 42, 45, 50, 53n3, 102; *Staging the People*, 83–84, 98; 'Ten Theses on Politics', 25; 'Who is the Subject of the Rights of Man?', 174
Ratcliffe, Tim, 228
Reacting to the Past, 147, 152, 154–55, 160, 163
redistribution of the sensible. *See* distribution of the sensible
representation, 3, 10, 18, 31–32, 35, 46, 51–52, 60, 81–82, 84–85, 88, 90–93, 96, 98, 125, 127–29, 138, 142, 172–73, 183, 188–90, 196–97, 206, 209, 222, 225, 227, 228, 232; democratic/ representative democracy, 82, 84, 89–91, 94, 98, 176, 186, 199; political/representational politics, 32, 84–85, 93, 177, 188; and presence, 81–85, 88–91, 93–95, 97–98; and presentation, 86, 88–89, 98; regime/ order of, 18–19, 35, 52, 81–84, 89–90, 97, 125, 127–28, 138; self-, 84, 91, 96; theatrical, 10, 84–87, 89–91, 93, 95–98, 103, 140, 188–90, 197, 203, 208
representational mediation, 216–17, 221
Rimini Protokoll, 181, 192n10; *100% City*, 90–94; *100% Salford*, 94, 98
role-immersion, 11, 147, 152–57, 159–61, 164. *See also* role-play
role-play, 69, 74–76, 108–9, 114, 153, 163
Rosler, Martha, 219, 221
rupture, 9, 11, 21, 24, 27–30, 35, 43–44, 101, 107–8, 177, 179, 186, 190, 196, 208, 219

Schiller, Friedrich, 19, 110, 225, 227
Scott, Nina, 196, 201
self-characterization, 71–74
sensus communis. *See* common sense
Situationist International, 217
slogans/sloganeering, 61, 63–64, 68, 70–71, 184, 195, 220
social reproduction, 196–97, 200, 203–5, 207–11. *See also* labour, socially reproductive
spectatorship, 4, 11, 27, 41–42, 46, 84–86, 96, 131, 172, 225, 231
spectators/the spectator, 1, 3–6, 8–12, 26–27, 43, 46–51, 85, 87, 96, 101, 103, 110, 112–13, 115, 117–18, 131, 138, 140, 171, 189, 202–3, 217–18, 220–21, 231. *See also* audience; spectatorship
Sprake, Herbert, 126, 129–30, 135
storytelling/storytellers, 10, 41, 46, 59–61, 63, 67–75, 77
subjectification, 81, 85, 93, 173, 183–84, 188

Tate Britain, 216, 220, 222–24, 226, 233
Tate Modern, 215–16, 222, 224, 226–29, 234
theatrocracy, 1, 3, 8, 12, 60, 84, 91, 96, 98, 125, 127, 142
'third thing', 112, 114, 117–19
Tom White's Street Arabs, 126, 132–36, 138, 140, 142
tragedy, 48, 52, 103–4, 154, 157, 172, 189
translation, 4, 8, 41, 46, 72–73, 76, 113–19, 131
Trump, Donald, 1–4, 178, 187

universal education. *See* education

visibility/the visible, 3–4, 24–25, 27, 31, 41, 44–46, 83, 87, 89, 125, 127, 142, 156, 172, 219–20; making visible, 3, 12, 24–25, 31–32, 40, 42–43, 92, 94–

95, 102, 131, 134, 161, 164, 196–97, 201, 205, 209, 212
void, 28

Walsh, Fintan, 185, 190
workers, 5, 25–26, 33, 61, 65–66, 70, 83, 105–6, 127–28, 143, 182, 196–97, 199–200, 204, 206–7, 210–11;

working class(es), 5, 11–12, 70, 83, 106, 128, 196–97, 202, 204–5, 208
workhouses/workhouse entertainments, 11, 126–27, 129–33, 135–43

You Should See The Other Guy, *Land of the Three Towers*, 12, 196–97, 200–202, 204, 207, 209–12

About the Contributors

Colette Conroy is the director of the Institute of Arts, University of Cumbria, UK. She has a background in theatre making, including time spent as associate director of Graeae Theatre Company, Europe's foremost professional theatre company of disabled people. Her contribution to Applied Theatre and Performance Studies includes current service as joint editor of the international refereed journal, *RiDE: The Journal of Applied Theatre and Performance* (Routledge). Colette has published widely on the connections between politics, bodies and performance. She is currently exploring ideas about political recognition and the cultural industries in the UK.

Nic Fryer is an academic, teacher and director. He is currently senior lecturer and course leader of the MA in Performance (Live and Digital) at Buckinghamshire New University. He researches into devised performance, performance pedagogy and performance philosophy. His work has been published in *Research in Drama Education* and *Reflective Practice* among others. He founded the award-winning Small Change Theatre, and has run workshops in a variety of theatrical and educational settings.

Ryan Anthony Hatch is an associate professor and the director of Graduate Studies in the English department at California Polytechnic State University, San Luis Obispo. His research theorizes the fraught relation of political and aesthetic forms as it bears on the field of art (modern drama, postdramatic theatre, interdisciplinary performance, contemporary art) and politics (the emancipatory/communist tradition from the French Revolution to the present). His writing has appeared in *CR: The New Centennial Review*, *Umbr(a): A Journal of the Unconscious*, *Correspondances: courrier de l'École freudienne du Québec*, *TDR*, the edited collection *Postdramatic*

Theatre and Form (Bloomsbury Methuen 2019) and *PAJ: A Journal of Performance and Art*, for which he serves as a contributing editor. He is currently working on two book projects: *Anyone Who Trembles Now*, on the antitheatricality of the revolutionary event, and a monograph, on the theatre of Young Jean Lee.

Jenny Hughes is professor of Drama at the University of Manchester. She has published on theatre and performance as responses to crisis and emergency, including a monograph, *Performance in a Time of Terror* (MUP, 2011), and co-authored book, *Performance in Place of War* (Seagull/Chicago, 2009). She has also published edited collections on applied theatre (*Critical Perspectives on Applied Theatre*, Cambridge 2016 – with Helen Nicholson), precarity, performance and welfare (*RiDE: The Journal of Applied Theatre and Performance*, 22:1, 2017), and activist performance (*Contemporary Theatre Review*, 25:3, 2015, with Simon Parry). At the time of writing, she is researching the national and colonial trajectories of popular, missionary and charitable theatres through the nineteenth century, and their legacies in twentieth- and twenty-first-centuries socially engaged theatre practice.

Adrian Kear is programme development director of Performance Arts at Wimbledon College of Arts, University of the Arts London. He is the author of numerous books and articles investigating the relationship between performance, politics and cultural practice. Adrian's books include *Thinking Through Theatre and Performance* (with Maaike Bleeker, Joe Kelleher and Heike Roms, Bloomsbury, 2019); *Theatre and Event: Staging the European Century* (Palgrave, 2013); *International Politics and Performance: Critical Aesthetics and Creative Practice* (with Jenny Edkins, Routledge, 2013); *Psychoanalysis and Performance* (with Patrick Campbell, Routledge, 2001); and *Mourning Diana: Nation, Culture and the Performance of Grief* (with Deborah Lynn Steinberg, Routledge, 1999).

Shulamith Lev-Aladgem, PhD, is an associate professor of theatre studies and former chair of the Theatre Arts Department at Tel Aviv University (2013–2017). She is a community-based theatre practitioner and researcher as well as a trained actress who uses her acting experience in both her research and teaching. Lev-Aladgem's main interests incorporate play theory, performance studies and cultural studies and their relation to community-based theatre, political theatre, alternative theatre, educational drama, drama therapy and feminist theatre. Her research on these subjects has been published in numerous leading periodicals in the United States, Europe and Israel. She has published two books: *Theatre in Co-Communities: Articulating Power*, published by Palgrave, Macmillan (2010), and *Standing Front Stage: Resistance*,

Celebration and Subversion in Community-Based Theatre, published by Haifa University Press and Pardes (2010) (in Hebrew).

Caoimhe Mader McGuinness is a lecturer in drama at Kingston. Her research and publications look at the politics of reception of contemporary theatre and live art through a Marxist, feminist, queer and postcolonial lens with a broad focus on the specific histories of Western liberalism as these apply to theatrical production and reception in Britain and France. Further interests include Marxist feminist approaches to performance and the relationship between theatricality and the state.

Liesbeth Groot Nibbelink is an assistant professor in Theatre and Performance Studies, Utrecht University, where she also coordinates the Master's programme in Contemporary Theatre, Dance and Dramaturgy. Her research interests include dramaturgy and scenography, spatial theory, performance ecologies, new materialism, and performance philosophy. She is the author of *Nomadic Theatre: Mobilizing Theory and Practice on the European Stage* (Bloomsbury 2019) and has contributed to (among others) *Contemporary Theatre Review*, *Performance Research* and to the volumes *Thinking Through Theatre and Performance* (Bloomsbury 2019), *Staging Spectators in Immersive Performances* (Routledge 2019), *Intermedial Performance and Politics in the Public Sphere* (Routledge 2018) and *Mapping Intermediality in Theatre and Performance* (Amsterdam University Press 2010).

Janelle Reinelt, emeritus professor of Theatre and Performance at University of Warwick, was president of the International Federation for Theatre Research (2004–2007). She has published widely on politics and performance, receiving the 'Distinguished Scholar Award' for lifetime achievement from the American Society for Theatre Research (2010) and an honorary doctorate from University of Helsinki in 2014. In 2012, she was awarded the 'Excellence in Editing' prize together with Brian Singleton for their Palgrave book series, Studies in International Performance. Recent books include *The Grammar of Politics and Performance*, edited with Shirin Rai (Routledge 2015), and *Gendered Citizenship: Manifestations and Performance* (Palgrave Macmillan 2017).

Stephen Scott-Bottoms is professor of Contemporary Theatre and Performance at the University of Manchester, UK. His books include *The Theatre of Sam Shepard* (1998); *Playing Underground: A Critical History of the 1960s Off-Off-Broadway Movement* (2004); *Small Acts of Repair: Performance, Ecology and Goat Island* (with Matthew Goulish, 2007); and

Sex, Drag and Male Roles: Investigating Gender as Performance (with Diane Torr, 2010). He is currently completing a new monograph under the working title *Incarceration Games*, with the support of a Major Research Fellowship from the Leverhulme Trust. From 2010 to 2017, Steve worked on a series of AHRC-funded projects exploring the uses of site-specific performance in relation to environmental citizenship and river stewardship. He remains active as a performer, director and dramaturge.

Dr Will Shüler is a lecturer in the Department of Drama, Theatre and Dance at Royal Holloway, University of London. There he serves as the director of Undergraduate Education for the School of Performing and Digital Arts and the director of the International Summer School. Will has recently been awarded teaching prizes for his collaborative work with the department of Media Arts on a digital Shakespeare initiative and for his web series, *Project Directing*, which investigates competition reality shows as a pedagogic model. Will's other publications include "The Greek Tragic Chorus and Its Training for War" in *War and Theatrical Innovation*, which argues that ancient Greek choral training functioned as a surrogate military education for young Athenian men.

www.ingramcontent.com/pod-product-compliance
Lightning Source LLC
Chambersburg PA
CBHW021848300426
44115CB00005B/61